Beunans Meriasek: The Life Of Saint Meriasek, Bishop And Confessor. A Cornish Drama

Whitley Stokes, Dominus Hadton

Nabu Public Domain Reprints:

You are holding a reproduction of an original work published before 1923 that is in the public domain in the United States of America, and possibly other countries. You may freely copy and distribute this work as no entity (individual or corporate) has a copyright on the body of the work. This book may contain prior copyright references, and library stamps (as most of these works were scanned from library copies). These have been scanned and retained as part of the historical artifact.

This book may have occasional imperfections such as missing or blurred pages, poor pictures, errant marks, etc. that were either part of the original artifact, or were introduced by the scanning process. We believe this work is culturally important, and despite the imperfections, have elected to bring it back into print as part of our continuing commitment to the preservation of printed works worldwide. We appreciate your understanding of the imperfections in the preservation process, and hope you enjoy this valuable book.

THE LIFE OF SAINT MERIASEK.

A CORNISH DRAMA.

BEUNANS MERIASEK.

THE LIFE OF SAINT MERIASEK,
BISHOP AND CONFESSOR.

A CORNISH DRAMA.

EDITED,
WITH A TRANSLATION AND NOTES,
BY
WHITLEY STOKES.

LONDON:
TRÜBNER AND CO., PATERNOSTER-ROW.
1872.

DUBLIN: PRINTED BY ALEXANDER THOM, 87 & 88, ABBEY-STREET.

PREFACE.

The following drama 'of the life of S. Meriasek, Bishop and Confessor,' was discovered about three years ago among the Hengwrt MSS. by Mr. Wynne of Peniarth. The first thirty-six lines were printed in the *Archaeologia Cambrensis* for 1869, p. 409, by the Rev. Robert Williams of Rhydycroesau, but the remainder is now for the first time published. I purpose in this preface, first, to describe the manuscript; secondly, to state the plot, and to print what I have found elsewhere concerning Meriasek; thirdly, to notice the names of the places mentioned in the play; and lastly, to make some remarks on the language and the metres in which it is composed.

1. *The Manuscript.*

The manuscript is a small paper quarto, measuring eight and a half inches by six, in an old brown leather binding now labelled on the back '310. Cornish Mystery,' and on the top side 'Legendary, &c. Lives of Saints, No. 2, 7 books, 310.' Inside the cover is a yellow label on which is printed 'R. WMES. VAUGHAN HENGWRT.' It contains 90 leaves paginated in pencil, and a leaf six and a quarter inches by six (marked 91ª, 91ᵇ), inserted immediately before the forty-sixth leaf. The versos of leaves 49 and 90 are occupied with rude plans of the stage. Half of p. 97, and three-fourths of p. 179 are blank. The colophon states that the MS. was finished by 'Dominus Hadton,' in the year 1504. The whole book is, I think, in his handwriting, but the MS. has been corrected in several places by a subsequent possessor,* who also inserted the stage-directions to which I have prefixed a

---

* Here follows a list of these corrections: *vyth*, 97, corrected *veth. an* 293, inserted. *esco* 511, *p* added. before 526, *kernov* inserted. *piiadou*, 560, made *peyadov. oma* 783 inserted. *flogh* 846, inserted. *athulh* 856, corrected *athuth. tev*, 936, corrected *tav. vy*, 936, inserted. *ovs*, 1051, corrected *ov covs. se*, 1056, corrected *serys. vyth*, 1073, inserted. *purwar*, 1114, corrected *purwhar. C* 1147, corrected *M. glowas*, 1160, corrected *glowes. movle* 1166 corrected *mevle. afaff* 1177 corrected *keuyn. an* 1180, inserted. *alemen* 1389 corrected *alema. wytsa*, 1760, corrected *wetsa. wyn* 2202, inserted. *prey*, 2352, corrected *preysys. presner kyns* 2462, corrected *eseth kens. vetynens* 2809 corrected *venitens. vetenens* 2886 corrected *ven·eten[en]s. vetenens* 2951 corrected *venetenes. benyth*, 2999, corrected *benytha. sur*, 3027, inserted. *han clehy* 3057 corrected *pur defry. moys*, 3204, corrected *sur devethys*, 3240, corrected *drehevys. rer pesy* 3440 corrected *rer y pery. gyyff* 3700 corrected *guyff. why*, 4252, inserted. *hag vohosogyen pur*, 4261, corrected *han v. pub. veth* 4448 corrected *vethe. gorth* 4535, corrected *gor.*

bracket, thus : [. The facsimile following this preface gives a good idea of the handwriting and of the mode in which these corrections and additions are made. The MS. has suffered little (ff. 11 and 13 have lost a small portion of the margin), and is carefully preserved at Peniarth, near Towyn, Merionethshire.

2. *The Plot.*

Mereadôcus, Meriadec (or, in Cornish mouths, Meriasek), son of a Duke of Britanny, is sent to school with his parents' blessing (lines 1-92). His studies and pious conduct are described (93-166). He returns home already renowned for learning, goodness, and courtesy (193-231). Conan, king of Armorica, wishing to wed him to a wealthy princess (168-192) goes with his nobles to the Duke's house (232-264), and after a feast (265-297) proposes the marriage (298-307). The parents gladly accept (308-319). But Meriasek refuses, declaring that he would be 'consecrated a knight of God' (320-355). After much vain expostulation from the king and Meriasek's parents (356-473), the king departs in anger (474-482); but the parents give their son their blessing, and he goes to a bishop who ordains him a priest (483-533). He thereupon performs his first miracles (534-568). Then with the bishop's blessing, he sails for Cornwall, and after saving the crew from shipwreck lands near Camborne (569-648). There he builds an oratory, makes a well spring up miraculously (649-677), and heals the sick, the maimed, and the leper (678-758). A pagan lord, Teudar, hearing of this, goes to Meriasek and, after discussing the doctrines of the Conception and the Redemption, requires him to deny Christ, and worship false gods (569-915). Meriasek refusing, Teudar sends his torturers to slay him (916-982). Warned of his danger by a vision, Meriasek hides under a rock, and escapes to Britanny (983-1096). After miraculously taming a wolf (1097-1131), he becomes a hermit, and builds a chapel on a bleak mountain near Pontivy (1132-1152).

The scene of the drama then shifts to Rome. The Emperor Constantine, still a pagan, sends forth his knights to persecute the Christians (1153-1287). The souls of two of the martyrs are received in heaven (1288-1305), and the persecutors scared by lightning. Pope Silvester and his clergy bury the martyrs, and flee to Mount Seraptyn (Soracte ?), while Constantine is stricken with leprosy (1353-1369), and seeks a cure from a doctor and a pagan bishop (1370-1439). The doctor cheats him (1440-1485), and the bishop prescribes a bath of children's blood (1486-1521). Constantine has three thousand children collected for slaughter (1522-1626), but takes pity upon them and their mothers and sets them free (1627-1682). The Apostles Peter and Paul appear in a vision to Constantine, and desire him to send for Silvester and get baptized (1689-1724). This is done: the emperor is healed by the baptismal waters, and establishes the Christian faith (1725–1865).

The scene shifts back to Britanny. Outlaws rob a merchant and a priest (1866–1935). The Earl of Rohan seeks Meriasek's hermitage (1936–1979), and after vainly trying to get him to return to the world (1980–2053), asks him to clear the land of robbers, and promises, thereupon, to establish three fairs (2054–2079). Meriasek agrees (2080–2084), and sends fire on the outlaws' forest (2085–2112). Then the outlaws calling on Meriasek are saved from death, and leave Britanny (2112–2204).

The Duke of Cornwall then for the first time hearing that Meriasek has been forced by Teudar to fly the country (2205–2277), marches with his men against that pagan (2278–2299). Teudar makes ready for battle (2300–2324), heartened by certain demons (2325–2356). After some parley Teudar is defeated (2357–2498), and the first part of the play concludes with a recommendation to the audience to drink and dance (2499–2512).

In the second part of the play the scene is laid first at Rome. Constantine announces the establishment of Christianity throughout his kingdom (2513–2521). The playwright then brings us to Brittany. A blind Earl Globus is led to Meriasek's hermitage, who rejects his offer of gold and land, but heals him for Christ's sake (2522–2627). Like miracles are also wrought on a demoniac and a deaf man (2628–2681). The Bishop of Vannes then dying, rich and poor desire Meriasek to succeed him, and the Earl of Vannes sends to Pope Silvester for the Bull authorizing Meriasek's consecration (2682–2762). Silvester gives the Bull (2763–2786); the messenger brings it to the Earl of Vannes, and the Earl, the Dean, and a Canon go to Meriasek and vainly endeavour to persuade him to accept the vacant bishopric (2787–2852). They return sorrowfully to Vannes, but at the instance of two Breton bishops, they and the Earl Globus make a second and successful attempt (2853–2909). Meriasek is led off to Dol and consecrated in St. Sampson's Church (2970–3030). He clothes the naked and heals lepers (3031–3155).

An episode from the *Miracula de Beato Mereadoco* is then introduced. The only son of a certain woman goes to the court of a King Massen, and joining in a hunting-party is taken prisoner by a heathen tyrant, who attacks and defeats the king (3156–3578). Tidings of her son's misfortune reach his mother, who entreats the Virgin on his behalf (3579–3600). The Virgin disregards the mother's prayer and the tyrant orders the son's execution (3601–3614). The mother, in revenge, carries off the child-Christ from the arms of the Virgin's image. Thereupon, the Virgin, with Christ's consent, descends from heaven, frees the prisoner, and restores him to his mother, who then takes back the stolen image of the bambino (3615–3802).

After this episode, the playwright returns to Meriasek, who miraculously restores a madman to his senses (3803–3853), performs severe penance, and is nourished by angels (3854–3895).

Again the scene is laid in Italy. Two heathen dukes go out to hunt, are attacked by a dragon, and flee to the Emperor Constantine. The heathen bishop before mentioned maintains that the existence of the monster must be due to Constantine's conversion. Pope Silvester is fetched and (heartened by S. Peter) he vanquishes the dragon and brings to life many whom it had slain. The heathen dukes are baptized and all go in procession to the Pope's palace (3896–4180).

Returning to Britanny and Meriasek, the playwright first sets forth a miraculous cure of a cripple (4181–4251), and then describes Meriasek's death, surrounded by his sorrowful clergy (4252–4330), and the reception of his soul in heaven (4331–4348). Bishops and earls, deans and canons bury the saint's body in a grave made and cleansed by those whom he had healed; and the second and last act concludes with a speech by the Earl of Vannes, in which, after invoking on the audience the blessing of Meriasek, of Mary of Camborne, and of the Apostles, he says—

> "Drink ye all with the play,
>   We will beseech you
>   Before going hence.
>   Pipers, pipe ye at once!
>   We will, every son of the breast,
>   Go to dance.
>   Go ye or stay,
>   Welcome shall ye be
>   Though ye be a week here."

The comic element necessary in all Cornish plays is here provided by Constantine's quack doctor (1408–1482), the *tortores* employed by Teudar (950–1040), Constantine and the tyrant (3245), the Breton outlaws and the bishops' crucifers.

It will be seen that the play is founded on three stories unskilfully pieced together, the legend of Meriasek, the legend of S. Silvester and Constantine, and the story of the Virgin's rescue of the *filius mulieris* (3156–3802). As to the origin of the last-mentioned episode I know nothing. Silvester's legend is widely spread and is well told by Mrs. Jameson in her Sacred and Legendary Art.[*] Meriasek's legend is thus given piecemeal by the Bollandists at June 7:—

DE SANCTO MERIADOCO.

episcopo venetensi in Britannia armorica.

Ex variis recentioribus, Vita antiquiori usis.

SEC. VII.] I*Nter Gallicanas civitates Britanniæ Armoricæ est Episcopalis urbs* Venetensis, Venetum *&* Venetiæ *etiam dicta, vulgo* Vannes,

---

[*] *See* Irish versions (hitherto unpublished) in the notes to the Félire of Oengus, Jan. 18, and in a life of Silvester preserved in the *Lebar Brecc.*

olim Ducum Sedes, quæ ad hunc diem vii *Junii cultu sacro veneratur* S. Meriadocum *vulgo* S. Meriadec, *suum Episcopum.*

Memoria ejus ut Sancti apud varios.] *Hujus aliquam Vitā Gallicè edidit Albertus le Grand, inter Vitas Sanctorum Britanniæ Armoricæ, jam altera vice recusas anno* MDCLIX: *& inter Auctores quibus se usum profitetur, sunt Augustinus du Pas, Joannes Chenu, & Claudius Robertus in Catalogo Episcoporum Venetensium.* Sed hi nudum nomen exprimunt, tantum titulo Sancti præfixo, & statuunt duodecimum aut decimum tertium hujus Sedis Episcopum. Sammarthani decimum quintum: de quo, inquiunt, consule Proprium Sanctorum dioecesis Venetensis, ubi fertur, ipsum obdormivisse in Domino vii Idus Junii.

cultus in Venetensi Proprio.] *Idem* Proprium *allegat etiam Albertus le Grand, quod nos habemus Veneti excusum anno* MDCXXX; *& inde subdimus aliquod Vitæ Compendium, in tres Lectiones parvas, ad secundum Nocturnum in Matutinis recitandas, distinctum: quibus alibi additur hæc Oratio:* Deus, qui de hujus mundi inedia, per mediū paupertatis, Beatum Meriadocum, Confessorem tuum atque Pontificem, abstraxisti ad patriam claritatis, tribue nobis quaesumus; ut, ipso pro nobis intercedente, dirumpas nostræ vincula pravitatis.

Legenda ex MS. Vita gallica.] 2. *Præterea idem Albertus allegat,* antiquum Legendarium manuscriptum detentum in ecclesia S. Joannis Traoume Meriadec, Poigt dicta, in parochia Plongaznau [leg. *Plou-*] dioecesis Trecorensis: *quam Vitam utinam sub finem edidisset: tunc certior fides adhiberi posset iis quæ refert, & in Lectionibus non habentur. Talia sunt, quod* S. Meriadocus anno 758 natus est: sed cifris transpositis opinamur legendum anno 578 aut 587, tunc autem valde senex fuisset circa annum 659, quando in Lectionibus *dicitur consecratus Sacerdos. Deinde, ait idem Albertus,* Meriadocum, post acquisitas inter studia scientias, à parentibus ablegatum ad aulam regiam, in eaque quinquennio vixisse à vitiis immaculatum, omni pietatis & sanctitatis exercitio deditum. Postea oblatum ab eisdem matrimonium recusasse & præelegisse sacros Ordines; Sacerdotioque suscepto secessisse in locum solitarium in Vicecomitatu Rohanensi, haud procul ab oppido Pontivio, ubi hoc tempore extat sacellum ejus nomini dicatum.

multa particularia continet.] Interim cum prædones vicina loca devastarent, eum instituisse apud Vicecomitem Rohanensem, ut dictos prædones pelleret: eique se id nequaquam posse efficere respondenti, promisisse, se id peracturum si tres celebres mercatus concederet in paroecia Noyal, scilicet die sexto Julii, octavo Septembris, & primo Octobris. Qua conditione à Vicecomite acceptata, dictos prædones solis S. Meriadoci apud Deum precibus fugatos fuisse. Denique, post administratum in omni sanctitate Episcopatum, vita functum esse & in ecclesia Cathedrali sepultum, ac tam in eo quam in loco solitudinis suæ claruisse miraculis: multas etiam in Britannia hac dicatas S. Meriadoco ecclesias, interque eas sacellum castri Pontivii, & aliud in paroecia Plou-gaznou, *supra indicato. Hæc inter alia Albertus le Grand.*

exhibetur elogium ex Saussaio.] 3. *Andreas Saussayus in Martyrologio Gallicano, hoc cum exornat elogio:* Apud Venetum in Armorica, S. Meriadoci Episcopi & Confessoris, qui ex regia stirpe Conani, provinciæ hujus Principis, editus, calcato temporalis gloriæ fuco, humilitatis Filii Dei imitator, sese, ne natalium fulgor spectabilem mundo redderet, indumentis vilibus tegens, in desertum locum, Deo soli ut serviret, recepit: ubi diu in omni sanctitate vitam ducens eremiticam, delituit. At deinde clara virtutum lucerna, ne sub modio esset diutius, divino indicio propalata, super candelabrum evecta est. Patefactus enim cælesti nutu Christi famulus, sublato è vivis Hinguthano Venetensi Episcopo, magna Cleri populi conspiratione, de solitudine dilectissima abstractus, electusque est Pontifex, atque Episcopus ordinatus: quamquam ipse subesse, non præesse, desideraret. Sic suscepto Pastorali munere, mores Episcopales ita induit, ut vix ullum, ante vel post ejus tempora, illa Ecclesia Praesulem viderit, qui majori solertia, doctrina, vigilantia, integritate, pietate, gregem rexerit commissum. Propter quarum virtutum excellentiam, & clara suae sanctitatis ac gloriae, quae cum vivus, tum defunctus prodidit, argumenta, à majoribus inter dioecesis hujus Tutelares praecipuos habitus, & in hunc usque diem à posteris sacris honoribus, qui beatis Opitulatoribus deferuntur, excultus, hoc ipso die, quo ad beatitudinem migravit, venerationis celebratur obsequiis.

& Lectiones novae] Haec Saussaius. Vitae autem Epitome ex propriis Ecclesiae Venetensis, est quae sequitur:

ubi narratur ejus ordinatio Presbyteralis, vita solitaria.] I. Meriadocus, illustri stirpe Conani minoris Britanniae Regis editus, à teneris annis sese ad virtutum omnium studium comparavit: humilitatem vero maxime in deliciis habuit, Christi Domini vestigiis insistens. Legitimam adeptus aetatem, sacris ordinibus ordinatur; et inania mundi nomina, quae suspiciunt homines, & junioribus animos faciunt, aspernatus, bonis omnibus et honoribus cessit, recepitque se in locum quemdam, non procul à Pontiviensi castro, in quo solus degebat, perturbationum expers, vitaeque compos securissimae.

miracula: electio ad Episcopatum] II. Aegrotos ibi plurimos, qui ad eum sanitatis recuperandae gratia confluebant, sospites restituit. Cumque insignis hujus virtutis & sanctitatis fama percrebuisset; Venetenses cives concilium cogunt, Capitulumque & universum Clerum impensius obsecrant, ut Meriadocum in Episcopi nuper defuncti locum sufficiant. Quibus in id convenientibus, datum est negotium quibusdam Canonicis, ut Meriadoco, ipsummet populi precibus & Cleri concordibus animis cooptatum Episcopum, renuntiarent.

in eoque virtutes.] III. Et licet sibi delatum onus deprecaretur; ita tamen ingeminatis omnium votis urgetur, ut iis tandem cesserit. Paucis post diebus in Ecclesia Cathedrali, celebri Episcoporum conventu, & magno populi concursu, fausta acclamatione plausuque consecratur circa annum sexcentesimum quinquagesimum nonum. Caritatem maxime & misericordiam erga pauperes et aegrotos exercuit, eorum inediam sublevando salutique consulendo. Cum verò pie & sancte vitam confecisset, miraculorum gloria celebris, septimo Idus Junii obdormivit in Domino.

Father Albert Le Grand, in his *Vies des Saints de Bretagne*, and D. Lobineau, in the second volume of his work bearing the same title, Paris, 1836, pp. 118–125, have translated or analysed in French the Bollandist legend.

D. Lobineau gives the name (Hingueten) of the bishop from whom Meriasek received priest's orders, and further states that there are many places in Brittany dedicated to him.

"Entre autres la chapelle du château de Pontivy, et une ancienne chapelle appelée *Traoun-Mériadec*, c'est-à-dire *le Val de Mériadec*, en la paroisse de Plouganou dans l'ancien diocèse de Tréguier, au lieu où est maintenant la chapelle de Saint-Jean-du-Doigt. Une autre chapelle du même saint se trouve dans la paroisse de Stival près de Pontivi. Cette chapelle est un lieu de pèlerinage assez fréquenté. On y conserve le chef du saint évêque, et l'on y montre une cloche de cuivre jaune, très-ancienne, de forme conique, et qu'on dit avoir appartenu à S. Mériadec; on la sonne sur la tête de ceux qui sont affligés de surdité. Enfin il y a encore une troisième chapelle dédiée à son honneur, et presque aussi fréquentée que celle de Stival, dans la paroisse de Plumergat.

'These' (writes Viscount de la Villemarqué), 'with the editors of the Propre du diocèse de Vannes, printed in 1660, and of the ancient breviary of Vannes (1589), are the only authors who, so far as I know, have concerned themselves, at least at any length, with St. Mériadec. Our contemporaries, such as abbé Tresvaux, in his new edition of D. Lobineau, M. de Kerdanet in his annotated reprint of Alb. Le Grand, M. de Garaby, *Vies de B. B.* or *Sts. de Bretagne*, and M. Levot, *Biographie bretonne*, have merely followed or corrected their predecessors.

'Ils les corrigent bien, je crois, en plaçant au viie siècle et non au xiiie, l'existence de St. Mériadec. Le *Catalogue* des évêques de Vannes, daté de l'an 1254, leur donne raison contre le légendaire du xve siècle qui fait mourir le saint en l'an 1302. On n'est pas moins dans le vrai en reléguant parmi les fictions inventées pour flatter les Rohan—qui n'existaient pas au viie siècle—tout ce qui est dit par ce dernier légendaire au sujet de la parenté et des rapports de St. Mériadec avec un Vicomte de Rohan et les foires franches obtenues de lui. Si le Saint y fut pour quelque chose, les Rohan n'y sont pour rien : leur illustre nom aura usurpé la place de je ne sais quel vieux nom obscur du pays de Porhoët.'

3. *The Names of Places mentioned in the Play.*

Except *Rome*, 1182, 2514, *Lumbardy*, 1534, *meneth Sereptyn* (Mount Soracte?), 1342, 1534, 1735, and *Poly* (Pola?), these relate either to Britanny (*breten* 2757, 2861, *bretyn* 4355, *breten byen* 517), or Cornwall (*Kernou*, 2294, 2860).

The Breton place-names are as follows :—

Kernou, 513, etc., now *Kerneé* or *Kerné*, 'la Cornouaille, un des quatres cantons de la Bretagne qui ont donné leur noms aux quatre dialectes principaux de la langue bretonne qu'on y parle.' (Legonidec).

an castel gelwys pontelyne ('the castle called Pontelyn') 1139, 1947. Of this Viscount de la Villemarqué writes as follows : 'There is no castle of Pontelyne,' au bord de la rivière, mais il y en avait un autrefois, nommé le *château du Thelem*. Je le trouve, après bien des recherches, et non sans un certain plaisir que vous comprenderez, cité dans une "Enquête" de l'an 1479, "touchant les droits et prérogatives de la Maison de Rohan." Voici le texte : "Le Sieur de Guémené mesme dépose que en la Vicomté de Rohan y avait anciennement plusieurs chasteaux et fortes places, scavoir est le *Chasteau du Thelem* .... esquelz on dit que anciennement y souloit avoir capitaine, guet et garde .... quelz par les Anglois furent ruinés et démolis."

'Ce vieux château du Thelem était situé à une lieue trois quarts de Josselin, au confluent de l'Oust et de la Lié (*aliàs* Eler) près du *Pont* du Camper (*aliàs* Kemper, confluentia). Il a donné son nom, sous la forme de *Pontelaine*, qui est à peu près celle de vôtre Mystère, à une famille dont je remarque un membre, en 1437, parmi les seigneurs châtelains de la Vicomté de Rohan."

an ryuer a Josselyne, 1142. Of this M. de la Villemarqué says —" Il n'y a pas de 'rivière de Josselin,' proprement dite, mais une rivière qui passe à Josselin; c'est l'Oust (*Ult* alias *Ulto* fluvius, *Ultum*, Cartul. de Redon, A. 834, 859—*Ost*,—D. Morice, 1205). Elle prend sa source dans le département des Côtes du Nord, et arrose un grand nombre de lieux de l'ancienne Vicomté de Rohan. Toutefois on ne peut douter que l'auteur de votre Mystère ait voulu l'indiquer."

Rohan 1936.

plu voala (leg. *plu noala*) 2078, 2202. "Le pays appelé *Plu-Voala*" (writes M. de la Villemarqué) "dans le mystère de St. Mériadec (lisez *Noala*, N au lieu de V) est le Plebs Nuial du Cartulaire de Redon, ad ann. 1082, le Noal de l'Abbaye de Bonrepos, ann. 1204; le Noyal d'un texte de 1219 cité par D. Morice, le Noual d'un autre texte de 1274, et pour ne pas reproduire toutes les formes de ce nom, la paroisse de Noyal d'aujourdhui, dite Noyal-Pontivy. Composée de 4 trèves et du Château de Pontivy, dans la Vicomté de Rohan, elle faisait partie du doyenné de Porhoët et est maintenant la plus grande commune du canton de Pontivy, département de Morbihan."

Venetens 2682, 2761, 2809 'Vannes.'

eglos sent Sampson (the first archbishop and metropolitan of Brittany): this church is in the town of Dôl.

The Cornish place-names are as follows:—

Cambron 644, 687, 730, 965, 982, 4293, now Camborne, a market town and parish in the hundred of Penwith, on the road from Redruth to Penzance. The late Dr. Oliver has shown that the patron saint of the church is Mereadocus. The Saint's Well is still known, and, according to Mr. Hunt, persons who washed in it were called *Merrasickers*.

Penwyth 783, *Penwith* 2217, now a hundred in Cornwall.

Carnebre 784, *Carnbre* 966, 'the cairn-hill,' near the sea, N.W. of Redruth, noticeable both from the English Channel and the Atlantic.

Castel an Dynas 2210, there is one place so named, 'an eminence' (729 ft.) 'crowned with an embankment,' near S. Columb Major, and another north of Penzance.

Peddre 2211, now Pidar, one of the hundreds of Cornwall.

Tyndagyel 2214, now Tintagel, Arthur's birthplace, on the Bristol Channel, N.W. of Camelford.

Menek, 2267, 2288, now Meneage, a peninsular district in Kerrier hundred, south of the town of Helston, with the Lizard for its extreme southern point.

Les Teudar 2267, 2284, now Les-teader, in the parish of S. Keverne, Meneage.

Porder 2288, now Powder, one of the hundreds of Cornwall.

Goddren 2289, now Goodren, in the parish of Kea, hundred of Powder, on a branch of the Truro river.

Morvelys 3415, has not been identified.

Tamer 2208, is the river Tamar.*

4. *The Language and Metres of the Play.*

Except a few English, French, and Latin oaths, curses, and other phrases scattered through the play, its language is Middle-Cornish, but rather more modern than that of the *Passion*, and of the dramas published by Mr. Norris. Thus loanwords from the English are somewhat more numerous than they are in Mr. Norris's dramas. Again, the vowels *e* and *o* have often become *a* (exalty*a* 15, wos*a* 22, my3tern*as* 154, th*a*n 1370, t*a*rthennou 1423, bohosogy*an* 472, soudory*an* 1354, calcory*an* 1375; maryasek 262: *y* sometimes occurs for *e* (beth*y*ns 818), and *e* for *i* (pr*e*nce 924). In two or three instances a mute *th* is written for *gh* (botho*th*ek 779, my3ternas 154, berthu*th* 1376). In *pethy* (for *pethyth*) and *forna* 1104 (for *forthna*) *th* is dropt. In one word (bedne*th* 198, 224) *nn* has become *dn*. In *falge* 777, *calge* 2046, and *felge* 1273, *s* has become soft *g*, as in the Italian *Ambrogio* from *Ambrosius*; *v* for *f* occurs in goth*v*os 28, goth*v*as 104, o*v*e 248, arveth 3201. But these are mere phonetic corruptions. The grammar of the language is pure Middle-Cornish. The infixed and suffixed pronouns are regularly used. The verb is unimpaired. The syntax is that of the older dramas, save that the future of the verb substantive is sometimes used for the present. On the whole, the play may be regarded as filling the gap between the fourteenth century Oxford plays and the modern Cornish *Creation of the World*.

Most of the interesting Cornish words and grammatical forms are mentioned in the Notes: the following additional remarks may be useful to students of the text.

The long vowels are expressed in three ways—1st, by adding *y* or *i*, 2nd, by duplication, 3rd, by adding a mute *e*. Thus—

1st, ta*y*s 295, ra*y*s 319, ma*y*s 534, be*y*s 340, bre*y*s 342, pe*y*th

---

* For information regarding these places I am indebted to the kindness of the Rev. Dr. Bannister, vicar of St. Day, Scorrier.

445, *weyll* 466, *voys* 312, *doy* 457, 610, *oys* 462, *moys* 689,=*mois* 130, *groyt* 3326, *goyt* 3325. In *glowaes* 1160 an *e* is added.

2nd, *glaan* 1719, *lees* 663, *jugleer* 921, *meen* 1406, *ree* 1509, *feer* 2195, *ree* 2308, *ree* (faciet) 2836, *pee* 3264, *lyynnyou* 4446.

3rd, *aye* 6, *myterne* 4, *scole* 10, *wore* 19, *corfe* 148, *wyre* 205, *ove* 248, *ole* 366, *meske*, 434, *hovle* 853, *toule* 1168.

c is sometimes used for *s*: *vecyl* 1519, *gemercys* 1837, *cydyr* 1969, *cervyes* 3595, *cervons* 3651, *grac* 215: *fecycyan* 1484: *s* for *c*: *reeves* 452.

ȝ has two powers, *dh* (W. *dd*, English soft *th*) and *y* (ȝurl 1937, ȝesseys 2162, ȝethewon 2602, ȝehes 4231).

g is either hard, or equivalent to English *j* (an *geffa* 20, *martege* 61).

sch in loanwords is sometimes for *sc* (*omschumunys* 1249), but generally for *sh*.

th has two powers: *dh* (*clethethyou* 1266, *thefy* 2475), or that of the sharp English *th*.

u is often = the consonant *v* (*seuys* 2). It is sometimes = *i* (*y*) (*crustunyon* 539, *muter* 3010, *turont* 3206), or *e* (*ugoreff* 3689, *yurlys* 294, *purfeth* 1546, *truspys* 1116): conversely *e* for *u* occurs in *forten* 1424, *stethya* 1495.

v is either = the vowel *u* (*vhell* 4), or the consonant *v*.

w is generally a vowel (*yw* 1, *gwlascur* 3), or semi-vowel; but it is sometimes = *v* (*barwow* 2309 *deworijs* 4178, *wur* 668, *wryens* 3963).

The stage-directions contain some curious words. Thus, the mediaeval Latin verb *pompo, kalus*, p. 32, *exulatores*, p. 106 (which would perhaps have been better rendered 'exiles' or 'fugitives'), *cardinale* p. 158, *crosser* (if this be intended for Latin) p. 164, *tentum* p. 192, *stallum* p. 200. *processonant* p. 242, *processconabiliter* p. 106. Except in one or two instances, I have allowed the scribe's wonderful Latin to remain uncorrected. The English *beryth* p. 76, *urnell* p. 80, *yledyt* p. 172, *bagyll* p. 174, *forling*, *suagynk* p. 220, *soudrys* p. 228 are also noteworthy. Some of the strangest English loanwords are mentioned in the notes.

The Metres.

These are numerous and elaborate, and may be divided into ten classes—

I. The seven-syllabled rhyming couplet, e.g. 2536, 2537.

II. Quatrains. Of these there are several kinds, in one the lines are seven-syllabled and the rhymes run thus: *abab* (e.g. 168-171). In another the first line has four syllables, the rest seven, and the rhymes are thus: *abba* (e.g. 126-129). See also 391-394.

III. Five-lined stanzas: see 4324-4328, where the rhymes are thus: *aabab*.

IV. Six-lined stanzas. Examples are 25–30, 31–36, 258–262, 813–818, 819–824.

V. Seven-lined stanzas. Examples are 99–105, 264–271 (where the rhymes are thus: *aababab*) 519–525 (where the rhymes are thus: *aabaaab*). See also 4349–4355, 4386–4392, 4198–4204.

VI. Eight-lined stanzas. Examples: 9–16 (where the rhymes are thus: *abababab*), 118–125 (*ababcddc*), 278–285 (*aabccbcb*). There is a curious form in which the fifth line has four syllables, the others seven syllables, and the rhymes run thus: *ababcddc*. See 1–8, 17–24, 37–44, 45–52.

VII. Nine-lined stanzas: e.g. 90–98 (rhymes *aab ccb ddb*), 207–215 (rhymes *ab ab c ddd c*). And see 172–180, 363–371, 3179–3187.

VIII. Ten-lined stanzas: e.g. 154–163, 474–483.

IX. Eleven-lined stanzas: 632–642.

X. Twelve-lined stanzas: 142–153 (rhymes *ababab ab cddc*), and see 848–859.

In conclusion, a few words as to the mode in which I have edited the text and made the translation. The MS. abounds in contractions. These I have extended, but always printed the extensions in italics. The scribe uses capital letters capriciously. I have employed them only to denote the commencement of a stanza. He sometimes wrongly joins two words, and wrongly divides a single word, namely in the following instances:—

clapsens 936. *kewar* 1048. *mapguirhas* 1125. *speryssans* 1317. *empertek* 1411. *pendraleueryth* 1486. *whybath* 1512. *mylflogh* 1657. *gasabev* 1661. *lynebras* 1993. *warnalosal* 2413. *gulym* 2604. *roythym* 2847. *dothekynsu* 2934. *my nnoghoma* 3199. *hawarbarthom* 3244. *poby* 3311. *dywhylescyans* 3463. *fydis* 3509. *venentha* 3579. *polgeov* 3655. *dyulwethygov* 3690. *saban* 3711. *reeovleferel* 3739. *nefrebetheheb* 3802. *gorthe* 3837. *thymokea* 4017. *braysogh* 4311. *halsebewe* 4466. *moyden* 4492. *duavan* 4548.

Teu dar 759, 1048. *ar luth* 1430. *hel myv* 1522. *trem myl* 1776. *so yth* 2292. *at lyan* 2477. *hawa reegrueys* 2767. *otho mogyan* 3137. *guar nyany* 3272. *du a* 3976. *kyn sol* 4170.

I have corrected these errors. In other respects I have spared no pains to reproduce the text with exactitude. For ample opportunities to do this I am indebted to Mr. Wynne, who first at Peniarth gave me free access to the MS. for nearly a week, and afterwards, at my request, deposited it for three months in the library of Trinity College, Dublin.

The translation is merely intended to convey, line for line, to philologists the meaning of the original so far as I have been able to ascertain it. Hence, I have not only rendered the *chevilles* with which the Cornish text is intolerably overloaded, but I have often disregarded English idiom. I believe that my version is generally accurate, but there are some words and passages from which I have been unable to elicit any satisfactory meaning.* That these are not more numerous is due to the researches of Norris and Ebel and to the kindness of the Rev. Robert Williams, of Rhydycroesau, who read a proof of the work, and to whom I am indebted for many corrections and suggestions.

W. S.

5, MERRION-SQUARE, NORTH, DUBLIN,
　December 14, 1871.

---

* See lines 17, 103, 156, 293, 719, 908, 1035, 1044, 1307, 1475, 1476, 1901, 2328, 2385, 2419, 2681, 2738, 2883, 3303, 3927, 3983. Attention is requested to the Corrigenda at pp. 278, 279.

p[ate]r Inter dula dualdy ÷ ob mdp gmdff the somymud
kemd the pole thelhondy ÷ gul mdhoy mony alla / obbdumitgd
pater Amen pst qambdumeth ky
ob mdp poro thym thelldy
· ono pothok assoff dofye / ob tyborth sny theorthyd
hec ... mor ... kvorytt
hic Epc kernob hic pompabit ... ... gobm
... tt mo pb osto mbrety ÷ m conteth golwys kernob
mny pb ob pryd pnptmeny ÷ colwethe thyny pb tdnob
pnc ... // ... pstot nyspabt
mynsnd m brete kyow / ob pob pnygmy hobdobt

[179]

Anno xxiiij H viij

This noteu and memorandu is concerning
the holle and whole mariage of mastres Cesely
...
...
Recevyd for the holle talbottes
gate

BEUNANS MERIASEK.

ORDINALE DE VITA SANCTI MEREADOCI.

p. 1.

HIC INCIPIT ORDINALE DE VITA SANCTI MEREADOCI EPISCOPI ET CONFESSORIS∴

Pater mereadoci pompabit hic

[PATER MEREADOCI]

Me yw gylwys duk bryten
  ha seuys a goys ryel
ha war an gwlascur cheften
4   nessa ȝen myterne vhell
  kyng conany
aye lynneth purwyr y thof
gwarthevyas war gvyls ha dof
8   doutis yn mysk arlyȝy

Vn mab purwyr ȝyn y ma
  meriasek y hanow
ȝe scole lemmyn y worra
12   me a vyn heb falladow
  dysky dader may halla
mersyv gans du plygadow
y karsen y exaltya
16   may fo perhennek gwlasow

MATER

Arluth henna yv gwrys da
  y exaltye yredy
perfect ef a wore redya
20   grammer angeffa deffry
  y vyea tek
ha worshypp wosa helma
yv ȝe voth mos a lemma
24   lauer ȝynny ov map wek

MERIADOCUS

A das ha mam ov megyans
  yv bos gorrys ȝe ȝyskans
  rag attendie an scryptur
28 gothvos ynweth decernya
omna ynter drok ha da
  yv ov ewnadow pup vr

HERE BEGINS THE PLAY OF THE LIFE OF SAINT MERIASEK, BISHOP AND CONFESSOR.

Meriasek's father shall here parade.

MERIASEK'S FATHER.

I am called Duke of Brittany,
   And raised from blood royal,
And over the country chieftain
4   Nearest to the high sovran,
   King Conany.
Of his lineage right truly am I,
Warden over wild and tame,
8   Feared among lords.

A son right truly we have,
   Meriasek his name.
To school now put him
12   I will without fail,
That he may learn goodness.
   If it be God's pleasure,
I should like to exalt him
16   That he may be owner of countries.

MERIASEK'S MOTHER.

Lord, that is done well
   To exalt him readily.
Perfectly he can read:
20   Grammar, that he shall have soon,
   It would be fair,
And worship after this.
Is thy will to go hence,
24   Tell to us, my sweet son?

MERIASEK.

O father and mother, my delight
Is to be put to learning,
   To attend the Scripture.
28 Knowledge likewise to discern
Here between evil and good
   Is my desire always.

PATER

    Beneth du ȝys meryasek
32 pup vr ty yv colonnek
      parys rag dysky dader
    meseger scon alemma
    kegy gans ov mab kerra
36   bys yn mester a grammer

PRIMUS NUNCIUS

    Arlud ȝe voth a vyth gvrys
    my a wor pur wyre yn ta
    py ma an mester trygis
40 hag yȝyv marthys densa
    sur worth flehys
    meryasek pan vynnogh why
    an forth dalleth yredy
44   ny a vyn ha pur vskys

MERIADOCUS

    A das ha mam kekyfrys
    pesef agis bannothow
    maym beus the well grays
48 benyȝa yn ov dyȝyow
      desky dader
    rag agis benneth[ow] why
    yv moy treasur ȝymmo vy
52   es pyth an bysma neb vr

PATER

    Ov mab wek ȝys benneth du
    ham benneth vy benyȝa
    ny fylleth hedre ven bev
56 ath porpos gene neffra
    lemmen squyer
    keȝegy gans ov map dy
    ha gveyth warnotho defry
60 ena ty a yl dysky
    martegen the vrys mur dader

MATER

    Ov map benneth varya
    dys ham bennath vy neffra
64 thethe ganov mannafi amma
    ewne yv ȝyn ȝeth leuf kara
    meryasek wek

FATHER.

    God's blessing to thee, Meriasek!
32 Always thou art hearty,
      Ready to learn goodness.
    Messenger, forthwith hence
    Go thou with my dearest son
36   Unto the master of grammar.

FIRST MESSENGER.

    Lord, thy will shall be done.
    I know right truly well
40 Where the master is dwelling,
    And he is wondrous kind
      Surely to children.
    Meriasek, when you wish
    The way readily begin
44   We will, and right quickly.

MERIASEK.

    O father and mother also
    I beseech your blessings
    That I may live made the better
48   Ever in my days
        To learn goodness.
    For your blessings
    Are a greater treasure to me
52   Than the wealth of this world any time.

FATHER.

    My sweet son, God's blessing to thee,
      And my blessing ever,
    Thou shalt not fail whilst I may be alive
56   Of thy purpose by me always.
      Now squire,
    Go thou with my son thither,
    And take care of him truly.
60 There thou canst learn,
      If it be thy wish, much of goodness.

MOTHER.

    My son, Mary's blessing
      To thee and my blessing for ever.
64 Thy mouth I would kiss it:
      Right is it for us to love thee dearly,
      Sweet Meriasek.

       my a dryst yn du avan
68 pan ven ny sur coth ha gwan
         gvreth aga*n* revlys tek

ARMIGER DUCIS

Meryasek ale*mm*a due*n*
gervyth a scryve pluven
72   whath me ny won ʒe redya
nag aswen ov leʒerow
me a bys du karadow
    roy ʒy*n*ny ynta spedya

p. 4.   *Hic magister pompabit*

MAGISTER

76 My yv mayster a g*r*amer
gvrys yn bonilapper
    vni*v*ersite vye*n*
my a wor m*ur* yn dyvyn
80 pa*n* ve lue*n* ov ʒos a wyn
    ny gara covs mes laten

PRIMUS NUNCIUS

Hono*ur* ʒyvgh mast*er* worthy
ha benytha m*ur* reuerens
84 duk conan pur yredy
y vab rag cawas dyska*n*s
    sur da*n*venys
ateva ʒyugh doctor wek
88 dyskovgh ef yn ma*ner* dek
    ha wy a vyth rewardeys

MAGISTER

Messeger na ʒovt an cas
my an dysk na vo y*n* gvlas
92   gramario*n* v*t* ay p*ar*ov
devgh seʒovg mereasek
yn myske an flehys p*ur* dek
    ha merovgh ag*is* leffrov
96 pe dyth munys kewsovghwy
let veth orth ag*is* dysky
    ha m*ur* ny*n*syv an gobrov

PRIMUS SCOLAR[IS]

Du gveras a b c
100 an pen ca*n* henna yv d
    ny won na moy yn liu*er*

    I trust in God above
68 When we shall be old and feeble
    Thou wilt observe our rules fair.

     THE DUKE'S SQUIRE.

  Meriasek, let us go hence.
  Never a word of pen-writing
72   Yet can I read.
  I know not my letters.
  I beseech loveable God,
    May he grant to us well to speed.

    Here shall the Master parade.

     MASTER.

76 I am a master of grammar
  Made in .... (?)
    Of a small university.
  I know much in citation:
80 When my tot may be full of wine
    I love not to speak (aught) save Latin.

     FIRST MESSENGER.

  Honour to you, worthy Master
    And ever much reverence.
84 Duke Conan right readily
    His son to have learning
     Surely hath sent.
  Here he is for you, doctor sweet.
88 Teach him in a beautiful way,
    And you shall be rewarded.

     MASTER.

  Messenger, fear not the case.
  I will teach him so that there will not be in the country
92   Any grammarian of his peers.
  Come, sit ye, Meriasek,
  Amongst the children very fairly,
    And look at your books.
96 If it be a little saying that ye speak,
  There will be hindrance to teaching you,
    And the rewards are not great.

     FIRST SCHOLAR.

  God keep A, B, C,
100 The end of the song, that is D.
    I know no more in the book.

ny vef yn scole rum levte
bys ynnewer gorʒewar
104 ʒum gothvas wosa lyfye
me a ʒysk moy ov mester

p. 5.   SECUNDUS SCOLAR[IS]
E s t henna yv est
pandryv nessa ny won fest
108   mur na reugh ov cronkye
rag my ny veʒaf the well
vnwyth a caffen hansell
me a russa amendie

MAGISTER
112 Dyske moy gans ʒe coweʒa
pan vynnogh eugh ʒe lyvya
meryasek wek eugh gansa
rag wy yv tender yn oys
116 ha flehys yonk a gar boys
ham bevnans vy yv henna

MERIADOCUS
Me a lever ʒyvgh mester
ha na vewy dysplesys
120 heʒyv sur yv dugwener
da yv sevell worth vn pris
ha predery an ena
rag kerensa an passyonn
124 a porthes ihesu ragon*
pynys hyʒyv y fanna

Ha pub gvener
a vo sur drys an vlyʒan
128 gul peyadov my a vyn
kyns eva na ʒybbry mevr

ʒen chappell me a vyn mois
ʒe crist a scolyas y woys
132   ʒe vʒyll ov peiadow
ha ʒe varye y vam
kyns eva na dybbry tam
helma yv ov vsadow

p. 6.   MAGISTER
136 Ov map gvra ʒe vlonogeth
tevlys os ʒe sansoleth
meriasek gon gvyr lemmyn

* MS. ragan.

I was not at school, by my loyalty,
    Until late (?) yesterday evening.
To my knowledge, after dining
    I will learn more, my master.

SECOND SCHOLAR.

E, s, t, that is *est*.
What thing is next I know not quite.
    Do not beat me greatly,
For I shall not be better.
Once if I got a handsel
    I should amend.

MASTER.

Learn thou more with thy comrades.
When you will, go to dine,
    Sweet Meriasek, go with them,
For you are tender in age,
And young children love food,
    And my life is that.

MERIASEK.

I say to you, Master,
    And be not displeased,
To-day surely is Friday:
    Good it is to arise for a while
    And think of the soul.
For love of the Passion
Which Jesu bore for us.
    Penance to-day I desire.

And every Friday,
Which shall be surely throughout the year,
Make prayer I will,
    Rather than eat or drink much.

To the chapel I will go,
To Christ who shed his blood,
    To make my prayer,
And to Mary his Mother,
Before drinking or eating a bit:
    This is my usage.

MASTER.

My son, do thy will.
Designed art thou for holiness,
    Meriasek, I know truly now.

          ke ha due pan vy plesyes
140   myns may hyllen sur esyes
          ty a vyth yn pup termyn
                   descendat solus ad capellam

        MERIADOCUS *in capella*
        Ihesu arlud nef han bys
        ʒys y raf ov peyadow
144   iesu arlud my ad pys
        orth temtacyon dewolow
        iesu crist gvyth vy pupprys
        lel ʒeth servye om dyʒyow
148   ihesu ov corfe ham spyrys
        ol ov nerth ham cowgegyow
        rof ʒeth gorthye
        hag ath peys vvel ha clour
152   nefra na veus yn nor
        trelyes ʒe lust an bysme

        Marya myʒternas nef
        a vagas crist gans ʒe leth
156   maria drefa ʒe luef
        ʒen mab a skyentoleth
        marya whek peys genef
        byth nangeffa an iovl keth
160   warnaf power
p. 7.   nan beys ov escare arall
        ham kyke yv escar teball
        pur ysel me an temper

164   gans golyas ha gans pynys
        me a garsa
        crist ʒe plesya
        a new[t] hag a henys
                  et tunc ad magistrum

        Hic pompabit rex conanus
        REX CONANUS
168   Gelwys yʒof conany*
        mytern yn bryton vyan
        han gvlascor pur yredy
        me a bev ol yn tyan
172   Der avys ov arlyʒy
        mones y fannaf lemmyn
        the duk pen an chevalry
        nesse ʒymmo yn certan
176   par del yv ef

        *MS. Conanus.

Go and come when thou mayest be pleased.
140 All we can, surely eased
Thou shalt be at every time.
Let him go down alone to the chapel.

MERIASEK *in the chapel.*
Jesu, Lord of heaven and the world,
To thee I make my prayer.
144 Jesu, Lord, I beseech thee
Against devils' temptations.
Jesu Christ, keep me always
Loyally to serve thee in my days.
148 Jesu, my body and my spirit,
All my strength and my thoughts
I give to worship thee,
And I pray thee, humble and pure,
152 That I never be on earth
Turned to the lust of this world.

Mary, queen of heaven,
Who fed Christ with thy milk,
156 Mary, upraise (?) thy hand
To the child of knowledge!
Mary sweet, pray with me
That never may the caitiff Devil have
160 Power over me,
Nor the world, my other enemy,
And my flesh is an evil enemy,
Full low I will tame it

164 With watching and with penance.
I would like
To please Christ
In youth and in old age.
And then to the Master.

Here King Conan shall parade.
KING CONAN.
168 I am called Conany,
King in little Britain;
And the country right readily
I possess altogether.
172 By advice of my lords
I would go now
To the Duke, head of chivalry,
Next to me certainly
As he is.

yma maryag galosek
cowsys ȝyn rag meryasek
mergh ȝe vyghtern gallosek
180 nynses brassa yndan nef

PRIMUS DOMINUS

Maryasek yv flogh fur
cortis hag vvel yn sur
drys oll flehys an powma
184 my a lever arlud flour
y terfensa myrgh emperour
ȝy par kefis mara peya

SECUNDUS DOMINUS REGIS

Meriasek yv kerys
188 anotha y ma notyes
mur a ȝadder yn povma
me a leuer ȝyvgh heb flows
ay cowt ny clowys cows
192 moy gracyus flogh yn bysma   [finit

MERIADOCUS

Me agis pesse mester
mar a pewy sur plesijs
mones ȝe dre heb awer
196 ȝe vyras ov ȝas vskys
hav mam kefrys
bedneth ȝyvgh am vestrigy
me a yl lour y bysy
200 genovgh tek yȝof dyskys

MAGISTER

Banneth crist ȝys meriasek
ham benneth pur colonnek
luen os a venegycter
204 yn ov scole ny ve bythqueth
ȝyso gy purwyre cowyth
yn discans nag yn dader
descendit cum armigero et redit ad patrem

MERIADOCUS

Lowena ȝum tas worthy
208 ha reuerens bys bynyȝa
lowena ȝum mam defry
enour ha dader neffra
pesef agys leun vanneth

>   There is a mighty marriage
>   Spoken of to us for Meriasek.
>   A daughter to a mighty sovran.
> 180   There is not a greater under heaven.

FIRST LORD.

>   Meriasek is a wise child :
>   Courteous and humble surely
>   Beyond all the children of this country.
> 184   I say, flower of lords,
>   He would deserve an emperor's daughter
>   For his mate, if she were found.

SECOND KING'S LORD.

>   Meriasek is loved,
> 188   Of him is noted
>   Much of goodness in this country.
>   I say to you, without a flout,
>   Of his comrade I never heard tell.
> 192   The most gracious child in this world !

MERIASEK.

>   I would beseech you, Master,
>   If you would be surely pleased,
>   To [let me] go home without sorrow
> 196   To see my father forthwith
>   And my mother likewise.
>   A blessing to you for my schooling!
>   I can enough beseech it.
> 200   By you well am I taught.

MASTER.

>   Christ's blessing to thee, Meriasek.
>   And my blessing right hearty.
>   Full art thou of blessedness.
> 204   In my school never was there
>   To thee truly a comrade
>   In learning nor in goodness.

He goes down with the squire and returns to his father.

MERIASEK.

>   Joy to my worthy father,
> 208   And reverence for ever !
>   Joy to my mother truly,
>   Honour and goodness!
>   I beseech your full blessing.

14

212 lemmyn grace an spyrys sans
re woloways ov skyans
yma ȝym perfect dyskans
grac the crist pen an eleth

p. 9.

PATER

216 Meryasek welcum yn tre
ham luen vanneth y rof ȝys
mar kyssys ynta spedie
me yv sur ȝe well plesijs
220 an keth trana
marrogyon parusugh wy
haneth omma yredy
mytern connan sur a thua

MATER

224 Meriasek bedneth crist ȝys
ha bedneth ȝe vam neffra
gvyf os the vos welcummys
hag enoris gans henna
228 rag ȝe ȝadder
ahanas vs ȝyn cowsys
du asota mur presijs
dres ol breton : heb awer

CONANUS REX *ad ducem*

232 Reuerens ȝyvg ser duk worthy
par del ovgh corf a galloys
me redeth omma defry
drefen agen bos vnwoys
236 ȝe kestalkye
lowena ȝyvgh arlothes
ha ȝen map ker vs genes
meryasek ov goys nesse

p. 10.

PATER MEREADOCI

240 Wolcum ogh ov lyche worȝy
wolcum ogh omma deffry
wy hag ol agis pobell
ȝe lowenna rag blythan
244 me a vyth yn pur certan
agis gvelas om castell

MATER MEREADOCI

Welcum ogh agan soueran
yn keth plassma pur certan
248 plesijs one agis gwelas*

* MS. gwielas.

212 Now the grace of the Holy Ghost
Hath enlightened my knowledge,
I have perfect learning,
    Thanks to Christ the head of the angels.

FATHER.

216 Meriasek, welcome home,
    And my full blessing I give to thee.
If thou leftest to speed well
    I am surely the better pleased
220   Of that same thing.
Knights, prepare you.
To-night here readily
    King Conan will come.

MOTHER.

224 Meriasek, Christ's blessing to thee,
    And thy mother's blessing ever.
Worthy art thou to be welcomed,
    And honoured therewithal
228   For thy goodness.
Of thee it is told to us,
Pardie, that thou art much praised
    Throughout all Brittany, without grief.

KING CONAN *to the Duke.*

232 Reverence to you, worthy Sir Duke.
    As you are a body of might.
I have come here indeed,
    Because of our being one blood,
236   To talk together.
Joy to you, lady,
And to the dear son that is with thee,
    Meriasek, my nearest blood!

MERIASEK'S FATHER.

240 Welcome are you, my worthy liege!
Welcome are you here indeed,
    You and all your people.
The gladder for a year
244 I shall be very certainly
    To see you in my castle.

MERIASEK'S MOTHER.

Welcome are you, our sovran,
In this same place very certainly
248   Pleased are we to see you.

welcumma* den benary
nefre ny ʒue yn ov chy
kynteffov ʒas am denes

MEREADOCUS

252 Welcum omma lych ryall
del ogh pen ha princypall
dreson ny ol yn tyan
worthy rag cawas reuerens
256 drefen agis governens
rewlys on brays ha byan

REX CONANUS

Gramercy ʒywy warbarth
my a vyn kyns es dybarth
260 muvye omma certan tra
rag dader hag honester
ʒe varyasek heb awer
ow goys nessa

PATER MEREADOCI DUX

264 Ny a vyn purwyr kensa
mones warbarth ʒe ʒybry
dun yn palys ʒe setha
bras ha byan pub huny
268 spencer yv parys pub tra
lauer ʒym del om kerry
ma yllyn mos ʒe lyfya
ov lych gans y arlyʒy

descendunt omnes in placeam

PINCERNA DUCIS BRITANIE

272 Pup tra oma yv parys
an arlythy desethys
bethens genogh meriasek
ny a kergh vytel in chy
276 trompys cleryons wethugh wy
lemen then fest lowenek

MERIADOCUS

Ov arluth lich a esa
omma purguir an kynsa
280 hav thays theragtho inweth
ham mam ger in pen an voys
orlyans duk a galloys
esethugh oma purfeth
284 han arlythy yonk ha loys
ran arak ran aberveth

* MS. welcumma ma.

More welcome man never
Will come into my house,
    Though may come my father that reared me.

MERIASEK.

252 Welcome here, royal liege,
    As you are head and principal
        Over us altogether
    Worthy to receive reverence
256 Because of your governance
        Ruled are we, great and small.

KING CONAN.

Gramercy to you altogether!
I will before separating
260   Move here a certain thing,
For goodness and decency,
To Meriasek, without grief,
    My nearest blood.

MERIASEK'S FATHER THE DUKE.

264 We will, truly, first
    Go together to eat.
Let us come into the palace to sit,
    Great and small, every one,
268 Spencer, is everything ready?
    Tell me as thou lovest me,
That we may go to dine,
    My liege with his lords.

All go down into the open space.

THE SPENCER *of the Duke of Brittany.*

272 Everything here is ready.
Let the lords seated
    Be by you, Meriasek.
We will seek victual within.
276 Trumpets, clarions, blow ye
    Now to the joyous feast!

MERIASEK.

My liege lord shall sit
Here right truly the first.
280   And my father before him also.
And my mother dear at the head of the table.
Orleans, Duke of power,
    Sit ye here perfectly,
284 And the lords, young and gray,
    Part before, part in the middle.

DUX ORLYANS

     Gromercy meryasek wek
     agis norter yv mar dek
288   maythogh keris gans lues
     hagis manerov a plek
     kefrys the letrys ha lek
        parov thyugh in bys nynsues
               Hic mimi ludent melodiam

MERIADOCUS

292 Ov lich kyng bethugh mery
     inweth oll an kyff nywy
        dukis 3urlys marogyon
p. 12.   ov thays hav mam am denys
296 omgersyogh me agis peys
        a luen golon

CONANUS REX

     Gromercy meryasek wek
       mar luen oys a corteysy
300 me ath ra den galosek
       trest am bus pur eredy
     me a wor py kefyth gruek
       neb yv mergh mytern worthy
304 ha gensy y feth tra dek
       maners trefov castylly
     theth tus ha dyso mar plek
     me a leuer pyv ew hy

PATER MERIADOCI DUX

308 Gromercy agen lych da
     mur gras y wothen nefra
       thywy agis bolnogeth
     the greffe y fyen ny
312 y voys maryys eredy
       ha moghheys agen roweth

MATER

     Ny yv plesijs hag a vyn
     boys revlijs drethogh certeyn
316   ha meriasek kekefrys
     ken the vlamya y fyen
     why yv pen agen ehen
       gouerner lich a fur rays

DUKE OF ORLEANS.

    Gramercy, sweet Meriasek,
    Your nurture is so sweet,
288   That you are loved by many,
    And your manners are pleasing
    Likewise to lettered and to layman.
        Peers to you in the world are not.
        Here the mimes shall play a melody.

MERIASEK.

292 My liege lord, be you merry:
    Likewise all shall have gaiety (?),
        Dukes, Earls, Knights.
    My father, and my mother who suckled me,
296 Comfort yourselves, I beseech you,
        From a full heart.

KING CONAN.

    Gramercy, sweet Meriasek,
        So full art thou of courtesy,
300 I will make thee a mighty man,
        Trust have I right readily,
    I know where thou wilt find a wife,
        Who is a worthy king's daughter,
304 And with her will be a fair thing—
        Manors, houses, castles.
    To thy people and thee, if it pleases,
        I will say who she is.

MERIASEK'S FATHER THE DUKE.

308 Gramercy, our good liege!
    Much thanks I give ever
        To you for your wish.
    We should be the stronger
312 Were he married readily,
        And our sway greatened.

THE MOTHER.

    We are pleased and we will
    Be ruled by you certainly,
316   We and Meriasek likewise:
    Otherwise to blame we should be.
    You are head of our tribe,
        Governor, liege of great grace.

p. 13.
MERIADOCUS

320 Ov arluth lich thyugh mur grays
thym agis bolnogeth da
ha na vewy dysplesijs
peseff aragogh omma
324 ov ascusia
wy ham tays hav mam kefrys
ny vanna omry then beys
na domethy benytha

PATER

328 Tav dymmovy meryasek
ty a thommeth ov map wek
the neb arlothes worthy
ha ny a veth the creffa
332 der an maryach benitha
hag ol the lynnyeth defry

MATER

Domethy mar ny reva
tus ara agen scornya
336 meriasek na govs folneth
wath bythqueth in bysma sur
acontis y fus flogh fur
gvyth the hanov da rag meth

MERIADOCUS

340 Na govsogh ger war an beys
benytha ov domethy
the ken forthov sur ov breys
yma syttis eredy

PATER

344 Pan forthov yv an rena
meryasek thym lauer
lemen mar mynnyth dotya
trueth vya ov map ker

p. 14.
MERIADOCUS

348 Na vanna dre grath ihesu
me a leuer ov thays wek
ov bolnogeth purguir yv
rag gorthia crist galosek
352 bones sacris marrek du
an order mar thym a plek
benitha hedre ven byv
me a garse lowenek

MERIASEK.

320 My liege lord, to you much thanks
    For your good will to me.
And be not you displeased.
    I beseech before you all,
324   To excuse me,
You and my father and my mother likewise.
I will not give myself to the world,
    Nor marry me ever.

THE FATHER.

328 Be silent for me, Meriasek!
Thou wilt marry thee, my sweet son,
    To some worthy lady,
And we shall be the stronger
332 Through the marriage ever,
    And all thy lineage surely.

THE MOTHER.

If he do not marry him
Folk will scorn us.
336   Meriasek, speak not folly.
Still ever in this world surely
Thou hast been accounted a wise child,
    Keep thy good name for shame!

MERIASEK.

340 Speak ye not a word in the world
    Ever to marry me.
To other ways surely my mind
    Is set already.

THE FATHER.

344 What ways are those?
    Meriasek, say to me.
Now if thou wilt dote
    It would be a pity, my dear son.

MERIASEK.

348 I will not through Jesu's sake,
    I say, my sweet father.
My will right truly is
    To worship mighty Christ.
352 To be consecrated a knight of God,
    Of the order that pleases me,
Ever as long as I may be alive
    I should like gladly.

CONANUS REX

356 Pan othem vs thysogy
 a naha roweth an beys
ha ty genys eredy
 abarth tays ha mam kefrys
360 nynsyv worschyp theth ehen
the conseyt in pur certen
 ov map preder forthov guel

PATER

Ellas ov map meryasek
364 bythqueth ʒ° gora ʒ° scole
ty rum gruk vy morethek
 a skyans prest nynsus ole
ty the desky
368 ny a veth scorne ol an pov
pytha an tyr han trevov
us thynny heb feladov
 mar ny vynnyth domethy

MERIADOCUS

372 A das gruegh crist agis er
 bo ens y then goys nessa
pythellens nefre numduer
 ganse ny vanna melya

p. 15.
CONANUS REX

376 Me a greys sur meryasek
nagote re skyansek
 gul erbyn the days hath vam
ny won pendrussis in scoll
380 a thader byth nynsus oll
 ov map ty the dysky tam

MERIADOCUS

Crist indelma a leuer
 ov sywa neb a vynna.
384 forsakyans byen ha muer
teryov trefov an bysma
y days hay vam
y nessevyn hay cothmans
388 hag eff a gvayn roov cans
bys benitha an bevnans
 in neff awartha heb nam

warlergh sen luk
392 me an kyff lell
thyugh in awell
screfis yv kepar del yn gruk

KING CONAN.

356 What need is there to thee
    Of refusing the sway of the world?
And thou (well-) born surely
    On side of father and of mother likewise.
360 It is not respect to thy tribe
Thy conceit very certainly.
    My son, think of better ways.

THE FATHER.

Alas, my son Meriasek,
364   That thou ever wert put to school!
Thou hast made me sorrowful.
    Of knowledge there is now nought at all
    To teach thee.
368 We shall be the scorn of all the country.
Where will go the land and the villages
That are ours without fail,
    If thou wilt not marry thee?

MERIASEK.

372 O father, make Christ your heir,
    Or let them go to the nearest blood,
Whither they may go concerns me not:
    With them I will not meddle.

KING CONAN.

376 I believe surely, Meriasek,
Thou art not overwise
    To act against thy father and thy mother.
I know not what thing thou didst in school:
380 Of any goodness there is not,
    My son, that thou learnest aught.

MERIASEK.

Christ thus saith:
    Whoso would follow me
384 Let him forsake small and great,
Lands, houses of this world,
    His father and his mother,
His kinsmen and his friends,
388 And he shall gain a hundred gifts
For ever of life
    In heaven above without fault.

According to Saint Luke
392   I will find it loyally
    For you in the gospel:
It is written as he made it.

CONANUS REX

      Pyraga na ylta gy
396   domethy oma in beys
      del fue lius den worthy
      ha gans y du purgerys
      ran sens in neff
400   genes ythoff dysplesijs
      gul theth tus bones gesijs
      kemeres duen ha greff

MERIADOCUS

      Rag kerense crist an neff
404   me a vyn agis pesy
      na gemerre denv' greff
      na duwen am govys vy

CONANUS

p. 16.   Coyl ortheff vy meryasek
408   me ath desyr dre tekter
      bonyl ty a feth edrek
      open dys me a leuer
      preder inta
412   the days ha me ny a yl
      statya an tyr dyogeyl
      mar mynen the den areyl
      na thefo dis benytha

416   In vrna avel begyer
      ty a veth sur heb awer
      sensys in pov
      hag ol the kerens blamys
420   ellas mar pethen schamys
      wath preder a guel forthov

MERIADOCUS

      Mar peth stat the den arel
      grueys annotho dyogel
424   ov liche wek me yv plesijs
      henna thymo ny ra greff
      mar calla cafus tyr neff
      fy the plos lustis an beys

CONANUS REX

428   Mur a varth yv genevy
      pan fyghythrychyth an beys
      bewe pel ny elte gy
      heb peth na denvyth genys

KING CONAN.

Why canst thou not
396 Marry thee here in the world,
As were many worthy men,
  And by them God was purely loved?
By the saints in heaven,
400 With thee I am displeased,
To cause thy folk to be jeered,
  To take dole and grief!

MERIASEK.

For love of the Christ of the heaven
404 I will beseech you
That no one take grief
  Or dole because of me.

CONAN.

Listen to me, Meriasek,
408 I desire thee through fairness,
Or else thou wilt have repentance,
  Openly I say to thee.
     Consider well.
412 Thy father and I, we can
Limit the land, certainly,
If we will, to another man,
  That it come not to thee ever.

416 Then as a beggar
Thou wilt be surely without grief
  Held in the country,
And all thy kinsmen blamed.
420 Alas, if we be shamed!
  Yet think of better ways.

MERIASEK.

If an estate to another man be
Made thereof certainly,
424 My sweet liege, I am well pleased.
That to me will not cause grief.
If I can find heaven's land
  Fye on the foul lusts of the world!

KING CONAN.

428 Much marvel have I
  When thou *fyest* the riches of the world.
Live long thou couldst not
  Without wealth, nor (could) any one born.

		dre rychyth ha chevalry
	432	dre rychyth ha chevalry
		den a veth degemorys
		inban in meske arlythy
		ha ganse prest enorys

p. 17.
432 dre rychyth ha chevalry
    den a veth degemorys
    inban in meske arlythy
    ha ganse prest enorys

p. 17.   436 Der y peth grueys den ryel
             ha gorys then stat vhel
             pendra dal an bohosek
             kyn fo brays y devethyans
         440 ef a dryk pennoth in hans
             nynguel an rych galosek

MERIADOCUS

         Na govsugh a chevalry
         byth moy rychys numdur man
    444 tollys yv lues huny
         der peyth an beys yn certan

         A dyves del redyn ny
         rych lour o in pup termen
    448 py theth y ena defry
         the yfern then peyn belen

         Lasser o den bohosek
         a thuk lavyr pur anwek
    452   abraham an reseves
         pan o marov dotho eff
         hag in y hascra heb greff
             in golovder an gvythes

CONANUS REX

[*surrexit circa placeam*

    456 Serys kemerugh in ban
         drog yv gena doys oma
         a meryasek guas belan
         dar soposia a reta
    460   den rych nefra
         mones then neff da ny yl
         me a greys dotyys oys vyl
             ha muscugys rum ena

p. 18.   ### MERIADOCUS

    464 An scriptor* leferel grua
         den rych then neff dyogel
         mage fur weyll yv dotha
         moys avel capel gorhel
    468   der trov nasweth

* MS. scripctor.

432 Through riches and chivalry
    A man will be accepted
Above amongst lords,
    And by them quickly honoured,

436 Through his wealth made a royal man,
And put to the high station.
    What thing is the poor man worth?
Though great be his lineage,
440 He will remain bareheaded down below:
    Him the rich powerful (man) will not see.

MERIASEK.

Talk you not of chivalry:
Never more do riches concern me:
444 Deceived is many a one
    By the wealth of the world certainly.

Of Dives as we read
Rich enough was he at every time.
448 Whither went his soul really?
    To hell, to the villanous pain.

Lazarus was a poor man
Who bore labour right unsweet:
452   Abraham received him,
When he was dead, unto him,
And in his bosom, without grief,
    Kept him in light.

KING CONAN.

[he rose (and walked) round the open space.

456 Sirs, get you up.
    I am sorry that I came here.
O Meriasek, villanous fellow,
    Dost thou suppose
460   That a rich man never
Can go to the good heaven?
I believe thou art doting vilely
    And distracted, by my soul!

MERIASEK.

464 The scripture doth say
    A rich man to the heaven certainly,
As great a labour is it for him
    To go as (for) a ship's cable
468   To go through a needle's eye.

       henna gans y destrowhy
       a yl boys spedijs defry
       indellan den rych besy
472 the vohosogyan guet ry
          in cheryte part ath peth

CONANUS REX

       Farwel ser duk
       re crist am gruk
476   the vap yv fol
       ganso omgrua
       ov herth oma
         galles the col
480   ham lafuryans
       the lee nefra
       war ov ena
         me an car in ov bevnans   [*finit*
           [*tranceat conanus*

PATER

484 Ov arluth dywy mur grays
       ov profia dotho dadder
       ellas ragos ov map rays
       na vennyth dre onester
488   bones revlys
       yma pensevyk an gluas
       dysplesijs purguir genas
         the days hath vam kekefrys

MERIADOCUS

492 Kynthogh geneff dysplesijs
       ythyv ol am anvoth vy
       trest ambus boys acordys
       orth ihesu crist a vercy
496 agys bannothov kefrys
       tays ha mam thymmo gruegh ry
       me a vyn mones uskys
       wath de thesky dadder moy
500 rag kerense an drensis
       na temptyogh vy the foly

p. 19.   ### PATER

       Inter dula du avan
       ov map gruaff the kemynna
504 kemer the rovle the honan
       gul nahen me ny alla
       ov banneth dis   [*finit*

That by destroying it
May be sped certainly.
So the rich busy man,
472 Take care to give to the poor
In charity part of thy wealth.

KING CONAN.

Farewell, Sir Duke,
By Christ who made me
476 Thy son is mad.
By him is caused
My journey here
To go to loss,
480 And my labouring.
To lessen thee ever,
On my soul,
I shall like it in my life.

[Let Conan pass off.

THE FATHER.

484 My lord, much thanks to you
Showing goodness to him.
Alas for thee, my son of grace!
Thou wilt not through decency
488 Be ruled.
The prince of the country is
Displeased right truly with thee,
Thy father and thy mother likewise.

MERIASEK.

492 Though you are displeased with me,
It is all against my will.
Trust have I that I am in accord
With Jesus Christ of mercy.
496 Your blessings likewise,
Father and mother, give ye to me.
I will go straightway
Yet to learn more goodness.
500 For love of the Trinity
Tempt me not to folly.

THE FATHER.

Between the hands of God above,
My son, I do commend thee.
504 Take thine own rule:
Do ought else I cannot:
My blessing to thee!

MATER

  Amen prest ham banneth vy
508 ov map dore thym the vay
  morethek assoff defry
    ov tyberth sur the orthys   [*finit*
    [*her meriasek weryth a prest ys gown*

  Hic episcopus kernov hic pompabit
  Me yv escop in breten
512 in conteth gelwys kernov
  mur yv ov rays pup termen
  cowethe thym yv tanov
   parlet mar stovt
516 prence war an vebyen lyen
  nynsus in breten vyen
   ov parov purguir heb dovt

MERIADOCUS

  Ser epscop thyugh lowena
520 agis pesy y fanna
   a ry dymmo vy ordys
  pronter boys me a garsa
  corff ihesu thy venystra
524 mar myn ov descans servya
   genogh pan ven apposijs
    [*descendit episcopus kernov in placeam*

EPISCOPUS KERNOV

  Wolcum oma meryasek
  me re glowes ov map wek
   ahanes covs mur thadder
528 ry dys ordys me a vyn
  in hanov ihesu lemyn*
   sacrys gena betheth suer
       [*genuflectit*
532 cryst roy dis in pup termyn
   omguythe prest in glander

CECUS

  Banneth du genogh tus vays
  me yv dal na yl guelays
536 regh dym agis alusyon
  ha ragogh y raff pesy
  the.crist ihesu a vercy
   selwadour an crustunyon

* MS. lemys.

THE MOTHER.

    Amen ever, and my blessing.
508 My son, give me thy kiss!
    Sad am I indeed
        At parting surely from thee.
            [*Here Meriasek wears a priest's gown.*

Here the Bishop of Kernou shall parade.

    I am bishop in Brittany
512   In a county called Kernou.
    Great is my grace always:
      Comrades are few to me
        A prelate so proud,
516 A prince over the sons of reading.
    There are not in little Britain
        My peers right truly without doubt.

MERIASEK.

    Sir Bishop, joy to you!
520 You I will beseech
        To give me orders.
    A priest I should like to be,
    Jesu's body to administer it
524 If my learning will serve
        By you when I may be appointed.

[*The Bishop of Kernou goes down into the open space.*

THE BISHOP OF KERNOU.

    Welcome here, Meriasek,
    I have heard, my sweet son,
528   Of thee much good spoken.
    Give thee orders I will.
    In Jesu's name now
        Consecrated by me thou wilt be surely.
            [*He kneels.*
532 May Christ grant to thee alway
        To keep thyself ever in purity!

A BLIND MAN.

    God's blessing (be) with you, good folk!
    I am a blind man who cannot see.
        Give me your alms!
536 And for you I will pray
    To Christ Jesu of mercy,
        The Saviour of the Christians.

KALUS*

540 Me yv inweth efrethek
am esely podrethek
gyllys in gron
schanlour y halla kerthes
544 me a pysse kynweres
the orthugh a luen golon

MERIADOCUS
                                                    [*genuflectit*

Ihesu arluth me ath peys
gueres an den ma yv dal
548 ihesu crist mytern glorijs
roy y syght dotho heb fal
ihesu arluth luen a rays
inweth sav an den arall
552 ihesu arluth map guirhays
dyswe the gallus ryall
lemen oma
in nomine patris et filij
556 virtu crist rebo yly
a dus gvan dyugh in torma

CECUS

Cryst ihesu dys ren tala
me a weyl lemen inta
560 benyges the peyadov†
me a wor bones oma
ha glorijs prest the geryov

p 21.
KALUS

Ha me yv sawys purdek
564 neb a fue sur efrethek
lues blethen in bysma
galer numbus
grays the ihesus
568 ha then denma   [*finit*
                          [*tranceat in placeam*

EPISCOPUS KERNOV

Meryasek dyso reuerans
keris gans du a seluans
gon guir lemen the vota
572 me ath peys trych genevy
ha sur nefre thysogy
me ny falla

---

* Leg. χωλός or claudus?
† The original scribe wrote *piiadov*, but this is crossed out and *peyadov* written over it.

A CRIPPLE.

540 I am also maimed,
    My limbs rotten
        Become in a heap.
    Scarce enough can I walk.
544 I would beseech a common cure*
        From you with a full heart.

MERIASEK.   [*He kneels.*

    Lord Jesu, I beseech thee,
        Cure this man who is blind!
548 Jesu Christ, glorious King,
        Give his sight to him without fail!
    Lord Jesu, full of grace,
        Heal the other man likewise.
552 Lord Jesu, son of a virgin,
        Display thy royal power
            Now here.
In nomine Patris et Filii.
556 May Christ's virtue be a salve,
        O weak folk, to you this turn!

THE BLIND MAN.

    Christ Jesu repay it to thee!
    I see now well.
560   That thy prayer blessed
    Is here, I know,
    And glorious ever thy words!

THE CRIPPLE.

    And I am healed right well,
564 (I) who was surely maimed.
        Many years in this world
    Sickness I had.
    Thanks to Jesus
568   And to this man!

BISHOP OF KERNOU.

    Meriasek, reverence to thee!
    Loved by God of salvation
        I know truly now that thou art.
572 I pray thee dwell with me,
    And thee surely never
        Will I fail.

---

* A cure in common with the blind man.

MERIADOCUS

  Ser epscop dywy mur grays
576 lafurya sur the ken gluas
   avesijs off alemma
  banneth genogh oll an sens
  han sansesov myns del ens
580   hagis compny ben(itha)

CROCIFER EPISCOPI KERNOV

  Banneth du thys meryasek
  ny a vya lowenek
   a mynnes oma tre(ga)
584 erbyn the voth
  thynny ny goth
   sur the lettya
    [ascendit episcopus kernov

MERIADOCUS

  Marners dorsona dywy
588 the kernov mar segh defry
   mones genogh y carsen
  the ry nammur me numbus
  sav me a beys crist ihesus
592   thagys socra pup termen

p. 22.
NAVTA

  Wolcum oys genen dremas
  ny ath wor the pen an gluas
   dre voth du kyn pen sythen
    [ascendit in navim
596 dus aberveth oma scon
  hav marners tennogh dyson
   an goyl thym in ban lemen

SERVUS NAVTE

  At eve fast bys in top
600 nov mata make fast the rop
   yma an gvyns ov wetha
  han mor ov terevel fol
  me a greys kellys on ol
604   ha buthys pur guir oma

(NAV)TA

  A gony pan vuen genys
  warbarth ny a veth kellys
   ens pup the ȝeys thy gela
608 nynsus oma forth nahen
  ahanan ny vev vn den
   tru gony doys then pletma

MERIASEK.

Sir Bishop, to you much thanks
576   To go onward surely to another country
    I am advised hence.
The blessing of all the saints
And the saintesses as many as there are
580   With you and your company ever!

THE BISHOP OF KERNOU'S CROZIER-BEARER.

God's blessing to thee, Meriasek!
We should be glad
    If thou wouldst stay here.
584 Against thy will
It behoves us not,
    Surely, to hinder thee.
        [*The Bishop of Kernou goes up.*

MERIASEK.

Mariners, a blessing to you!
588 To Cornwall if you are going now
    I should like to go with you.
To give I have not much,
But I will beseech Christ Jesus
592   To succour you always.

THE SAILOR.

Welcome art thou with us, honest man.
We will put thee to the end of the country,
    Through God's will, before a week's end.
        [*He goes up into the ship.*
596 Come thou in here at once;
And, my mariners, quickly haul
    The sail up for me now!

THE SAILOR'S SERVANT.

Lo it is quite up to the top.
600 Now mate, make the rope fast.
    The wind is blowing,
And the sea rising madly.
I believe we are all lost
604   And drowned right truly here.

THE SAILOR.

Ah woe is us that we were born!
Together we shall be lost!
    Let every one go to confess to his fellow.
608 Here there is no other way.
Of us not one man will live.
    Sad, woe is us, to come to this plight!

MEREADOCUS

   A bethugh a confort da
612 crist agen gueres a ra
    ha me a vyn y pesy
   mar pe y voth indella
   na rella den peryllya
616 in tyr na mor in bysma
    mar creya war crist ha my

p. 23.   ### NAVTA

   Meryasek gorthys reby
   drethos ol sawys on ny
620 a peryl sur in torma
   kegy in tyr a dremas
   in kernov the ihesu gras
    theth desyr ty re dufa
       [*descendit in cornubia*

MEREADOCUS

624 The ihesu rebo grasseys
   the pov astrange devethys
    me yv oma
   kerthes in tyr me a vyn
628 ihesu arluth cuff colyn
    the teller da rum gedya
   gorthya crist ker may hallen
    han werhes flour maria

632 Devethys off in tereth
    ha squeth me yv ov kerthes
   maria mam ha maghteth
    mara sus dis chy na plaes
636 oges oma
   grua ov gedya vy bys dy
   rag mur y carsen defry
   guthel thymmo oratry
640 in herw⁺ chy maria
   densa lowena dywhy
    pan a chapel yv henna

p. 24.   ### DOMESTICUS

   Me a leuer dys dyson
644 chapel maria cambron
    gelwys yv an keth chyna
   a py le in govynnyth
   lauer henna dymo weyth
648 a cow⁺ da

MERIASEK.

  O be ye of good comfort!
612 Christ will save us,
   And I will beseech him,
  If his will be thus
  That no one shall be in danger
616 On land nor sea in this world
   If he cry on Christ and me.

THE SAILOR.

Meriasek, worshipped be thou!
Through thee we all are saved
620   From peril surely this turn.
Go thou on land, O honest man!
In Cornwall, thanks to Jesu,
  According to thy desire thou hast come.
       [*He lands in Cornwall.*

MERIASEK.

624 To Jesu be thanks!
  To a strange country come
   Am I here.
  Walk on land I will,
628 May Lord Jesu, dear heart,
   To a good place guide me,
  That I may worship dear Christ,
   And Mary, the flower of maidens!

632 I am come on land,
  And weary am I walking.
  Mary, mother and maiden,
   If thou hast a house or place
636   Near this,
  Do guide me even unto it,
  For much I should like really
  To make me an oratory
640   Near Mary's house.
  Kind (sir), joy to you!
   What chapel is that?

A HOUSEHOLD SLAVE.

  I will tell thee at once.
644 Mary of Camborne's chapel,
   That same house is called.
  From what place dost thou ask it?
  Say that to me yet,
648   O good fellow!

MEREADOCUS

    A vreten sur then povma
    dresen mor me re dufa
        del vynnas du ov desky
652 hag omma gul me a vyn
    ryb chapel maria wyn
        thym oratry
    us dour omma in oges
656 rag nefre nahen dewes
        nynsa om ganov defry

DOMESTICUS

    Dour yv mur ascant oma
    reys yv polge da alema
660   mones certen thy gerhes
    corff bo gvyn a cafen vy
    dour ny effsen eredy
        na ny vye rag ov lees

MERIADOCUS

664 North yst then chapel omma
    me a vyn mos the guandra
        dour thymmo sur rag weles

        Tranceat ad pratum
            [*genuflectit*

p. 25.   Ihesu arluth me ath peys
    668 ihesu gront dovyr a wur speys
        ihesu dymmo der the graes
    del russys kyns the moyseys
        an men cales
          [*her ye wyll sprynggyth vp water*

DOMESTICUS

672 Densa benyges reby
    dovr oma ov try thynny
        mar dek thagen confortya
    kerys oys purguir gans du
676 prevys open oma yv
        the ragon in teller ma

HOMO FEBRICOSUS

    A thu ellas pendrama
    lader cleves thym yma
680   a veth gelwys an seson

MERIASEK.

From Brittany surely to this country
Over the sea I have come,
    As God teaching me willed.
And here I will make,
By blessed Mary's chapel,
    For me an oratory.
Is there water here at hand?
For never other drink
    Shall go into my mouth surely.

THE HOUSEHOLD SLAVE.

Water is very scanty here.
Needful is it a good bit hence
    To go certainly to fetch it.
Ale or wine if I could get,
Water I would not drink readily,
    Nor would it be for my good.

MERIASEK.

North-east of the chapel here
I will go to wander,
    Water for me surely to seek.

Let him go across to the meadow.
                    [He kneels.

Jesu, Lord, I beseech thee,
Jesu, grant water in great abundance,
    Jesu, to me through thy grace
As thou didst before for Moses
    From the hard rock.
        [Here the well springeth up water.

THE HOUSEHOLD SLAVE.

Kind (sir), blessed be thou,
Bringing here to us water
    So fair to comfort us!
Loved art thou right truly by God,
It is clearly proven here
    Before us in this place.

A FEVER-PATIENT.

O God, alas, what thing is it?
A thief of a disease I have,
    Which is called the season.

```
            ganso me ambeth schorys
            pup deth nansyv lues mys
                rag peyn feynt yv ov colon

                    CONTRACTUS
        684 Me yv efrethek heb fal
            du thym a sevya mal
                appeua marov an beys
            yma tregys in cambron
        688 den ov cul merclys dyson
                guel yv dyn moys dy us(kys)
            hay besy a luen colon
                thynny ny guthel guereys
                                    transit ad meriadocum
```

p. 26.
```
                    HOMO FEBRICOSUS
        692 Lowene dys meriasek
            ny yv dev then bohosek
                me grefijs gans an febyr
            han keth den ma sur yv mans
        696 na nyl susten na pegans
                ny yllen dendyl the guir
            grua gueres dynny dyblans
                rag kerense ihesu ker

                    MERIADOCUS [genuflectit
        700 Ihesu arluth neff han beys
                yehes dywy re grontya
            ihesu arluth me ath peys
                lemmen sav an keth tusma
        704 maria mam luen a rays
                peys theth vap arluth ragtha
            maria mam ha guerhays
                gueres ov pesy gena
        708 sevugh inban a tus vays
                fetel omglowugh omma

                    CONTRACTUS
            Gorthyans the crist me yv sav
            yagh yv ov corff ham garrov
        712     kerthes heb greff me a yll          [finit

                    HOMO FEBRICOSUS
            ha me yv yagh the crist grays
            meryasek wek luen a rays
                fortyn du dotho ny fyl
        716 thy worthya ny yv senses
                hag a vyn awos peryl              [finit
```

With me I have marks
Every day, now it is many months.
   For pain faint is my heart.

A CRIPPLE.

684 I am maimed without fail—
God for me has raised a desire
   If (only) I were dead from the world!
There is dwelling in Camborne
688 A man working miracles at once.
   Better is for us to go to him quickly
And to beseech him with a full heart
   To help us.

He goes across to Meriasek.

THE FEVER-PATIENT.

692 Joy to thee, Meriasek!
We are two poor men,
   I grieved with the fever,
And this same man surely is maimed.
696 Neither sustenance nor goods
   Can we earn of a truth.
Help us clearly
   For love of dear Jesu.

MERIASEK [*kneels.*

700 May Jesu, Lord of heaven and of the earth,
   Grant healing to you!
Lord Jesu, I beseech thee
   Now save this same folk!
704 Mary Mother full of grace,
   Beseech thy Son (the) Lord for them.
Mary Mother and Virgin,
   Help, beseeching with me!
708 Rise ye up, O good folk,
   How do you feel yourselves here?

THE CRIPPLE.

Worship to Christ! I am whole.
Healed are my body and my legs.
712   I can walk without grief.

THE FEVER-PATIENT.

And I am cured, thanks to Christ!
Meriasek, sweet, full of grace,
   God's fortune to him will not fail.
716 To honour him we are bound,
   And will, notwithstanding peril.

MERIADOCUS

  Grassegh the crist a tus vays
   adar trav⁺ dymmo vy
720 omma lemen fondya plays
   dre voth ihesu a vercy
    sur me a vyn

p. 27.
   awose helme eglos
724 the worthya crist deth ha nos
   y feth omma thum porpos
    ryb chapel maria wyn

MORB[OS]US

  Ellas ellas pendrama
728 in ov fays cothys yma
   cleves vthyk num car den
  in ca[m]bron me re gloways
  yma prest vn methek brays
732 ov sawya tus in certen
  me a vyn moys the verays
   gul gueres dymo mar men
         [*ad meriadocum*

  Lowene dis meryasek
736 thymo vy den bohosek
   awoys crist lemen gueres
  in ov fays cleves yma
  mana car tus an beysma
740 neb lues sur ov gueles

MERIADOCUS [*genuflectit*

  Arluth neff reth weresa
  naamam kyns es helma
   a sawyas an cleves mur
744 gans dour y raff the golhy
  ihesu crist du a vercy
   theth gueres mar tuth an nur

p. 28.
DOMESTICUS

  Ty then gylleth boys lowen
748 sawys tek oys in certen
   grasse the meryasek wek
  rag eff yv lenwys a grays
  ha kerys gans du a rays
752 del welyn letrys ha lek   [*finit*

MORB[OS]US

  Meryasek dywhy mur grays
  me a beys crist luen a rays

MERIASEK.

Give thanks to Christ, O good folk,
  Say nothing to me.
Here now found a place,
  Through the will of Christ of mercy,
    Surely I will.
After this, a church,
For worshipping Christ day and night,
Shall be here, to my purpose,
  By holy Mary's chapel.

A SICK MAN.

Alas, alas, what thing is this?
On my face is fallen
  A frightful disease, no one loves me.
In Camborne I have heard
There is now a great leech
  Healing folk certainly.
I will go to see
  If he will cure me.
                              [To Meriasek.

Joy to thee, Meriasek,
To me, a poor man,
  For Christ's sake now help.
In my face is a disease,
So that the folk of this world love not,
  Not many surely, to see me.

MERIASEK *[kneels.*

May Heaven's Lord help thee!
Naaman before this
  He healed of the great disease.
With water I do wash thee:
Jesu Christ, God of mercy,
  To help thee if he has come on the earth.

THE HOUSEHOLD SLAVE.

Thou, O man, mayst be joyful.
Well healed art thou certainly,
  Thank sweet Meriasek.
For he is filled with grace,
And loved by God of worth,
  As we see, lettered and lay.

THE SICK MAN.

Meriasek, to you much thanks!
I beseech Christ full of grace

    in neff thywhy ren tala
756 han wyrhes maria splan
    du assus lues den gvan
    sawys genogh in bysma   *[tranceat*
    [hic meriadocus expectat apud cambron

 hic tevdarus pompabit
    Tevdar me a veth gelwys
760 arluth regnijs in kernov
    may fo mahum enorys
     ov charg yv heb feladov
     oges ha pel
764 penag a worthya ken du
    y astev peynys glu
     hag inweth mernans cruel

     NUNCIUS
    Heyl dyugh ser a[r]luth tevdar
768 yma gena nowothov
    sav ny vethe sur heb mar
     y covsel thyugh gans ganov
     na vethe nes
772 del won inta
    war ov ena
     ny veth ov les

p. 29.   TEVDARUS
    Pyv an iovle us warfethys
776 lauer thymmo ty lorden
    ay covs ty falge negethys
     dar ny glov an plos iovden
    covs vnw ty bothosek
780 covs myscheff yth vryonsen
    ay covs ty map molothek
     an iovl rebo the worfen

     NUNCIUS
    Yma oma in penw
784 nebes a weyst the carnebre
    vn pronter ov cuthel guyth
     sawya tus dal in bysme
     bother ha mans
788 ha pup cleves ol in beys
    a thu ny vyn boys covsis
     mas a crist a thuk mernans
    pan o marov daserrys
792 y methe bue the vevnans

    In heaven to you may he pay it,
756 And the Virgin Mary bright.
   Pardie, there are many weak men
    Healed by you in this world. [*Let him go off.*
    [*Here Meriasek waits at Camborne.*

    Here Teudar shall parade.

   Teudar I am called,
760   Lord reigning in Cornwall.
   That Mahound be honoured
    Is my charge without fail,
     Near and far.
764 Whosoever worship another god,
   They shall have keen pains,
    And likewise a cruel death.

    A MESSENGER.

   Hail to you, Sir Lord Teudar!
768   With me are news,
   But it would not be safe without doubt
    To say them to you with a mouth
     That should be nearer.
772 As I know well,
   Upon my soul,
    It will not be my advantage.

    TEUDAR.

   What the devil is it that has happened?
776   Tell to me, thou lurdane.
   Ah, speak, thou false rascal!
    Ruin! the dirty scoundrel will not hear.
   Speak (at) once, thou beggar!
780   Speak! mischief in thy throat!
   Ah, speak, thou son accursed!
    May the devil be thy end!

    THE MESSENGER.

   There is here in Penwyth,
784   Somewhat west of Carnbrea,
   A priest doing a work,
    Healing blind folk in this world,
     Deaf and maimed,
788 And every disease in the world.
   Of [thy] god he will not that there be a thought,
    But of Christ who died.
   When he was dead, raised,
792   He says that he was, to life.

TEVDARUS

    Out govy rag galarov
      py dol an iovle ythama
    out govy na vuff marov
796   kyns doys a dor ov dama
      govi rag schame
    sovdoryan duen alemma
    may hallen ganso rekna
800   the develys name

PRIMUS MILES

    Ov arluth genogh ny a
    me re glowes an denna
      nansyv mysyov tremenys
p. 30. 804 tus dal eff a ra sawya
    ha tus vother mageta
      inweth gul dethe cloweys   [*finit*

SECUNDUS MILES

    Tevdar dyugh me a leuer
808 an keth denna grueys yv muer
      purguir yn pov
    mar ny vethe chastijs
    a vahum ny veth sensys
812   moy es ky heb feladov

TEVDARUS [*descendit*

    Duen ny in kerth
    gans mur a nerth
      ov marogyon
816 py ma tregys
    thym leferys
      bethyns dyson

NUNCIUS

    Sur me an guel
820 arluth ryel
      enos in plen
    mes an chapel
    pur thyogel
824   doys a ra len

TEVDARUS

    Ty bagcheler treyl war tuma
    the hanov thym lafara
      quik hath cregyans

TEUDAR.

Out, woe is me, for sorrows!
What devil's hole am I in?
Out, woe is me that I was not dead
796   Before coming from my mother's womb!
        Woe is me! for shame!
Soldiers, let us come hence
That we may reckon with him.
800   The devil's name!

FIRST SOLDIER.

My lord, we will go with you.
I have heard of this man,
    Now there are months past.
804 Blind folk he doth heal,
And deaf folk as well,
    Also he maketh them to hear.

SECOND SOLDIER.

Teudar, to you I say
808 That same man is made great,
    Right truly in the country.
If he be not chastised
Of Mahound there will not be thought
812   More than a hound without fail.

TEUDAR [*descends*.

Let us come away
With much of strength,
    My knights.
816 Where is he dwelling?
Said to me
    Let it be forthwith.

THE MESSENGER.

Surely I see him,
820 Lord royal,
    There in the plain.
Out of the chapel
Right certainly
824   He doth come loyally.

TEUDAR.

Thou bachelor, turn on this side!
Thy name to me tell
    Quick, and thy belief

	828	gothfes henna
		sur a vanna
		hath devethyans

p. 31.
MERIADOCUS

	Meryasek yv ov hanov
832	sevys a lyne conany
	in crist ihesu caradov
	ytheseff prest ov cresy
	y vos lel du
836	genys ay vam maria
	ha hy maght^t aywosa
	helma ov cregyans ythyv

TEVDARUS

	Sevys oys a woys worthy
840	meryasek beth avysyys
	rag dovt cafus velyny
	na govs tra na fue guelys
	me a leuer
844	erbyn reson yv in beys
	heb hays gorryth thymo creys
	bones flogh vyth concevijs
	in breys benen heb awer

MERIADOCUS

848	Nynsesos ov attendya
	an laha del vya reys
	omma an genegygva
	a ihesu crist war an beys
852	hay pascyon ker
	avel hovle der weder a
	heb y terry del wylsta
	indella crist awartha
856	a thuth in breys maria
	heb mostye iunt v^t in suyr
	der an sperys sans kerra
	concevijs y fue the guir

p. 32.
TEVDARUS

860	Na wyle gene flatra
	kynfes nefre ov clattra
	the ihesu ythese tays
	mage lel avel y vam
864	nynsus ger guir malbe dam
	wath in ol the daryvays

828 Know that
Surely I would,
And thy race.

MERIASEK.

Meriasek is my name,
832   Raised from Conan's line.
In Christ Jesu the loveable
   Am I ever believing.
     That he is true God
836 Born of his Mother Mary,
And she a maiden notwithstanding;
   This is my belief.

TEUDAR.

Raised art thou of worthy blood.
840   Meriasek, be advised,
For fear of getting disgrace,
   Speak not aught that has not been seen,
     I say.
844 Against reason it is in the world,
Without a man's seed, believe me,
That a child should ever be conceived
   In a woman's womb, without grief.

MERIASEK.

848 Thou art not considering
   The law as need should be,
Of the birth here
   Of Jesus Christ on the world,
852   And his dear Passion.
As (the) sun goes through glass
Without breaking it as thou seest,
So Christ above
856 Went into Mary's womb
   Without defiling any joint surely.
Through the Holy, dearest Spirit
   He was conceived, of a truth.

TEUDAR.

860 Seek not to talk with me.
Though thou wert for ever clattering
   To Jesus there was a father
Just as well as his mother.
864 There is not a true word, malbe dam,
   Yet in all thy declaration.

MERIADOCUS

  Du avan prest o y days
  a cothfes y attendya
868 rag prenna adam hay hays
   doys y fynnas then bysma
  mernans tyn eff a porthas
   eneff map den gruk sawya
872 ese in colmen satnas
  eff as dros the lowena

TEVDARUS

  Marso du avan y days
   me a leuer meryasek
876 eff a alse der y rays
   selwel rych ha bohosek
   heb boys marov
  ath daryvas schame ythyv
880 pan othem o the vap du
   boys lethys avel carov

MERIADOCUS

  Der pegh adam agen tays
  eff hay lynnyeth o dampnys
884 sav an devgys a vynnays
   arta y vones prennys
   the saluascon
  an map a fue concevijs
888 ha densis a kemereys
  rag na ylly an devsys
   gothe pasconn

p. 33.
TEVDARUS

  Ny thue les agen argya
892 kyn feny oma vyketh
  meryasek crist denaha
   ha the cothmen me a veth
   may fo guelys
896 epscop worthy me ath ra
  chyff peb les oll an povma
  na moy me ny deserya
   mas gorthya mahum pup preys

MERIADOCUS

900 Ima guel forth es honna
  grua thegy crist ker gorthya
   ken maner kyllys os suir

MERIASEK.

    God above was his father.
    Thou oughtest to consider it.
868 To redeem Adam and his seed
    He would come to this world.
    Sharp death he bore:
    Man's soul he saved
872 Which was in Satan's bond.
    He brought it to joy.

TEUDAR.

    If God above was his father
    I say, Meriasek,
876 He could through his grace
    Have saved rich and poor,
    Without being dead.
    Of thy assertion shame is!
880 What need was there for God's son
    To be slain like a hart?

MERIASEK.

    Through the sin of Adam our father
    He and his lineage were damned,
884 But the Godhead wished
    Again that he should be redeemed
    To salvation.
    The Son was conceived
888 And took manhood,
    For that the Godhead could not
    Suffer passion.

TEUDAR.

    Profit will not come of our arguing,
892   Though we be here for ever.
    Meriasek, deny Christ
    And I will be thy friend
    So that it may be seen.
896 A worthy bishop I will make thee,
    Chief of the whole breadth of this country.
    I desire nothing more
    But to worship Mahound always.

MERIASEK.

900 There is a better way than that:
    Do thou worship dear Christ,
    Otherwise thou art lost surely.

TEVDARUS

  Vn ger na campol a gryst
904 ha mar qureth me ath wra trest
   wath coyl orthef ha beth fuir
  rag pan deffen ha moys fol
  an iovle a thue mes ay dol
908   kyns es ov ruthy purguir

  Drok yv gena
  war ov ena
   meryasek wek
912 gul dis mas da
  ha gorthyans grua
   thum dewov tek

p. 34.
MERIADOCUS

  Theth dewov try mylw^t fy
916 rag sur dewolov ens y
   nys gorthya vy benytha
  ortheff na wyla pythays
  nahy mar mynnyth boys vays
920   foyl oys mar trestyth inna

TEVDARUS

  Out warnes ty fals jugleer
   defya ov dewov flour
  ty a crek in cloghprennyer
924   rag perel prence hag emperour
   omma the foyl
  the voy nefre me ath cays
  outlayer fyys ath wlays
928 covs vn geer erbyn ov rays
   ha ty an noyll

  Me yv empour
  ha governour
932   conquerrour tyr
  arluth worthy
  mur ov mestry
   gothfeth ha myr

MERIADOCUS

936 Tav thymo vy the clap sens
  speyna a reth mur a gvyns
   oma sur in sevureth
p. 35.   guel yv dis bones cristyan
940 gorthya crist a luen golan
   ha my lemmen ath vygeth

TEUDAR.

One word do not talk of Christ,
904   And if thou dost I will make thee sad.
      Yet listen to me and be wise.
   For when I should come and go mad
   The Devil will come out of his hole
908   Rather than make me easy (?) right truly.

Sorry am I,
On my soul,
     Sweet Meriasek,
912 To do thee aught save good.
Ah do worship
     To my beautiful gods!

MERIASEK.

On thy gods three thousand times fie!
916 For surely devils are they.
     I will never worship them.
Of me seek not affection,
If thou wilt refuse to be good.
920   Mad art thou if thou trustest in them.

TEUDAR.

Out on thee, thou false juggler,
   To defy my flower of gods!
Thou shalt hang in prison,
924   For peril of prince and emperor,
     Here, thou fool.
The more ever will I hate thee.
An outlaw thou hast fled from thy country.
928 Speak a word against my grace
   And thou shalt catch it.

I am emperor,
And governor,
932   Conqueror of land,
A worthy lord,
Great is my mastery.
   Know and see!

MERIASEK.

936 Silence for me! hold thy prate!
You do spend much of wind
   Here surely in seriousness (?)
Better is it for thee to be a Christian,
940 To worship Christ with a full heart,
   And I now will baptize thee.

TEVDARUS

Out govy gesugh thym spath
alema quik rag feya
944 deve an iovle the rag ov fath
3ᵉ vynnes ov begithia
marov off in kres an plath
na pel mar.trege omma
948 mahum darber hardygrath
3ᵉ neb a ruk ov throbla
                                                 [*ascendit*

Tormentoris dugh in plen
tormentoris marsogh len
952   tormentoris dugh dym scon
ay ay ay dar ny regh vry
                                         [*descendit*

reys yv age herhes y
    pan yv mogh ol ov duwon
            [*her yerdis aredy for tevdar and hys men*

956 Hov hov pythesogh matis
y besche reb your patis
    pendra reny dar napya
ay num clewugh ov kelwel
960 tannegh honthsel kyns sevel
    go to dalethugh frappia
                                          [*et verberabunt eos*

p. 36.   PRIMUS TORMENTOR

Ser arluth na cronk na moy
ha lauer the voth thynny
964   ny an grua purthyogel

TEVDARUS

Eugh thymo bys yn cambron
awest the carnbre dyson
ena wy a gyff in lel
968 guas ov theria heb questron*
esel yv then tebel el

Meryasek ythyv gelwys
in crist yma ov cresy
972 genogh why bethens sesijs
    gruegh y tormontya besy
crist mar ny veth denehys
pegh then horsen trewesy
976 genogh kynfove lethys
me agis menten defry

        * leg. question.

TEUDAR.

    Out, woe is me, leave me a space!
      Hence quick to flee (?)
944 The devil has come before my face
      To wish to baptize me!
    Dead am I in the midst of the place
      Any longer if thou stayest here.
948 Mahound, provide hard grace
      For him who hath troubled me!
                                          [He ascends.

    Torturers, come into the field.
    Torturers, if ye are loyal,
952   Torturers come to us at once!
    Ay, ay, ay, ruin, you don't regard
                                          [He descends.
    Need is it to fetch them
      Since all my grief is a mockery.
        [Here staves ready for Teudar and his men.

956 How, how, where are ye, mates?
    I will baste ye (?) by your pates.
      What thing shall we do . . . . . . (?)
    Ah, you hear me calling?
960 Take handsel before rising.
      Go to, begin striking!
                                   [And they shall beat them.

FIRST TORTURER.

    Sir lord, beat no more,
    And tell thy will to us:
964   We will do it full certainly.

TEUDAR.

    Go ye for me as far as Camborne
    Westward of Cambrea, quickly.
      There will ye find loyally
968 A lad tarrying: without question,
      A limb is he of the evil angel.

    Meriasek is he called:
      In Christ is he believing.
972 By you let him be seized
      Do ye torment him.
    If Christ be not denied,
      A thrust to the doleful whoreson!
976 Though he be slain by you,
      I will maintain you certainly.

SECUNDUS TORTOR

      Arluth henna ny a ra
      desempys duen alema
980   aspyans pup ay quartron
      me agis gyd rum ena
         pur uskis bys in cambron

              [*trancit tevder domum*

MERIADOCUS

      Then arluth rebo grasseys
984 dre besyon ythoff guarnys
         may thellen mes an povma
      arta the breten uskys
         han falge tevdar avodya
988 an porpos yv erverys
         wath eff a fyl annotha

p. 37. Omma me re fundyas plas
         ryb maria a cambron
992 ihesu crist darber 3° grays
         in keth chyma pup seson
      may fo prest an drensys tays
         inno enoris dyson
996   ha maria
      han sacrements vij
      kefris gol ha guyth
         menystrys wose helma

1000 Grefons ha cleves seson
      mar angeveth lel crystyan
         hav remembra in plasma
      ihesu arluth cuff colan
1004   y grefons gura sewagya

      Inweth an dour ov fenten
      rag den varijs in certen
         peseff may fo eff ely
1008 thy threy arta thy skyans
      ihesu arluth a selwans
         gront helma der 3° vercy

      Ov banneth genes a plas
1012 reys yv vodya a vur spas
         oges yma ov envy
      me a vyn guythe then won
      hag omma powes dyson
1016   indan an garrek defry

[*her meryasek schall hydde hym sylfe vnder ye rokke*

SECOND TORTURER.

Lord, that will we do.
Straightway let us go hence.
   Let every one spy from his quarter.
I will guide you, by my soul,
   Very quickly, as far as Camborne.

[Teudar goes away home.

MERIASEK.

To the Lord be thanks!
By a vision I am warned
   That I should go out of this country
Again to Brittany forthwith,
   And avoid the false Teudar.
The purpose is designed
   Yet he will fail thereof.

Here have I founded a place
   By Mary of Camborne.
Jesu Christ, provide thy grace
   In this same house, every season,
So that the Father's Trinity be always
   Therein honoured forthwith,
      And Mary,
And the seven sacraments
Likewise on feast and work (day)
   Administered after this.

Grievance and disease of the season,
If a loyal Christian have it,
   And remembers me in this place,
Jesu, Lord, dear heart,
   His grievance will assuage.

Likewise the water of the fountain
For a man insane certainly
   I pray that it be a salve
To bring him again to his sense.
Jesu, lord of salvation,
   Grant this, through thy mercy.

My blessing with thee, O place!
Need is it to quit (thee) in a short time,
   Near is my enemy.
I will keep to the field
And here stay quiet
   Under the rock certainly.

[Here Meriasek shall hide himself under the rock.

p. 38.
SECUNDUS TORTOR

A wylste gy meryasek
in cambron an lagasek
    nynsusy eff malbe dam

TERTIUS TORTOR

1020 bener regyffy the con
galles eff in mes then won
    rengeffo moleth y vam

CALO

Aspyen orthen buschys
1024 hag orth an karrek kefrys
mar asethe the cutha
gase ny vyn boys kefys
    duen ny the dre alema

PRIMUS TORTOR

1028 Py dol an iovle ythetha
tevder mes y skyans a
    pan glowe y vos scappys

SECUNDUS TORTOR

avesyans eff ahena
1032 praga na ruk y sesya
    orth y ganov pan govsis

TERTIUS TORTOR

                                                                         [*ad teuder*

Heyl tevder in agis tour
meryasek an povma dor
1036   galles ny ny wothen ken
in trefov hag in gonyov
ny ren welas sur heb wov
    annotho covs ny wor den

p. 39
TEVDARUS

1040 Out govy harov harov
    an pov mar sewe fyys
ny vensen heb feladov
    awoys dyv ran peth an beys
1044   na vensen* mes
a pennov methov
o^t in ov dythyov
    creyaff warnogh ladron drues

    * leg. vese?

SECOND TORTURER.

Sawest thou Meriasek?
In Camborne, the quick-of sight
    He is not . . . .

THIRD TORTURER.

1020 Never mayest thou have thy supper!
He has gone out to the field.
    May he have his mother's curse!

A DRUDGE.

Let us spy at the bushes
1024 And at the rock also.
    If he is sitting to hide.
He will not allow (himself) to be found.
    Let us go home hence.

FIRST TORTURER.

1028 What hole of the devil has he gone to?
Teudar will go out of his wits
    When he hears that he has escaped.

SECOND TORTURER.

Let him consider thereof
1032 Why he did not seize him (Meriasek)
    By his mouth when he spoke.

THIRD TORTURER.
                              [*To Teudar.*

Hail, Teudar in thy tower!
Meriasek from this country quite
1036   Has gone: we know not otherwise.
In villages and on downs
We have not seen him surely, without a lie.
    Of him no one can speak.

TEUDAR.

1040 Out! woe's me! *haro, haro!*
    If he be fled the country.
I would not, without fail,
    For sake of two parts of the world's wealth
1044   That he should be away.
Ah, drunken heads,
Out! in my days
    I cry on you bold thieves!

CALO

1048 Ay tevdar ke war the gam
    molleth du the vapp the vam
      pyraga na*n* guythte gy
      pan eses ganso ov covs
1052 ny vyn y thu eff heb flovs
      orto cafus belyny

                    [*descendit tevder*

TEVDARUS

    Yv helma ol an confort
      ambethe deworthugh wy
1056 ay serys yma thyugh sport
      pa*n* vs dewen dy*m*mo vy
      wel wel na for(s)
    re appolyn ov du splan
1060 kyns dyberth ny warth mas ran
      me a pe ʒen hebyhors
      hay cowetha
    have that iiij[ar] lorel
1064 hag arta perthugh coff guel
      pendrelle*n* the comondya

                    [*verberat eos*

p. 40.   #### MERIADOCUS

    The ihesu rebo grasseys
    o*m*ma me re poweseys
1068   pur guir inda*n* an me*n*ma
    ov envy in kerth galsons
    ov metya byth ny alsons
      du a vynnas indella
1072   carek veryasek holma
      gelwys vyth wose helma

    Me a vyn sensy the*n* mor
    the weles thy*m*mo tru mach
1076 dorsona dyugh mester flor
    du re wythe orth damach
    a*gis* lester
    mar mynnogh moys the vrete*n*
1080 me a bysse pur certe*n*
      mones genogh heb awer

NAVTA

    Ty a hevelsa dremas
    dus in hanov du an tas
1084   leme*n* aberveth gene*n*

A DRUDGE.

1048 Ah Teudar, go on thy way.
　　God's curse on thy mother's son!
　　　　Why didst thou not keep him
　　　　When thou wast with him talking?
1052 His God will not, without flout,
　　　　Have villainy upon him.
　　　　　　　　　　　[*Teudar goes down.*

TEUDAR.

　　Is this all the comfort
　　　　That I should have from you?
1056 O sirs, it is a sport to you
　　　　When it is grief to me.
　　　　Well, well, no matter!
　　By Apollo, my bright god,
1060 Before separating not a laugh but a cry.
　　　　I will pay to the hobby-horse,
　　　　　　And her comrades.
　　Have that, (ye) four lorels,
1064 And again remember better
　　　　What I may command.
　　　　　　　　　　　[*He beats them.*

MERIASEK.

　　To Jesu be thanks!
　　Here I have rested
1068　　Right truly under this stone.
　　My enemies have gone away.
　　Meet me they could never.
　　　　God willed so.
1072　　Meriasek's rock this
　　　　Shall be called hereafter.

　　I will hold to the sea
　　　　To seek for me true mates.
1076 A blessing to you, flower of masters,
　　　　May God keep from damage
　　　　　　Your ship!
　　If ye will go to Brittany,
1080 I would pray right certainly
　　　　To go with you without grief.

THE SAILOR.

　　Thou wouldst seem an honest man.
　　Come in God the Father's name,
1084　　Now on board with us.

   ten an gol inban mata
   an guyns thagen corse dufa
     cowel ny a weyl breten   [*finit*

SERVUS

1088 Tremenys yv dyogel
   lemen genen an chanel
     may fe holmyv spede dek
   devethys on bys in tyr
1092 lemen quik tha*gis* desyr
     grueghwy londia meryasek [*descendit*
   an men re ruk inclynya
   in tyr rag the receva
1096   gras the ihesu galosek

p. 41.   MERIADOCUS

   Du ren tala thyugh tus vays
   arluth ihesu luen a rays
     rum gedya in forth wella
1100 thum nessevyn mar a saff
   ganse temptijs ysethaff
     trohe ha lust an bysma

BRITTONNUS

   Dremas beth war pythylly
1104 blyth brays in forna defry
     purguir yma
   mar a tue in the ogoys
   eff a ra scollya the goys
1108   ellas at eve ena

MERIADOCUS

   Best thys me a worhemmyn
   thymmo na rylly dregyn
     na the crystyan benytha
1112 na gymmer ovn vyth dremays
   thy handla sur eff am gays
     myr purwhar in ketelma
   ov sywa eff a levays
1116   truspys vyth ny ra profia.

BRITTONNUS

   Sur ty yv den benygays
   lues den eff re lathays
     ha flehys prest in povma

Hoist up the sail, mate.
The wind has come to our course,
    Fully we shall see Brittany.

THE SAILOR'S SERVANT.

1088 Passed is safely
Now by us the Channel
    So that this was fair speed.
Come are we to shore
1092 Now quick to your desire
    Do you land, Meriasek.   [*He lands.*
The stone has bent down
On the shore to receive thee.
1096   Thanks to mighty Jesu!

MERIASEK.

May God pay it to you, good folk,
May Lord Jesu, full of grace,
    Guide me in the best way.
1100 To my kinsmen if I go,
By them I shall be tempted
    Towards them and the lust of this world.

A BRETON.

Honest man, be wary where thou mayst go.
1104 A great wolf in that way indeed,
    Right truly is.
If he come anear thee
He will spill thy blood.
1108   Alas, behold him there!

MERIASEK.

Beast, to thee I command
That to me thou do no mischief
    Nor to a Christian ever.
1112 Have no fear at all, honest man.
He will surely let me handle him.
    See, quite gently thus
He has ventured to follow me:
1116   Any violence he will not offer.

THE BRETON.

Sure thou art a blessed man!
Many men hath he slain
    And children ready in this country.

1120 thyso gy sensys asson
at eva kep*ar* hag on
a vo doff orth ʒ° sywa   [*finit*

p. 42.   MERIADOCUS

Gul truspys thym ny pro*fias*
1124   nag eff nyngeveth dregyn
in hanov c*ris*t map guirhas
thys best me a worhemyn
moys the*n* guelfos
1128 gans map de*n* na ra mellya
nefra a wose helma
aberth ihesu awartha
yth forth grua mos

1132 Me a vyn moys the*n* guylfoys
ena ermet purguir boys
may halle*n* gorthya ov du
na ve*n* tempt*is*
1136 gans t*us* an beys
hedre ve*n* byv

Omma sur ryb an castel
gelwys pontelyne defry
1140 war an meneth dyogel
hag orth an ryu*er* surly
a josselyne
chapel guthel me a vyn
1144 rag gorthya maria wyn*
kynthyv teller guyls ha yne
        [*ascendit ad montem*

Gorthyans the c*ris*t map maghteth
M pas sur yv an meneth
1148 the worth an grond byteweth
du am gueres
ov chy fundia
sur ha grondya
1152 manneff uskyes
  [*chappell aredy. Her a weryth a rosset*
      mantell and a berde.

p. 43.   HIC INCIPIT VITA SANCTI SILUESTRY
       Constantinus hic pompabit dicens

Drefen ov boys corff hep par
ha dovtijs gans an bobil
ov hanov in guir† heb mar
1156 yv costyntyn the nobil

* MS. *why*.   † MS. *guire*, but the *e* is in a later hand.

1120 To thee we are bound.
　　　Lo he is like to a lamb
　　　　　That may be tame following thee.

MERIASEK.

　　　He did not offer to do violence to me,
1124 　　Nor shall he have hurt.
　　　In the name of Christ, the Virgin's Son,
　　　　To thee, Beast, I command
　　　　　To go to the wilderness.
1128 With a son of man meddle not
　　　Ever hereafter.
　　　By will of Jesu above
　　　　On thy way do go.
1132 I will go to the wilderness
　　　There a hermit right truly to be,
　　　　That I may be able to worship my God.
　　　(And) that I may not be tempted
1136 By the folk of the world
　　　　Whilst I may be alive.

　　　Here surely by the castle
　　　　Called Pontelyne really
1140 On the mountain certainly,
　　　　And by the river surely
　　　　　Of Josselyn,
　　　A chapel I will make
1144 To worship blessed Mary,
　　　　Though it is a place wild and cold.

　　　　　　　[*He goes up to the mountain.*

　　　Worship to Christ the Maiden's Son!
　　　A thousand paces surely is the mountain
1148 From the ground ever.
　　　　God help me!
　　　Found my house
　　　Surely, and ground (it)
1152 　　I will forthwith.
　　　　　[*A chapel ready. Here he wears a russet
　　　　　　　mantle and a beard.*

HERE BEGINS THE LIFE OF SAINT SILVESTER.

Constantine shall here parade, saying,

　　　Because of my being a body without peer,
　　　　And dreaded by the people,
　　　My name truly without doubt,
1156 　　Is Constantine the noble,

        emperour worthy
        map then vyternes helen
        neb yv pen ol y ehen
1160   del glowas lues huny

        Yma in pov falge cregyans
        ov cul dym angyr an iovle
        mar tur na pel ov bevnans
1164   me as *temper* by my sovle
        hag as gor ol then mernans
        der eselder peyn ha mevle
        me re lathes lues cans
1168   hag indella yv ov thovle
        wath dyswul moy
        tormentoris guesyen fol
        tormentoris dugh thym ol
1172   aberth mahum ha soly

Hic pompabunt tortores [w swerdys

1172* Heyl costenten the nobil
        del onny* the lel bobil
        devethys ython warbarth
        rag enour dis ha gorthyans
1176   benitha the eskerans
        mar as keuyn sur ny warth

CONSTANTINUS

        Wolcum kynghtis euerych on
        reys yv dywy lafurya
1180   rag chastya an crustunyon
        drest ol an gluas rome alemma

p. 44.   Myns a greys in map maryon
        der peyn gruegh age latha
1184   byth na thovtyogh dampnasconn
        me agis menten nefra

SECUNDUS TORTOR

        Ny thovtyn peryl na pegh
        yma debron thum ij vregh
1188   mar bel ov boys ov powes
        heb moldra an crustunyon
        ornogh thynny sovdoryon
        na garra sevel in cres

CONSTANTINUS IMPERATOR

1192   Tus arvov genogh ytha
        ij cans purguir alemma
        guetyogh omprevy manly

* MS. *onneny*, but the *e* is in a later hand.
† The corrector has struck out the *s*.

             A worthy Emperor,
        Son to the queen Helena,
        Who is head of all his tribe,
1160   As many a one has heard.

        There is in the country a false belief
             Causing me the devil's anger.
        If my life no longer endures
1164   I will tame it, by my soul,
        And will put it all to the death
             Through baseness of pain and disgrace.
        I have slain many hundreds,
1168   And thus is my will
             Yet to undo more.
        Torturers, mad lads,
        Torturers, come ye all to me
1172   In behalf of Mahound and Sol.
           Here the torturers shall parade [with swords.

1172ᵃ Hail, Constantine the noble!
        As we are thy loyal people
             Come are we together.
        For honour to thee and worship.
1176 Thy enemies ever,
             If we take them, surely will not laugh.

                    CONSTANTINE.
        Welcome, knights, everyone!
             Need is it for you to go on
1180 To chastise the Christians
             Over all the kingdom of Rome hence.

        All that believe in Mary's Son
             By torment slay them.
1184 Never fear damnation.
             I will support you ever.

                    SECOND TORTURER.
        We fear not peril nor sin.
        There is an itching in my two arms
1188   That I should be resting so long
        Without murdering the Christians.
        Order for us soldiers
             That love not to stand quiet!

                    EMPEROR CONSTANTINE.
1192 Armed men shall go with you
        Two hundred right truly hence.
             Take care to prove yourselves manly,

                                          F 2

then cristunyan scollya goys
1196 na sparyogh yowynk na loys
eskerans ov du soly

TERTIUS TORTOR

Na ren purguir costyntyn
y asteveth torment tyn
1200 myns a worth crist an brebour
dueni in kerth scon cowetha
pup ay du gruens aspya
ov quandra mar sus treytour

CALO

1204 Me a weyl enos ij guas
sur orth fysmens age fays
crustunyon yth havalsens
p. 45. serys leferugh thynny
1208 pana cregyans us dywy
oma scon war beyn mernans

COMES

In crist ihesu ny a greys
awos ovn a then in beys
1212 ny forsakyn y hanow
neb na cresse in della
the peyn yfern sur ytha
the torment pan vo marov

PRIMUS TORTOR

1216 Out warnes ty plos brathky
na hanw crist theragon ny
ha mar qureth y feth mernans
rag dyswul an crustunyen
1220 danvenys gans costenten
ny yv then povma dyblans

DOCTOR IN FIDE*

Awoys ovn a costenten
nag a peynys neb termen
1224 ihesu ny ren dynaha
thynny mar quregh velyny
cryst yv pen an arlythy
a ra agys aquytya

* *in fide* added by the corrector here and before l. 1245.

    To spill blood for the Christians,
1196 Spare not young nor grey,
     Enemies of my god Sol.

      THIRD TORTURER.

    We would not do [so], right truly, Constantine.
    They shall have sharp torment,
1200   All who worship Christ the beggar.
    Let us come away forthwith, comrades!
    Let each on his side spy
     If there be a traitor wandering.

      A DRUDGE.

1204 I see there two lads.
    Surely by the semblance of their faces
     Christians they would seem.
    Sirs, say to us
1208 What belief you have
     Here forthwith on pain of death.

      THE EARL.

    In Christ Jesu we believe.
    For fear of man on earth
1212   We will not forsake his name.
    Whoso may not believe thus
    To hell's pain surely shall go,
     To torment when he shall be dead.

      FIRST TORTURER.

1216 Out on thee, thou foul hound!
    Name not Christ before us,
     And if thou dost thou shalt have death.
    To undo the Christians
1220 Sent by Constantine
     Are we to this country clearly.

      A DOCTOR IN THE FAITH.

    For dread of Constantine
    Or of tortures at any time
1224   We will not deny Jesu.
    If ye do outrage to us
    Christ, who is the head of lords,
     Will he acquit you?

SECUNDUS TORTOR

1228 Ty horsen agen* brag ny
thys mylw⁴ ha ʒᵉ crist fy
dynagh uskis y hanov   [y' galovs aredy

p. 46.   gorth quik iovyn ha soly
1232 bo ty a vyrwe eredy
oma dre peynys garov

COMES

Guel yv genen ny merwel
es gorthya devle dyogel
1236 in bysma yv grueys apol
tru a thu asogh goky
na worthyogh crist a vercy
a thuk mernans ragon oll

TERTIUS TORTOR

1240 Rag covs geryov mar velen
in cloghprennyer purcerten
oma y fetheth cregys
inweth an treytour arall
1244 ryb the scoth kepar ha gal
genevy a veth hangys

DOCTOR IN FIDE

Maria myternes neff
maria agen eneff
1248 peys mengeffo saluasconn
a pobyl omschumunys
remembrogh agis sperys
rag dovt cafus dampnasconn   [finit

CALO

1252 Tav gays thym the ombrene
pur a wylsta war an kee
gesys yn bysma enaff
p. 47. kynfo porthov neff degeys
1256 wath yferne a veth aleys
peneyl ellen fors ny raff

COMES

Ihesu arluth cuff colon
ihesu grond thyn saluasconn
1260 rag oma reys yv merwell

* leg. nagen?

SECOND TORTURER.

1228   Thou whoreson, insult us not.
    On thee and on Christ a thousand times fie!
      Deny his name forthwith.
                    [*The gallows ready.*
    Worship quickly Jove and Sol,
1232   Or thou shalt die at once
      Here through rough pains.

THE EARL.

    Better is it with us to die
    Than to worship a devil certainly.
1236   In this world Apollo is made.
    Pity, O God, you are (so) foolish
    That you do not worship Christ of mercy,
      Who bore death for us all!

THIRD TORTURER.

1240   For saying words so villainous
    In a prison right certainly
      Here thou shalt be gibbeted.
    Likewise the other traitor
1244   By thy shoulder like a villain
      By me shall be hung.

A DOCTOR IN THE FAITH.

    Mary, queen of heaven,
    Mary, pray that our soul
1248   May have salvation.
    O accursed people
    Remember your spirit
      For fear of getting damnation!

A DRUDGE.

1252   Be silent, leave me to redeem myself.
    Hast thou really seen on the way
      A soul left in this world?
    Though heaven's gates be shut
1256   Yet hell will be wide open.
      Unto which of the two I may go I care not.

THE EARL.

    Jesu, Lord, dear heart,
    Jesu, grant us salvation,
1260   For here need is to die.

    benyges rebo an preys
    ihesu dyso ov sperys
      me a gemen dyogel   [*finit*

PRIMUS TORTOR

1264 Lemen pan vsons in crok
    vskys moghheen age drok
      duen drethe gans clethethyov
    an tenewen thy gela
1268 mar guir an iovle res pela
      helme at eve marov

SECUNDUS TORTOR

    Der y gela me a reys
    ny gara sevel in creys
1272   atta hy der y pottis
    me an felge a drus then pen
    may teffo y ompynnen
      ha skynnya avel mottis

p. 48.   ### TERTIUS TORTOR

1276 Parys on ny the gul drok
    neb na vo rengeffo crok
      cothys then doyr attonsy
    age corff warbarth yv trogh
1280 dyghtys ens kepar ha brogh
      a vo squerdis gans mylgy

CALO

    Nefre cosker ongrassyas
    menogh a ra bostov bras
1284   neb tebel dorne pan vo grueys
    mas hap drok orthugh askyn
    gase farwel me a vyn
      molleth du in cowetheys

    [*trancit calo et tortores expectant in placea*

IHESUS *in celo dicens**

1288 Ov eleth gvyn avel grueys
    an enevov mertherijs
      drewhy scon the lowena
    rag age lauer in beys
1292 grontis yv dage sperys
      an ioy a thur bys nefra

* In the corrector's hand: the original scribe wrote *Deus*.

Blessed be the time!
Jesu, to thee my spirit
    I commend certainly.

FIRST TORTURER.

1264 Now since they are on the gallows
Quickly let us greaten their evil.
    Let us come through them with swords
From one side to the other.
1268 So truly may the devil peel them!
    This one, look, is dead.

SECOND TORTURER.

Through the other I will run.
I like not standing quiet.
1272   Look at it through him put!
I will slit him across to the head
So that his brains may come
    And ascend like motes.

THIRD TORTURER.

1276 Ready are we to do evil:
May he who is not have the gallows!
    Look at them fallen to the ground!
Their bodies together are broken:
1280 Dighted are they like a badger
    That may be torn by a greyhound.

THE DRUDGE.

Ever an ungracious set
Often will make great boasts
1284   When any evil turn may be done.
But an ill hap will fall on you.
I will leave a farewell.
    God's curse on the company.

[*The drudge goes off and the torturers wait in the open.*

JESUS *in heaven saying.*

1288 My angels white like crystal!
The martyred souls
    Bring ye soon to joy.
For their labour in the world
1292 Granted is to their spirits
    The joy that dureth for ever.

MICAEL

   Ihesu the voth a veth grueys
   neb yv in beys mertherijs
1296   y a due de lowena
   del yv dynny comondys
   lel pup vr ol y feth grueys
   hag y tegoth in della

p. 49.   ### GABRIEL

1300 A enevov mertherijs
   ioy neff yma dyugh grontys
    gans crist ihesu awartha
   drefen an torment in beys
1304 thagis corfov rebue grueys
    why agys beth lowena

          [her yͤ sovlys aredy

PRIMUS TORTOR

   Out duen in kerth cowetha
   the neb hensy rag cutha
1308   ken warbarth ython leskys
   in neys rum caradevder
   yma cothys golovder
    dretho maythoff amuwys

Hic Sanctus Siluester Incipit dicens

1312 Gefugh* creys vfel ha clovr
   in hanov du dy lawe
   neb a formyas neff ha novr
   in bysma gans y dule
1316   map den a pry
   tays ha map ha sperys sans
   iij ferson hag vn substans
   henna yv an lel cregyans
1320   del deske sans eglos dynny

   Lemen warbarth ov flehys
   ny a vyn moys alemma
   the anclethias an dus vays
1324 us mertherijs del glowa
   gans drok pobyll
p. 50. tus an empour costenten
   gasa crystyen byv ny ven
1328   in povma purthyogel

          [*descendit*
          [yͤ tumbe aredy

* Perhaps *Gesugh*.

MICHAEL.

  Jesu, thy will shall be done.
  Whoso are martyred on earth
1296   They shall come to joy.
  As is commanded unto us
  Loyally always it shall be done,
   And thus it behoveth.

GABRIEL.

1300 O martyred souls,
  Heaven's joy is granted to you
   By Christ Jesu above.
  Because of the torment on earth
1304 Which was done to your bodies
   You shall have joy.
        [*Here the souls ready.*

FIRST TORTURER.

  Out! let us come away, comrades!
  To some ways (?) to hide,
1308   Else together we are burnt.
  Anear, by my loveableness,
  Is fallen lightning
   So that I am startled thereby.

  Here Saint Silvester begins, saying,

1312 Ye shall have peace, lowly and clear.
   In God's name, praise to Him
  Who made heaven and earth,
   In this world with his two hands,
1316   The son of man of clay.
  Father and Son and Holy Ghost,
  Three Persons and one Substance,
  That is the true faith,
1320   As holy Church teaches us.

  Now together, my children,
   We will go home
  To bury the good folk
1324   Who as I hear are martyred
    By evil people.
  The folk of the Emperor Constantine
  Will not leave a Christian alive
1328   In this country right certainly.
         [*He descends.*
         [*The tomb ready.*

CARDINALE

  Seluester agen tays wek
  ihesu arluth galosek
    pup vr regen gueresa
1332 at oma an dus varov
  goren y scon in bethov
    ha fyyn quik alemma

        [*her they beryth them*

SILUESTER

  Lemmen pan vsons in beth
1336 ihesu crist pen an eleth
    gorw^t age enevow
  ny a vyn polge avodya
  mar a kyllyn omguytha
1340 orth costentyn in torma
    ken ganso bethen marov

  Then meneth a seraptyn
  mones purguir ny a vyn
1344 in rome dyn ny dal trege
  gena ov mebyen lyen
  dugh lemen bras ha byen
    mar kyllyn polge omguythe

      [*ascendit ad montem seraptyn*

   [*a vysour aredy apon Constantyn ys face*

51. SECUNDUS TORTOR [*ad constantinum*

1348 Heyl ser arluth costynten
  crustunyon marov genen
    yma sur neb try vgans
  ran cregys ran debynnys
1352 ran orth lostov mergh draylys
    ran leskis in tan dyblans

        [*tranceat*

CONSTANTINUS

  Eugh the dre ov sovdoryan
  an iovle thagis covya
1356 yma ortheff lovrygyan
    cothys ha ny won fetla
    ellas ellas
  ythoma gyllys leper
1360 del leuer pup ol hager
    ny gar den gueles ov fas

A CARDINAL.

Silvester, our sweet Father,
May Jesu, (the) mighty Lord,
    Always help us!
1332 Lo here are the dead folk:
Let us put them forthwith in tombs,
    And let us flee quickly hence.
                  [*Here they bury them.*

SILVESTER.

Now, since they are in the tomb,
1336 Jesu Christ, the head of the angels,
    Preserve their souls!
We will for a little while go away,
If we can keep ourselves
1340 From Constantine this turn,
    Else by him we shall be dead.

To the mountain of Soracte
Right truly we will go:
1344   In Rome it behoves us not to stay.
With me, my disciples,
Come now, great and small,
    If we can for a little while keep ourselves.
              [*He goes up to Mount Soracte.*

    [*A mask ready upon Constantine's face.*

SECOND TORTURER *to Constantine.*

1348 Hail, Sir Lord Constantine!
Christians dead with us
    There are surely some three score.
Some hung, some beheaded,
1352 Some dragged at horses' tails,
    Some burnt in fire clearly.
                    [*Let him pass off.*

CONSTANTINE.

Go home, my soldiers,
    The Devil to remember you!
1356 There is leprosy on me
    Fallen, and I know not how.
    Alas, alas!
I am become a leper,
1360 As every one says, ugly.
    No one loves to see my face.

A govy pendra yv guel
    ortheff lemmen the voys grueys
1364 a me revue ree cruel
    orth crustunyan me a greys
a tekter rychys farwell
    nebes ioy ambus an beys
1368 mensen stak omma merwell
    in meske tus na ven guelys

JUSTUS

Danvenogh than epscobov
    han doctours bras doys oma
1372 y a lefer der lyfryov
    marsus savment in bysma
    orth an cleves
rag y yv calcoryan vrays
1376 ha na berthuth ovn in cays
    then deseys y a gueres

p. 52.
CONSTANTINUS

Maseger a thesempys
    kergh thym an epscop omma
1380 han doctour brays kekefrys
    yv gelwys flour an bysma
    sur in clergy
mar cothens dym leferel
1384 boys neb gueres dyogel
    orth an cleves ambus vy

SECUNDUS NUNCIUS

Heyl ser emperour costentyn
    oma ythese parys
1388 rag lafuria pur ylyn
    alema in the nygys
    ny raff strechya
an epscop han doctour flour
1392 me as kergh uskis theth tour
    moys a raff in vn trettya

Hic pompabit Episcopus Poly* vel Doctor

SECUNDUS NUNCIUS

Heyl ser epscop in the dour
heyl inweth dywhy doctour
1396   metijs da ogh in vn chy

* *poly* here and elsewhere is added by the corrector.

    Ah woe is me, what thing is best
     To me now to be done?
1364 Ah, I have been overcruel
     To Christians, I believe.
    Ah beauty of riches, farewell!
     Little joy have I of the world.
1368 I would wish for a tether here to die:
     Amongst folk I would not be seen.

      A JUSTICE.

    Send ye to the bishops
     And the great doctors to come here.
1372 They will say by books
     If there be salve in this world
      For the sickness.
    For they are great caulkers;
1376 And have you no fear in the case:
     They will cure the disease.

      CONSTANTINE.

    Messenger, straightway
     Fetch to me the Bishop here,
1380 And the great Doctor, likewise,
     That is called flower of this world
      Surely in learning.
    If they can tell me
1384 That there is any aid certainly
     Against the sickness that I have.

      SECOND MESSENGER.

    Hail, Sir Emperor Constantine!
     Here I was ready
1388 To go on right clean
     Hence in thy business.
    I will not walk slowly.
    The Bishop and the flower of doctors
1392 I will fetch them quickly to thy tower.
     I will go in a turn.

Here the Bishop of Pola or the Doctor shall parade.

      SECOND MESSENGER.

    Hail, Sir Bishop in thy tower!
    Hail, also to you, Doctor!
1396   Ye are well met in one house.

    the costenten reys yv doys
    prederugh inta kyn moys
      gorthebov fur reys yv ry

      EPISCOPUS POLY

1400 Wolcum maseger ylyn
    oys oma war ov ena
    pendra wer the costyntyn
    dar nynsusy in poynt da
1404   lauer thynny
    mar a sywe dyscrasiis
    meen drethon a veth kefys
     may fo purlowen defry

p. 53.   DOCTOR

1408 Mayl at eua bargyn da
     maseger tek
    lauer thymo in preytha
     then emper tek
1412   pendrus werys

     SECUNDUS NUNCIUS

    claff deberthys eff yv sur
    ny welys in beys na mur
     denvith del ywa dyghtijs

      DOCTOR

1416 A haha me a wothya
    bakcheler ienkyn in preytha
     heth ov lefer a fysek
    dokhy indan the gasel
1420 ha grua thegy ov gormel
     ov boys fecycyen connek

     [*erthyn pott. ye bovke aredy And
      the vrnell enspektad*

     CLERICUS IANKYN*

    Rag esya an pedrennov
    ha rag stopya tarthennov
1424   yma thywy forten tek
    a caffogh sur benewen
    polge ryb agis tenewen
     why a proffse den connek
        [*descendit ad constantinum*

   * *jankyn* is added by the corrector.

To Constantine need is to come.
Consider well before going.
    Answers wise need is to give.

BISHOP OF POLA.

1400 Welcome, fair messenger,
    Thou art here on my soul.
What has happened to Constantine?
    Is he not in good point
1404   Say thou to us.
If he be disgraced
Means through us will be found
    So that he may be very glad really.

DOCTOR.

1408 *Mal*, lo here is a good bargain,
    Sweet messenger,
Say to me, in good time,
    To the fair emperor
1412   What thing has happened?

THE MESSENGER.

A separated leper he is surely.
I have not seen on earth or sea
    Any one as he is dighted.

DOCTOR.

1416 Ah, haha, I knew.
Bachelor Jenkyn, in good time
    Fetch my book of physic,
Carry it under thy armpit,
1420 And do thou praise me
    That I am a cunning physician.

        [*An earthen pot: the book ready;
        and the urinal* [*to be*] *inspected.*

CLERIC JANKIN.

For easing the buttocks,
And for stopping tertians,
    You have good luck.
1424 If you got a woman
For a while by your side
    You would prove a cunning man.
        [*He goes down to Constantine.*

EPISCOPUS POLY

1428 Gorthyans in se
ha lowene
    thyugh arluth gluas
omma wharee
1432 ny redufe
    gans an gannas

p. 54.
CONSTANTINUS

A wolcum *ser* epscop flour
wolcum inweth *ser* doctour
1436   dugh inban me ag*is* peys
ov cleves *pr*est wy a weyl
nynsyv grefons me an geyl
    a wothogh gul dym guereys

DOCTOR

1440 Mannaff gueles agys dour
hag in vrna an empour
    angeveth gorthyb in cays

JUSTUS

me a prederys henna
1444 y vryn atta oma
    tovle in the wedyr glays

DOCTOR

Hoc vrum malorum
et nimis rubrorum
1448   aha me a wor inta
dus oma bacheler ienkyn
myr warvan drefe the vyn
    ay lok up byscherev tha

1452 Annotho na gy*mm*er gloys
kynthus ganso sawer poys
    gor dotho nes the frygov
helma yv mater tykly
1456 leme*n* me a wor defry
    pendra yv an clevegov

p. 55.
Pendra vynnogh dym the ry
ha sawys pur eredy
1460   costentyn bethugh gena
dre weres ov du soly
me a vyn gul drynk dywhy
    mar cafa stoff the perna

BISHOP OF POLA.

1428 Worship on (thy) seat
And joy,
To you, lord of the kingdom!
Here anon,
1432 We have come
With the messenger.

CONSTANTINE.

O welcome, sir flower of bishops!
Welcome, also sir doctor!
1436 Come ye up, I pray you.
My disease at once you shall see:
It is not a grievance I conceal:
Can ye do me a cure?

DOCTOR.

1440 I will look at your water
And then the emperor
Shall have an answer in the case.

JUSTICE.

I thought of that.
1444 His urine lo is here:
Throw it into thy blue glass.

DOCTOR.

Hoc urum malorum
Et nimis rubrorum,
Aha, I know well.
1448 Come here, bachelor Jenkyn
Look up, raise up thy lip!
O look up, beshrew thee!

1452 Thereof do not take pain
Though there be with it a heavy savour.
Put thy nostrils nearer to it.
This is a ticklish matter.
1456 Now I know certainly
What are the diseases.

What thing will you give to me,
And cured full readily,
1460 Constantine, you will be by me?
Through aid of my god, Sol,
I will make a drink for you,
If I get the stuff to buy (it).

CONSTANTINUS

1464 Tan at omma thys x puns
in dalleth an rema syns
    grua vy sav hag y feth guel
benithe in the vevneyns
1468   me ath ra parlet vhel

DOCTOR

Mayl an rema a ra les
me a vyn pesy cumyes
    rag mones dre
1472 arta me a thue deth yov
oma dyugh gans dewosov
    a relle agis sawye
    descendit cum clerico. [*Expectat episcopus*
    poly ibidem

Rum fay ny alla peragh besse
1476 teka pemont nansyv wesse
    re du soly numdarfa
sav malbe dam a won vy
gueres the cleves defry
1480   byteweth reys yv bewa
mar ny weres falsury
    fecessyon ny thereff nefra   [*finit*
    [*tranceat domum*

p. 56.   ### CLERICUS

Me ny won guel losowen
1484 in bysma rag fecycyen
    by my troyth es del yv gov   [*finit.*
    [*trancit domum*

CONSTANTINUS

Epscop pendra leueryth
ny won us methegyeth
1488   am gruelle sav der lyfryov

EPISCOPUS POLY

Nag us arluth rum lovta
me rebue sur ov stuthya
    in lyfryov nansyv tremmys
1492 why ny vethugh sav nefra
marnes golhys in bysma
    a vewhy purguir in goys

CONSTANTINE.

1464 Take, lo here ten pounds for thee!
    In the beginning, hold these.
        Heal me and thou shalt have better
    Ever in thy life.
1468   I will make thee a high prelate.

DOCTOR.

Mál, these will do good!
I will beg leave
    To go home.
1472 Again I will come on Thursday
Here to you with potions
    Which will heal you.

    He goes down with the clergyman. [*The Bishop of Pola waits in the same place.*

By my faith I cannot . . . .
1476 Fairer payment, now is a . . .
    By god Sol, has not happened (?) to me.
But, *malbe dam*, if I know how
To heal thy disease certainly.
1480   Ever need is to live.
If falsehood helps not
    A physician will never rise.

CLERIC.

I know not a better herb
1484 In this world for a physician,
    By my troth, than falsehood is.

        [*He goes off home.*

CONSTANTINE.

Bishop, what sayest thou?
I do not know through books
1488   That there is medicine that would heal me.

BISHOP OF POLA.

There is not, lord, by my loyalty.
I have been surely studying
    In books, it is now three months.
1492 You will never be whole
Unless washed in this world
    You be right truly in blood.

PRELATUS

  Ny revue ov stethya sur
1496 a pegh golhys dre goys pur
   wy a fya tek sawys
  ha benitha ken maner
  del govs thynny an lefer
1500   ny yllogh bones yaghheys

CONSTANTINUS

  Pana goys a veth henna
  na sparyogh best in bysma
   mar a kylla boys kefys
1504 othommek me a vya
   del welogh the voys sawys

p. 57. **EPISCOPUS POLY**

  Ny dal dotho boys goys best
  flehys purreys yv dyugh fest
1508   the kuntel dres ol an pov
  ha specyly ree ov tena
  goys glan yma then rena
   a dremen pup elyov
1512 gruegh why bath in lycorna
   hag y fethugh pur salov

PRELATUS

  Danvenogh sovdrys in pov
  the kuntel an flehyggyov
1516   ea numbyr a tremmyl
  han rena bethens lethys
  hage goys pur ysawys
   tek a glan yn vn vecyl
1520 pan vegh in henna golhys
   ythegh gvyn avel crystel   [*finit*

CONSTANTINUS

  Helmyv tra a yl boys grueys
  torment*oris* desempys
1524   torment*oris* scon thym dugh
  torment*oris* gans mur greys
   torment*oris* dufunugh

PRIMUS TORTOR
       [*ad constantinum*

  Heyl ov arluth costentyn
1528 kekefrys gal ha brentyn
   oma ython devethys

PRELATE.

We have been studying surely.
1496 If you were washed in pure blood
You would be healed fair,
And never otherwise,
As saith the book to us,
1500 Can you be cured.

CONSTANTINE.

What blood will that be?
Spare ye not a beast in this world
If it can be found
1504 Wanting I would be,
As you see, to be healed.

THE BISHOP OF POLA.

It ought not for him to be a beast's blood,
Children very needful is it for you
1508 To gather over all the country,
And specially some a-suckling.
Pure blood, those have,
Which excels every salve.
1512 Bathe in that liquor
And you will be quite whole.

PRELATE.

Send soldiers into the country
To gather the children,
1516 Yea, a number of three thousand,
And let them be slain,
And their pure blood be saved
Fair and clean in a vessel.
1520 When you shall be washed therein
You shall go white as chrystal.

CONSTANTINE.

This is a thing that may be done.
Torturers, straightway,
1524 Torturers, come quick to me!
Torturers, with much strength.
Torturers, awake!

FIRST TORTURER.
[*To Constantine.*

Hail, my lord Constantine!
1528 As well rascal as noble,
Here we are come.

del grese awoys gul da
ny russugh agen creya
1532   na thywhy nynso vsijs
        [ye wymmen aredy w^t ther chyldryn

p. 58.   CONSTANTINUS

Eugh thymo dres ol an pov
kefrys rome ha lumbardy
kuntullugh an flehyggyov
1536   a vo pur certen achy
the try blythy
dens omma hage mammov
tremmyl orth nyver heb wov
1540   nynsus forse kyn fens cans moy

Ens pup oll in y quartren
parcel tus arvov certen
intrethogh rennys a veth
1544 neb a kuntel an moghya
angeveth an grays brassa
ea ha reward purfeth
           [armatores aredy

SECUNDUS TORTOR

Arluth the voth a veth grueys
1548 quart[r]on meyny desempys
dugh genavy alemma
benen gans the flogh byen
hath kentrevoges certen
1552 trussogh quik the costentyn
bo my agis lath omma.

TERTIUS TORTOR

Namsus thym vj vgons flogh
dywans then empour trussogh
1556   may hallons boys dewogys
kepar ha porhel bo lugh
lemen sovdoryen waryogh
na schappya benen in beys

CALO

1560 Kuntullys gena yma
viij vgons flogh rum ena
lour yv henna thum parte vy
serrys yv age mammov
1564 pan vo an rema marov
wegennov ny a ra moy

   As I should believe, for sake of doing good
   You would not have cried to us:
1532   Not for you is this usual.
     [The women ready with their children.

      CONSTANTINE.
   Go ye for me all over the country,
    Likewise Rome and Lombardy,
   Gather the children,
1536   That may be right certainly at home
     Up to three years.
   Let them and their mothers come here,
   Three thousand by number without a lie—
1540   It is no matter though they be a hundred more.

   Let every one go into his quarter
   A parcel of armed folk certainly
    Among you shall be divided.
1544   He that gathers the most
   Shall have the greatest thanks,
    Yea, and a perfect reward.
      [Armed men ready.

     SECOND TORTURER.
   Lord, thy will shall be done.
1548   A quarter of the household straightway
    Come with me hence.
   Woman, with thy little child
   And thy neighbouress certainly
1552   Pack ye quick to Constantine,
    Or I will slay you here.

     THIRD TORTURER.
   Now I have six score children!
   Quickly pack to the emperor
1556   That they may be bled
   Like a porker or a calf.
   Now, soldiers, take care
    That not a woman in the world escape.

      A DRUDGE.
1560 Gathered by me are
   Eight score children, by my soul!
    Enough is this for my part.
   Troubled are their mothers.
1564 When these shall be dead
    We will make more sweetlings.

PRIMUS TORTOR
[ad constantinum cum mulieribus et [pueris] plurimis

  Heyll costentyn in the dour
  lafuryys rag the pleysour
1568   a dro in pov me revue
  at oma xix cans flogh
  y feth sur colonov trogh
   pan weller age lathe

SECUNDUS TORTOR
1572 Costentyn devethys dre
  me yv hag yma gene
   vi *cans* flogh inweth y tek
  parys thage dewosa
1576 me a veth ov arluth da
   merugh an babyov wek

p. 60.
TERTIUS TORTOR
  Heyl costentyn the nobyl
  mblothov mur a bobyl
1580   rag the plesya me rumbue
  malbev an flogh a scappyas
  colonov ran a crakkyas
  viij *cans* sur me re gavas
1584   gruegh scon age dewose

CALO
  Heyl costentyn in the dour
  xj *cans* flogh theth enour
   ha moy me re ruk kuntel
1588 aban ethe mes a dre
  me re ruk flehys ievvje
   ragas tevery ancoel

PRIMA MATER
  Ellas emperour debyta
1592 mar mynnyth oma latha
   flehys bythqueth na pehes
  yma dywhy guan cusel
  a du an neff tayl dyel
1596   warnogh a tus ongrassyes   *[finit*

p. 61.
JUSTUS
  Na vragyogh brays lafarov
  y a veth purguir marov
   rag cafus sur age goys

FIRST TORTURER.

*[To Constantine with the women
and very many children.*

 Hail, Constantine in thy tower.
 Laboured for thy pleasure
1568   About in the country have I.
 Lo, here are nineteen hundred children!
 There will be surely broken hearts
   When their slaughter is seen.

SECOND TORTURER.

1572 Constantine, come home
 Am I, and here with me
   Six hundred children likewise I have brought.
 Ready to bleed them
1576 I am, my good lord.
   See ye the sweet babes!

THIRD TORTURER.

 Hail, Constantine the noble!
 Curses great from the people
1580   For pleasing thee I have had.
 . . . . the child has escaped
 Hearts of some have brok'en:
 Eight hundred surely I have found
1584   Have them bled at once.

THE DRUDGE.

 Hail, Constantine, in thy tower!
 Eleven hundred children to thy honour
   And more have I gathered.
1588 Since I went out from home
 I have made for thee, *je vous dis*,
   Children really dying.

FIRST MOTHER.

 Alas, Emperor pitiless!
1592 If thou wilt here slay
   Children that never sinned,
 This is to you a weak counsel.
 O God of heaven wreak vengeance
1596   On you, O graceless folk!

JUSTICE.

 Do not brag big words!
 They shall right truly be dead
   To get their blood, surely,

1600 an empour flour they golhy
may fo tekkeys eredy
kefys yv der an clergy
 sav in delma y hyl boys

CONSTANTINUS

1604 Py sul yv sum an flehys
us kuntullys thym *o*mma
ythyv sur mur a ponfeys
mar peth reys age latha
1608 trueth ambus ov queleys
age mammov ov thola
ha lowen certe*n* ʒeheys
thu*m* corff me a geme*r*sa

PRIMUS TORTOR

1612 Ima oma iij myl flogh
thu*m* gothfes ha vij vgans
bethens marov na sparyogh
ha wy a veth purthyblans
1616 in ag*is* lee me as lath
heb ovn oma na truath
moy es earov gvyls a coys

SECUNDUS TORTOR

Me a vyn dewose myl
1620 trehy age bryonsen
an corfov ny a ra pyl
hag as gor in dor ce*r*ten
the develys name
1624 ny sense moy latha flogh
es dyswul gau*er* py bogh
rag in mat*er* ny coth schame

p. 62.   CONSTANTINUS

Dynyte an goys ryel
1628 yv in rome pur thyogel
del recorde agen latha
neb a lath flogh in batel
sensys y feth de*n* cruel
1632 ov geryov gruegh attendya
poys yv gena dyswuthel
heb ken an keth flehys ma
ny won awose m*er*wel
1636 a vetha peyn thu*m* ena

1600 (And for) the flower of emperors, to wash him,
That he may be beautified readily.
Found is it through our learning
That he may be whole.

CONSTANTINE.

1604 How many is the sum of the children
That are gathered for me here?
It is surely much of trouble
If needs be to slay them.
1608 Pity have I seeing
Their mothers wailing,
And gladly certainly health
For my body I should get.

FIRST TORTURER.

1612 Here are three thousand children,
To my knowledge, and seven score.
Let them be killed! spare ye not!
And you shall be very clear.
1616 In your place I will kill them
Without fear here nor pity
More than (for) a wild hart of the wood.

SECOND TORTURER.

I will bleed a thousand
1620 (And) cut their throats.
The bodies we will strip,
And put them in earth certainly.
The devil's name!
1624 I would not hold killing a child more
Than destroying a goat or a buck,
For in the matter shame is not becoming.

CONSTANTINE.

Dignity of the blood royal
1628 Is in Rome right clearly.
As our law records:
Whoso shall slay a child in battle
Will be held a cruel man.
1632 Consider ye my words.
Heavy am I to destroy
Without pity these same children.
I know not, after dying,
1636 Whether there will be pain to my soul.

TERTIUS TORTOR

Ser emperour bethens lethys
 rag savment dywhy lemen
mar ny vyn du the coweys
1640 an iovle a vyn pur lowen
wose helma
omgolhough in age goys
sav nefre mar mynnogh boys
1644 ha ny as lath knak oma

CALO

Pan gol us awoys latha
 an chettis mowes ha mav
in vn noys mar lefara
1648 me a russe dywhy ix
an keth sort ma
mar mynnogh arluth brentyn
me a dregh y vreonsen
1652 hag an dewoys knak oma

   [*tranceunt tortores et mulieres
    expectant in placea*

p. 63.
CONSTANTINUS

A wek wegov agys mam
thywhywy y fye cam
 boys lethys am govys vy
1656 trueth vye del wothogh
latha omma iij myl flogh
 awoys sawya vn body

Guel yv genavy merwel
1660 in cleves bras indelma
ha gasa bev dyogel
 an iij myl flogh us omma
es del yv gena purlel
1664 gul mernans mar thebyta
me a vya den cruel
 mar lathen oll an re ma

Regh an flehys thage mam
1668 war beyn tenna ha cregy
me a charge na ve heb nam
 flogh vyth lethys eredy
ha me a vyn
1672 then benenes ry mona
boys ha dewes the perna
ha then flehys delles da
the dre mammethov tota
1676 why hagis flehys vyan

THIRD TORTURER.

Sir Emperor, let them be slain
   For healing to you now:
If God will not aid thee
   The devil will right gladly.
     After this
Wash yourself in their blood
If you will ever be healed,
     And we will slay them here, snap!

A DRUDGE.

What loss is it for slaying
   The chits, girl and boy!
In one night, so I say,
   I would make for you nine
     Of this same sort.
If you will, Lord sovran,
I will cut their throats
     And bleed them here, snap!

        [*The torturers go off and the women
            wait in the open.*

CONSTANTINE.

O sweet sweets of your mothers!
To you it were a wrong
   To be slain because of me.
Pity were it, as you know,
To slay here three thousand children
   For sake of healing one body.

I had liefer die
   In great disease thus,
And leave alive certainly
   The three thousand children that are here,
Than by me right truly
   Do a death so pitiless.
I should be a cruel man
   If I slew all these.

Give ye the children to their mothers.
   On pain of drawing or hanging
I charge that there be not, without exception,
   Any child slain verily;
     And I will
To the women give money
To buy food and drink,
And to the children good raiment.
Home, nurses, quickly,
     You and your little children!

p. 64.

SECUNDA MATER

    Ser emperour dywhy mur grays
    agys boys mar pytethays
        orth benenes bohosek*
1680 rag sawya agen flehas
    du re tharbara ȝehas
        thywhy arluth galosek   *finit*

CONSTANTINUS

    Me a vyn moys thum guely
1684 nansyv noys pur eredy
        squyth off omma am bevnans
    thum corff am beua ȝehas
    y rosen hanter ov gluas
1688   hag ol ov mebyl dyblans
            [*claudat hostium*

IHC.

    Pedyr ha povle eugh lemen
    then norveys the costenten
        dren pyte a gemeras
1692 orth flehys gruegh ha byen
    seluester in pur certen
        dotho ef a ree ȝehas

PETRUS

    Arluth the voth ny a ra
1696 broder povle duen alema
        the confortya costenten
    rag na scollyas
    goys an flehas
1700   gueresys y feth certen
        [*descendunt petrus et paulus ascendit
           in turrim constantinus*

p. 65.

PAULUS

    Constentyn mar qureth cosca
    golsov orthen ny oma
        danvenys dys rag ȝehas
1704 drefen kemeres pyta
    an flehys gruergh† del rusta
        ihesu a vyn the weras

    * perhaps *vohosek*.   † leg. *gruegh* ?

SECOND MOTHER.

    Sir Emperor, much thanks to you
    That you are so pitiful
        Towards poor women.
1680 For saving our children
    May God provide health
        For you, mighty Lord!

CONSTANTINE.

    I will go to my bed,
1684 Now it is night, right readily:
        Weary am I here of my life.
    For my body that I might have health
    I would give half my kingdom,
1688   And all my chattels clearly.
            [*Let him close the door.*

JESUS.

    Peter and Paul, go now
    To the earth unto Constantine:
        Through the pity he has had
1692 Towards children tiny and little
    Silvester very certainly
        Shall give him health.

PETER.

    Lord, thy will we shall do.
1696 Brother Paul, let us come hence
        To comfort Constantine,
    For he spilt not
    The blood of the children.
1700   He shall be healed certainly.
        [*Peter and Paul descend. Constantine
          goes up to the tower.*

PAUL.

    Constantine, if thou dost sleep
    Hearken to us, here
        Sent to thee for healing,
1704 Because of taking pity
    On the tiny children, as thou hast done,
        Jesu will cure thee.

PETRUS

      Drefen na russys scollia
1708 goys then ynocens oma
        crist dys agen danvonas
      pur salov grueys may festa
      the syluester donfon grua
1712   may teffo eff theth gueras

PAULUS

      An pap syluester defry
      in meneth sur neb vsy
        seraptim hennyv gelwys
1716 eff a ra prest the golhy
      may festa sav eredy
        heb moldra floghv^t in beys   [*finit*

PETRUS

      Ha pan vesta sav ha glaan
1720 gueyt dustruya in tyan
        ol templys an falge dewov
      grua socour ha menteyna
      myns may hylly in bysma
1724   the ihesu crist eglosyov

              [*tranceat ad celum*

p. 66.   CONSTANTINUS

      Benedicite pana syght
        ambuevy haneth in noys
      thymo y tuth ij den vryght
1728   degeys an darasov cloys
      hag a covsis
      donfon wa[r]lergh seluester
      hag y fethen heb awer
1732   a oll ov cleves sawys

      Maseger gans mur a greys
      kergh seluester thym uskys
        in mont sareptim yma
1736 ov cuthe gans y clergy
      lauer dethe eredy
        may teffons dymmo omma

SECUNDUS NUNCIUS *ad constantinum*

      Arluth costentyn pup preys
1740 the volnogeth a veth grueys
        genevy a fur termyn

PETER.

Because thou didst not spill
1708 The blood of the innocents here,
  Christ has sent us to thee,
Right sound that thou mayst be made.
To Silvester send
1712   That he may come to cure thee.

PAUL.

The pope Silvester, certainly,
Who is surely on a mountain,
  Soracte that is called,
1716 He will readily wash thee,
So that thou wilt be whole at once
  Without murdering any child in the world.

PETER.

And when thou shalt be whole and clean,
1720 Take care to destroy completely
  All the temples of the false gods.
Succour and maintain,
As many as thou canst in this world,
1724   Churches for Jesu Christ.
    [*Let him pass to heaven.*

CONSTANTINE.

Benedicite, what a sight
 I had this very night!
To me came two bright men,
1728 The doors shut close,
  And said
To send after Silvester
And I should be without grief
1732   Healed of all my disease.

Messenger, with much strength,
Seek Silvester for me quickly.
  On Mount Soracte he is,
1736 Hiding with his clergy.
Tell them at once
  That they come to me here.

SECOND MESSENGER [*to Constantine.*

Lord Constantine, always
1740 Thy will shall be done
  By me in a short time.

    marogyen duen alema
    me ny won in fays pyma
1744 an keth meneth na certyn
      [*ad siluestrem in monte seraptim*

    Heyl seluester hath clergy
    na fella cuthe defry
     wy ny regh in keth plasma
      [*The ymagis aredy w^t sylvester
       of pyter and povle*

p. 67. 1748 the costyntyn an emperour
    reys yv dyugh lafurya dour
    eff a erhys indella

      SELUESTER

    Arluth neff rebo gorthys
  1752 me a wor lemen inta
    gothe mernans dyn a reys
    byth ny yller y sconya
    ov bredereth
  1756 duen alema kescolon*
    ihesu map a saluasconn
     regen guerese pup deth
      [*ad constantinum*

    Heyll costentyn in the dour
  1760 me a wor ty a wetsa
    bones grueys dyso enour
    ha the cregyans a pe da
    ny an grussa
  1764 rag the voys in dysgregyans
    awos ovn gothe mernans
    inclenya dys ny vanna
      [*ascendit*

      CONSTANTINUS

    Seluester wolcum owhy
  1768 nynsyv awos drokcoleth
    ythogh kerhys dymovy
    repreff na cam nygis beth
    desesijs bras off defry
  1772 kekefrys ha nos ha deth
    cusullys der ov clergy
    o tus a fur skentoleth
    sur me a fua
  1776 tremmyl flogh gruergh the latha
    bath may rellen in v[r]na
    in goys tum an flebys na

     * MS, kescolen.

   Knights, let us come hence.
   I know not well where is
1744   That same mountain certainly.
       [To Silvester on Mount Soracte.
   Hail, Silvester, and thy clergy!
   Hide any longer
    You shall not in this same place.
      *[The images of Peter and Paul ready
        with Silvester.*
1748 To Constantine the emperor
   Need is it for you to go on vehemently:
    He has ordered so.

SILVESTER.

   Heaven's Lord be worshipped!
1752   I know now well
   To suffer death he has given to us.
    Never can it be refused.
     My brethren,
1756 Let us come hence with one heart.
   May Jesu, Son of salvation,
    Protect us every day!
        [To Constantine.
   Hail, Constantine, in thy tower!
1760   I know thou deservest
   That honour be done to thee,
    And that thy belief should be good
     We would cause it.
1764 Because of thy being in unbelief,
   For fear of suffering death
    Incline to thee I will not.
        [He goes up.

CONSTANTINE.

   Silvester, you are welcome:
1768   It is not on account of an ill deed
   That you are fetched to me.
    Reproof nor wrong ye shall not have.
   Greatly diseased am I,
1772   Likewise day and night
   Counselled by my clergy,
    Who were folk of much knowledge,
     Surely was I
1776 Three thousand tiny children to slay,
   Bathe that I should then
    In the warm blood of those children.

p. 68.

	Tremmyl a fue kuntulys
1780	thymo oma rag an cays
	mur trueth y kemerys
	latha prest kemys flehas
	awoys vn den
1784	me as ornes in fyv dre
	sav noswyth a thyuvne
	syght coynt y welys certen
	Dev then a thuth dym in nos
1788	gans nerth bras a wo[lo]vde[r]
	han darasov degeys clos
	ny won rum caradovder
	pyv ens y suer
1792	dymo y a covsis cler
	donfon warlergh seluester
	may renlen quik heb awer
	eff ath wolgh purlan kyn moys
1796	may fo sav the cleves mur
	pyv ylly an rema boys
	a wothogh wy seluester
	ov guarnya vy
1800	del grese dev thu ens y

SELUESTER

	Nynso an rena dewov
	me a leuer costentyn
	ij abostel caradov
1804	y o ʒᵒ crist cuff colyn

p. 69.

	Myr age ymach heb wov
	mar syns y havel certyn
	ha thyso age hanov
1808	me a leuer pur ylyn

CONSTANTINUS

	Ren ena us om body
	poren an rena ens y
	henna gans an alwethov
1812	hay cowᵗ a thek cletha
	in nos y a fue gena
	teka syght war ov ena
	ny welys in ov dethyov
1816	mercy war crist y creya
	boys crystyan menna heb wov

SELUESTER

	Me ath wra* cathecumynys
	ha lemen ty a penys
1820	vn sythen heb feladov

* Seems *vora*.

    Three thousand were gathered
1780   To me here for the case.
    Much pity I took
     To slay so many children
      On account of one person.
1784 I ordered them alive home:
    But at night-time I awoke:
     A strange sight I saw certainly.

    Two men came to me at night
1788   With a great strength of radiance,
    And the doors shut close.
     I know not, by my loveableness,
      Who they were surely.
1792 To me they said clearly
    Send after Silvester
    That I should quickly without grief—
    "He will wash thee full clean before going,
1796   So that thy great disease shall be healed."
    Who could these be,
     Know ye, Silvester,
      Warning me?
1800   As I believed, two gods were they.

      SILVESTER.

    Those were not gods,
     I say, Constantine.
    Two loveable apostles
1804   They were to Christ the dear heart.
    Behold their images without a lie
     If they are like them certainly,
    And to thee their names
1808   I will tell very fairly.

      CONSTANTINE.

    By the soul that is in my body
    Exactly those they were!
     That one with the keys,
1812 And his comrade bore a sword.
    At night they were with me.
    Fairer sight, on my soul,
     I have not seen in my days.
1816 Mercy I cry on Christ.
     Be a Christian I will without a lie.

      SILVESTER.

    I will make thee a catechumen,
    And now thou shalt do penance
1820   A week without fail.

war lergh henna begythys
ty a veth sur ha golhys
may fy salov

CONSTANTINUS

p. 70.

1824 Penys purguir yv ov luyst
ha creya pup vr war crist
mercy rag ov fehosov
then guan ha tus omthevas
1828 in dewelyans am pehas
manneff ry alesonov

SELUESTER

[*descendit. holy water aredy*

Lemmen gruaff the vegethya
in hanov map maria
1832 omma atte ty golhys
neb a vyrwys in grovs p[r]en
re gronntya dyso lemen
del in peseff luen yehey(s)

[*ye vysour away*

*Cum in aquam descendisset baptismatis
mirabilis enituit splendor lucis Sic inde
mundus exiuit et christum se vidisse asseruit*

IHC.

1836 Costentyn rag the pyte
a gemercys an flehys
han tregereth warnethe
age lathe na vynsys

[*ye processyon aredy*

1840 me a vyn sur the sawye
a pegh pan ota golhys
mercy neb a gemerre
mercy an gueres pup preys

CONSTANTINUS

1844 Benedycite pan wolov
revue oma sollebreys
ihesu crist pen elyov
pur thefry me re weleys
1848 aleys ol y wolyov
the ragoff sur disquetheys
ys guelys cleth a dyov
ha tek eff am confortyeys

After that baptized
Thou shalt be surely, and washen,
 That thou mayst be healed.

CONSTANTINE.

1824 To do penance right truly is my desire,
And to cry always on Christ
 Mercy for my sins.
To the weak and orphan folk
1828 In atonement of my sin
 I will give alms.

SILVESTER.

[He descends. Holy water ready.

Now I do baptize thee
In the name of Mary's Son.
1832 Lo, here thou art washen.
May he who died on the cross-tree
Grant to thee now,
 As I beseech him, a full healing!
[The mask away.

When he went down into the water of baptism there shone forth a marvellous splendour of light. So thence he came forth clean, and declared that he had seen Christ.

JESUS.

1836 Constantine, for thy pity
 Which thou tookest on the children,
And the mercy upon them
 That thou wouldst not slay them
[The procession ready.
1840 I will surely heal thee
 When thou art washen from sin.
Whoso may have mercy
 Mercy shall heal him always.

CONSTANTINE.

1844 Benedicite, what a light
 Was here some time ago!
Jesus Christ, head of healing,
 Right certainly I have seen.
1848 Widely all his wounds
 Before me surely uncovered,
I saw them left and right,
 And fairly he comforted me.

SILUESTER

1852 Ty a yl boys lowenek
    kyntheste claff anhethek
        grasse the crist ythoys sav
nyn fus teka
1856 den na weka
        thum gothfes in the dethyov

CONSTANTINUS

The crist ihesu ingrassaff
    ha thys seluester nefra
1860 theth palys lemen manaff
    gans processyon the gora
dres an gluas y comondyaff
    du mas crist gorthys na ve
1864 ha me a ra mar pewaff
    the lays ihesu cresyae

        ad palacium pape procesc[i]onabiliter
        [*et postea tranceat domum*

[And John ergudyn aredy a horse bakke yt was yt
Justis wt constantyn ffor to play yt marchont*

p. 72. *Exulatores hic pompabunt vel vnus pro omnibus*

PRIMUS EXULATOR

Me yv outlayer in coys
moy reovte in ov oys
    1868 bythqueth purguir numdarfa
pan vo due ov stoff achy
ware me a provy moy
    nynsyv marnes sportt raffna

SECUNDUS EXULATOR

1872 Nansyv preys aspya pray
due yv an mona rum fay
    mester in agen mesk ny
aspyen gvas gans pors poys
1876 mar kyllyn den sans eglos
    whare y a kuntel moy

PRIMUS EXULATOR

In sol matis duen in kerth
aspyogh gans mur an nerth
1880   py fo marchont ov quandra

---

* Here, in a third hand, follow the words: *Pax vos omnes nos sumus melyores vyrgilius.*

SILVESTER.

1852 Thou mayst be joyous.
Though thou wert a loathsome leper,
Thanks to Christ, thou art whole.
There has not been a fairer
1856 Man, nor a sweeter,
To my knowledge, in thy days.

CONSTANTINE.

To Christ Jesu I give thanks,
And to thee, Silvester, ever.
1860 To thy palace now will I
With a procession put thee.
Throughout the kingdom I will command
That no god but Christ be worshipped,
1864 And I will cause, if I live,
Belief in Jesu's laws.

To the pope's palace in procession-wise,
[and thereafter let him go home.

[And John Ergudyn, who was the Justice with Constantine, on horseback ready to play the merchant.

Outlaws shall here parade, or one for all.

FIRST OUTLAW.

I am an outlaw in the forest.
More sway in my age
1868 Never right truly has fallen to me.
When my stuff at home shall be ended
Soon I will try more.
Naught save sport is it to rob.

SECOND OUTLAW.

1872 Now's (the) time to look out for prey.
Ended is the money, by my faith,
Master, amongst us.
Let us look out for a lad with a heavy purse,
1876 If we can, a man of holy Church.
Anon they will gather more.

FIRST OUTLAW.

Up, mates, let us come away.
Look out with much of strength
1880 Where a merchant may be wandering.

    y dalhenna na sparyogh
    me a omgem*er* ragogh
      hag*is* men*ten* benytha

               descendit

TERTIUS EXULATOR

1884 Me a weyl guas war geyn margh
    na fella ny vanna p*a*rgh*
      gene at eve sesijs
    deyskyn then dor mata
1888 ha the borse mes ath ascra
      me ambeth hath margh usk*is*

MERCATOR

    A serys clowugh ov leff
    dovtyogh drok thag*is* eneff
1892   pan dremennogh an bysme
    agys sp*erys* sur an pre*n*
    in anken ha m*ur* a peyn
      a thu go ef an ene

            [*ye prest aredy*

PRIMUS EXULATOR

1896 Pur a wylste war an kee
    eneff map de*n* in bysmae
      ov repentya rag y throk
    mar nu*m*kem*er* du certen
1900 an iovle a ra purlowen
      inagefery† avel hok

QUARTUS EXULATOR

    Me a weyl guas in gon hyr
    pron*ter* ef a hevel suyr
1904   yma mona gans henna
    ser p*a*rson bona dyes
    me a vyn changya porses
      be my fay kyns mos lema

PRESBITER

1908 A te then p*r*eder ath du
    y volnogeth byth nynsyv
      bones grueys in ketelma
    terry y wormenadov
1912 a regh why heb feladov
      gothvethugh y attendya

* MS. paragh.   † MS. perhaps *inagesery*.

To lay hold of him spare not.
I will betake myself before you,
    And support you ever.
                                       [*He goes down.*

THIRD OUTLAW.

1884 I see a lad on horseback.
No further will I forbear.
    By me behold him seized.
Get down to the ground, mate,
1888 And thy purse out of thy bosom
    I will have, and thy horse quickly.

MERCHANT.

O sirs, hear my voice!
Fear evil to your soul,
1892   When ye pass from this world
Your spirit surely shall pay for it
In grief and much of pain
    O God, woe is it the soul!
                                   [*The priest ready.*

1896   ### FIRST OUTLAW.

. . . hast thou seen on the way
The soul of a son of man in this world
    Repenting for her sin.
If God will not take me certainly
1900 The devil will very gladly
    Into his number (?) like a . . . .

FOURTH OUTLAW.

I see a lad in a long gown.
A priest he seems surely :
    There is money with that one.
1904 Sir parson, *bona dies*,
I will change purses
    By my faith before going hence.

THE PRIEST.

1908 Ah thou man, think of thy God!
His will is not at all
    To be done thus.
Break his commandments
1912 You do without fail,
    Ye know (how) to attend to him.

PRIMUS EXULATOR

  Neb a gem*er* ovn y thu
  ny sew*en* henna neb tu
1916   mata orthen ny na set
  sav dascor ol the vona
  bo annyl the quartrona
   oma me a ra heb let

PRESBITER

1920 Galles genogh me*ns* ambus
  ter*men* a thue *cr*ist ihe*s*us
   inter*t*hon a ran an gvyr
  prederugh helma deth brus
1924   pemo*nt* thy*mm*o gruegh in suyr

PRIMUS EXULATOR

  A vethe preys* bys deth brus
  ny thue henna in trogel
  ty a gel moy an pyth us
1928   adro dyso dyogel
   streppyogh y queth
p. 75. eff re ros thyn deth hyr lour
  pan vo an vrus wy a wour
1932   an pement na hyns ny veth

SECUNDUS EXULATOR

  At eve strepys in noth
  in delma guthel y coth
   then guesyon astefe peth

       [*expectant in placea*

HIC COMES ROHANI

1936 Me yv chyff arluth rohan
  ʒurl worthy na*n*geves par
  meryasek in certa*n*
  o thymo pur oges car
1940   in kerth galles
  forsak*is* y das hay vam
  ha ny won py theth heb nam
   ragtho may thoma *s*erres

PRIMUS NUNCIUS

1944 Ser ʒurle arluth galosek
  yma purguir meryasek
   devethys oma the*n* pov

    * Perhaps *peys.*

FIRST OUTLAW.

  Whoso has fear of his God
  He will not succeed on any side.
1916   Mate, do not set (thyself) against us,
  But deliver all thy money,
  Or else quarter thee
   Here I will without hindrance.

PRIEST.

1920 Gone with you is all I have.
  The time of Christ Jesus will come
   Between us the True will divide.
  Think of this, on doomsday
1924   You will surely make payment to me.

FIRST OUTLAW.

  Should there be time until doomsday,
   That will not come in the body.
  Thou shalt lose more, the wealth that is
1928   Around thee surely.
   Strip off his garment!
  He has given to us a day long enough.
  When the Judgment may be you know.
1932   The payment will not be before.

SECOND OUTLAW.

  Lo, he is stript naked.
  Thus ought to be done
   To the lads who have wealth.

    [*They wait in the open space.*

HERE THE EARL OF ROHAN.

1936 I am a chief, lord of Rohan,
   A worthy earl, who has not a peer.
  Meriasek certainly,
   Who was to me a very near relation,
1940   Went away,
  Forsook his father and his mother,
  And I know not where he went, without mistake,
   So that for him I am vexed.

FIRST MESSENGER.

1944 Sir Earl, mighty Lord,
  Meriasek right truly is
   Come here to our country:

ryb pontelyne eredy
1948 avel hermyt purthevry
speyna a ra y dethyov

p. 76.   COMES ROHANI

Me a vyn mones dotha
hay cothmens purguir gena
1952   y temptya mar a kyllyn
rag treyla thy eretons
y nessevyn sur ymons
serris dretho in certyn

COGNATUS COMITIS ROHANI

1956 Yma eff in meneth bras
del glowevy sur myl pas
theworth an grond a woles
hag ena prest nos ha deth
1960 y honen ol eff a veth
y vos hay susten nebes

[*descendit* [leg. *ascendit*] *comes ad montem*
et cognatus et agnatus

MERIADOCUS

The ihesu rebo grasseys
omma ythese tregys
1964   avel hermyt in guelfos
in le ov delles ourlyn
purpur pannov fyn certyn
lemen me a wesk queth los

1968 In ov nesse hevys ruen
ny eve cydyr na gwyn
na dewes marnes dour pur
hag erbys an goverov
1972 a veth ov bos thum preggyov
na vo ree fors ov nattur

p. 77.   AGNATUS

Oma yma meryasek
ov corthya du galosek
1976   poren in top an meneth
myl pas in ban alemme
then chapel purguir ymae
acontis gans tus purgoeth

By Pontelyne indeed
1948 As a hermit full really
He doth spend his days.

THE EARL OF ROHAN.

I will go to him,
And his friends truly with me,
1952 If we can tempt him
To return to his inheritance.
His kinsmen surely are
Vexed through him certainly.

A RELATION OF THE EARL OF ROHAN.

1956 He is on a great mountain,
As I hear, surely a thousand paces
From the ground at the bottom.
And there always, night and day,
1960 He himself is,
His food and his little sustenance.

[*The Earl goes up to the mountain, with the relation, and the agnate.*

MERIASEK.

To Jesu be thanks!
Here I have been dwelling
1964 As a hermit in the wilderness.
In lieu of my raiment of silk,
Purple cloths fine certainly,
Now I wear a grey garment,

1968 Nearest me (is) a shirt of horsehair.
I quaff not cider nor wine
Nor any drink, unless pure water,
And herbs of the brooks
1972 Are my food for my meals,
So that my nature be not overstrong.

THE AGNATE.

Here is Meriasek,
Worshipping mighty God,
1976 Right on the top of the mountain.
A thousand paces up from hence
To the chapel right truly is it
Accounted by folk full old.

I

COMES ROHANI

1980 Meryasek lowene dys
omma duthen theth vereys
 hag inweth theth confortia
ha gul dyso aswonfos
1984 the nessevyn in ponfos
 y mons ragos in bysma

MERIADOCUS

Prag ymons y in ponfos
ny ruk truspus thum gothfos
1988 dethe na the den in beys
myns may hallen omguythe
na ny garsen benythe
 gans weres du benegeys

COMES ROHANI

1992 Trueth mur yv ahanas
den yv sevys a lyne bras
 ty the vynnes mar sempel
p. 78. bones omma in ponvos
1996 the car the honen nynsos
 me a veth y leferel

MERIADOCUS

Da dym ythyv.
nesse the du
2000 hay gorthya eff
guthel y voth
kepar del goth
 may hallen dendyl gluas neff

COGNATUS COMITIS ROHANI

2004 Ty a also gorthya du
del us lues den hythyv
 ov pewe tek hag onest
dus alema genen ny
2008 ellas trueth ambus vy
 the vos oma avel best   [finit

MERIADOCUS

Bohogogneth abreth du
remoconn then cur ythyv
2012 wose helma

THE EARL OF ROHAN.

1980 Meriasek, joy to thee!
Here we have come to see thee,
  And likewise to comfort thee,
And to cause thee to know
1984 Thy kinsmen in trouble
  Are for thee in this world.

MERIASEK.

Why are they in trouble?
I have not done violence, to my knowledge,
1988   To them, nor to anyone on earth.
To go that I may worsen myself
I should never like
  With help of blessed God.

THE EARL OF ROHAN.

1992 Great pity is of thee,
A man that is raised of a great line.
  That thou wishest so simply
To be here in trouble.
1996 Thine own friend thou art not,
  I shall be to say it.

MERIASEK.

Good to me it is
To draw near to God,
  And to worship Him,
2000 To do His will,
As behoveth,
  So that I may earn heaven's kingdom.

THE RELATION OF THE EARL OF ROHAN.

2004 Thou mightest worship God
As there are many men to-day
  Living fair and decently.
Come thou hence with us
2008 Alas, pity have I
  That thou art here like a wild beast.

MERIASEK.

Poverty on behalf of God
Is removal to the Court (of heaven)
2012   After this,

        hag inweth mam a yehes
        ny wothogh why ov flehes
            pendryv ol boys an ena

p. 79.   **COMES ROHANI**

2016 Meryasek nynsos fur
      gorthya du ty alse sur
          kyn fy reoute an beys
      meth yv gans ol the cufyon
2020 the vones omma dyson
          avel begyer desethys

              MERIADOCUS

      A war agys cam why pobyl
      helma yv bevnans nobyl
2024   termen a thue
      ha then ena sur megyans
      ythyv rag cafus selwans
          ol then ene

2028 Lust an kyk y ra vodya
      han beys eff a ra gasa
          the trettya indan y dreys
      byth ny ra cam the neb den
2032 gallus an iovle pup termen
          dretho a veth confundijs
      megyans then ena certen
          ha ioy neff dretho guanys

p. 80.   **COMES ROHANI**

2036 Ima lues den heb greff
      a theseff mones then neff
          ha wath a gar peth an bys
      indelle te a alse
2040 gul worschyp* mur theth nesse
          ha boys selwys

              MERIADOCUS

      Pyth an beys ha reovte
      ha rychyth bras rum lovte
2044   benithe me nys care
      nynsyns the trestye mas falge
      annethe kyn feste calge
          war na ra fethye inne

          * MS. worsthyp.

And also a mother of healing.
Ye know not, my children,
   What is all the food of the soul.

THE EARL OF ROHAN.

2016 Meriasek, thou art not wise
Worship God, thou mightest surely
   Though thou shouldst have sway of the world.
Shame is with all thy dear ones
2020 That thou art here at once
   Like a beggar seated.

MERIASEK.

Go on your way, you people.
This is a noble life.
2024   An end will come,
And to the soul a sure delight,
It is to have salvation
   All to the soul,
2028 The lust of the flesh it will expel,
And the world it will leave
   To be trodden under its feet.
Never do wrong to any one.
2032 The devil's power always
   Thereby will be confounded.
Delight to the soul certainly
   And joy of heaven gained thereby.

THE EARL OF ROHAN.

2036 There are many men, without grief,
Who desire to go to the heaven,
   And yet love somewhat the world.
In like manner thou mightest
2040 Do much worship to thy nearest,
   And be saved.

MERIASEK.

Wealth of the world and sway,
And great riches, by my loyalty,
2044   Never have I loved them.
They are not to be trusted, but false.
Of them though thou hast many,
   Beware that thou confide not in them.

AGNATUS

2048 Na temptyogh na moy an den
reys yv the crist cuff colen
thy lel servye
na ve y vose guir sans
2052 mar lues merkyl dyblans
byth ny russe   [*finit*

COMES ROHANI

Ny vannef y annye
rag thym ny ammont defry
2056 meryasek me ath pease
a wul vn dra ragovy
del oys ov goys
p. 81.   laddron mur us in povma
2060 lues den ov tustruya
grua then rena avodya
par del yv mur the galloys

Ny yl den mones then fer
2064 na vova robijs in suer
dustruys ha corff ha peth
certen feryov in breten
cafus y fensen certen
2068 ov gueres mar a mynneth

An wehes deth
in gortheren
an kynse feer
2072 han gela veth
mys est certen
orth ov deser
an viijth deth
2076 han tresse mys gvyn gala
dugol myhal yv henna
in plu voala* neffrea
an keth feriovma a veth

MERIADOCUS

2080 Helma dis a veth grontis
poren del yv deserijs
dre grath du ha tra nahen
an ladron a veth pelleys
2084 ran the guel forthov treylys
mercy du mar crons goven
    [*comes rohani trancit domum et
      meriadocus expectat ibidem*

* leg. noala.

THE AGNATE.

Tempt the man no more.
Need is Christ, dear heart,
    To serve him loyally.
If he were not a true saint
So many miracles clearly
    He would never work.

THE EARL OF ROHAN.

I will not annoy him,
    For me it concerns not really.
Meriasek, I would pray thee
    To do one thing for me.
        As thou art my blood.
Robbers many there are in this country,
Many persons destroying:
Make those go away,
    As thy power is great.

No one can go to the fair
Without being robbed surely,
    Ruined both body and wealth.
Certainly fairs in Brittany
I would have certainly
    If thou wouldst help me.

The sixth day,
    In July,
        The first fair,
And the other will be,
    In the month of August certainly,
        By my desire.
            The eighth day,
And the third month September,
Michael's feast-day is that.
In the parish of Noala ever
        These same fairs shall be.

MERIASEK.

This to thee shall be granted
Just as is desired
    Through God's grace and nothing else.
The robbers shall be banished,
Some turned to better ways,
    If they ask God's mercy.

    [*The Earl of Rohan passes home and Meriasek
      waits in the same place.*

p. 82.
PRIMUS EXULATOR

     Nov mat*is* merugh adro
     mar quelogh so mot y go
2088   den ryb an coys ov quandra
     gedyogh dymo quik y pors
     eff angeveth god ys cors
        neb a covs erbyn raffna

          Hic ignis venit super illos

SECUNDUS EXULATOR

2092 Out gony bras ha bye*n*
     yma ol an coys gans tae*n*
        the lusu ython leskys
     dufe warnan anfusy
2096 hennyv rag an devlugy
        a russyn oma in beys

TERTIUS EXULATOR

     Ay tav an iovle theth lesky
     praga pe*n*dryv an fesky
2100   us genes han terlemel
     an golovder me a wor
     nynsyv eff leme*n* an lor
        pan vsy ov trehevel

QUARTUS EXULATOR

2104 Out oᵗ fyyn ny
     yma ov lesky
        an coys the vn tanges lel   [*horse aredy*
     out oᵗ ny a veth skaldys
2108 alema fye uskys
     me a vyn mar a calla
p. 83. ha molleth du in gorel
     pyma thym ov margh morel
2112   an iovle mur re*n* ancumbra

        [*tranceat iiij*ᵗᵘˢ *exulator super equum*

PRIMUS EXULATOR

     A me*r*yasek me*r*yasek
     del ote sans galosek
        peys ragovy
2116 na veua leski*s* in tan
     ha the se*r*vont in certan
     me a veth bys venary

FIRST OUTLAW.

 Now mates, look around!
 If ye see, so mote I go,
2088   Any one wandering by the wood,
 Guide his purse to me quick.
 He shall have God's curse
  Who speaks against robbing.

   Here fire comes upon them.

SECOND OUTLAW.

2092 Out! woe's us! great and small!
 All the wood is on fire!
  We are burnt to ashes!
 Misfortune has come on us:
2096 That is for the devilry
  That we have done here in the world.

THIRD OUTLAW.

 Ah be silent! the devil to burn thee!
 Why, what is the hurry
2100   That is with thee, and the skipping?
 The light I know:
 Is it not now the moon
  Since she is rising?

FOURTH OUTLAW.

2104 Out, out, let us flee.
 The wood is burning
  To a real blaze.   [*a horse ready.*
 Out, out, we shall be scalded
2108 Hence fly forthwith
  I will if I can.
 And God's curse on the work!
 Where for me is my black horse?
2112   May the great devil encumber him!

  [*Let the fourth outlaw go off on a horse.*

FIRST OUTLAW.

 O Meriasek, Meriasek,
 As thou art a mighty saint,
  Pray for me
2116 That I be not burnt in fire,
 And thy servant certainly
  I will be for ever.

SECUNDUS EXULATOR

  Meryasek sav vy heb flovs
2120 marsyv guir a glowys covs
   the voys galosek oma
  thyso omry
  y fannavy
2124   bys venary mar pewa   [*finit*

TERTIUS EXULATOR

  Meryasek del oys guir sans
  leme*n* p*re*st sav ov bevnans
   ha thys y fanaff omry

QUINTUS EXULATOR

2128 me a greys in m*er*yasek
  y vones eff galosek
   se*r*vont dotho bethevy
  ha rag ov fehas mosek
2132   mercy ihe*s*u me a gry   [*finit*

PRIMUS EXULATOR

  Gras the c*r*ist ha m*er*yasek
  sawys on ny glan ha tek
   the orth mys[ch]eff in torma
p. 84. 2136 mones dotho ny a vyn
  hay deserya p*u*r ylyn
   pesy c*r*ist dyny gava

         [*ad meriadocum in monte*

  Meryasek lowene dys
2140 omma ython devethys
   rag pesy the cusel p*re*yst
  ny revue t*us* ongrasyas
  ha re vsias hage*r* gas
2144   raffna ladra p*ur* lues feyst

  Pan esen dethwyth in coys
  ov mones sur a porpos
   the laddra t*us* p*ur*guyryon
2148 warne*n* y tuth bum a tan
  ha luehes in pur certan
   in hevelep lesk*is* glan
    ny a vethe pur dyson

2152 Me a greys truethek
  gueres thymo m*er*yasek
   der hen*n*a y fuff sawys

SECOND OUTLAW.

Meriasek, save me without a flout,
If it be true, as I have heard say,
    That thou art mighty here.
Give myself to thee
I will
    For ever if I live.

THIRD OUTLAW.

Meriasek, as thou art a true saint
Now quickly save my life,
    And to thee I will give myself.

FIFTH OUTLAW.

I believe in Meriasek
That he is mighty,
    A servant to him I will be,
And for my stinking sin
    Mercy, Jesu, I cry.

FIRST OUTLAW.

Thanks to Christ and Meriasek,
Saved are we clean and fair
    From mischief this turn.
We will go to him
And desire him right fairly
    To beseech Christ to forgive us.

        [To Meriasek on the mountain.

Meriasek, joy to thee!
Here we are come
    To beseech thy counsel quickly.
We have been graceless folk,
And have used, an ugly case,
    To rob, to plunder very many indeed.

When we were on a day in the wood
Going surely on purpose
    To plunder full righteous folk
On us came a blow of fire
And lightning in very certain.
Apparently clean burnt
    We were right surely

I cried out piteously
'Help me, Meriasek!'
    By that I was saved.

ha part am felschyp gena
2156 ran in kerth re ruk feya
ran ny won pythens gyllys
maythovy ameys oma
ellas mar pethen dampnys

p. 85.   MERIADOCUS

2160 Pesugh mercy war ihesu
ha remembrogh agis du
guetyogh may fegh glan zesseys
na dreylogh the pegh na moy
2164 ha ragogh pur eredy
the ihesu crist me a beys

PRIMUS EXULATOR

A meryasek meryasek
an enevov bohosek
2168 kemer trueth mar kyl boys
na ve creya warnogh why
kellys ol y fyen ny
yowynk ha loys   [*finit*

MERIADOCUS

2172 Byth na gothugh in dysper
mercyabyl yv du ker
the vyns a vyn y pesy
pan us dywhy edrega
2176 y raff agis benyga
*in nomine patris et filii
et spiritus sancti amen*
the pup gruegh restorite
myns may hallogh pub termen

COMES ROHANI

2180 The ihesu rebo grasseys
hag inweth 3ª veryasek
p. 86.   thyn ol ythyv coselheys
kefrys rych ha bohosek
2184   purguir a yll
lemen mones then feryov
an laddren pel mes an pov
gyllys yns purthyogeyll

2188 Grays the ihesu galosek
dre peiadov meryasek
oll yv helma

And part of my fellowship with me.
2156 Some away did flee,
    Some I know not where they are gone.
So that I am without here.
    Alas, if I should be damned!

MERIASEK.

2160 Ask mercy of Jesu,
And remember your God.
    Take care that you be clean confessed.
Turn not to sin any more.
2164 And for you very readily
    To Jesu Christ I will pray.

FIRST OUTLAW.

O Meriasek, Meriasek!
On the poor souls
2168   Take pity, if it can be.
Had there not been crying on thee,
We should all have been lost,
    Young and gray.

MERIASEK.

2172 Never fall into despair.
Merciful is dear God
    To as many as will beseech him.
Since you have repentance
2176 I will bless you
    In the name of the Father and the Son
    And of the Holy Ghost, amen.

To every one make restoration
    All that you can always.

THE EARL OF ROHAN.

2180 To Jesu be thanks,
    And likewise to Meriasek!
For us all is quieted.
    At the same time rich and poor
2184   Right truly may
Now go to the fairs.
The robbers far away from the country
    Are gone right certainly.

2188 Thanks to mighty Jesu,
Through Meriasek's prayer
    All this is.

an treffer a veth sensys
2192 meryasek as grontyeys
gorthys rebo benytha
vi deth in mys gortheren
vn feer a veth in certen
2196 thum desyr in ketelma
in meys est an viij^{ves} deth
an secund feer sur a veth
sensys in pov benytha
2200 han tresse meys gvyngala
dugol myhall byth henna
in plu wyn voala* sensys
ha meryasek benytha
2204 inna purguir campollys

p. 87. *Hic Dux Cornubie pompabit dicens*
Me yv duk in oll kernow
indella ytho ov thays
hag vhel arluth in pov
2208 a tamer the pen an vlays
tregys off lemen heb wov
berth in castel an dynas
sur in peddre
2212 ha war an tyreth vhel
thym yma castel arel
a veth gelwys tyndagyel
henna yv o[v]fen tregse

2216 Leferys yv thymmo vy
bones in keverang penweth
den grassyes pur eredy
dres an mor dy eff a thueth
2220 nynsyv na pel
ov styward a glosugh why
cows annotho in tefry
leferugh dym dyogel

p. 88. SENESCALLUS DUCIS
2224 Clowys arluth galosek
eff yv gelwys meryasek
den grassyes in y dethyov
gans pup ol ythyv kerys
2228 inweth del yv leferys
dadder mur y ruk in pov

CAMERARIUS DUCIS
Arluth me a leuer guir
gallas henna the ken tyr
2232 nansyv sythyn tremenys

*leg. noala

The third fair shall be held :
2192   Meriasek has granted it.
       Worshipped be he ever.
Sixth day in the month July
A fair shall be certainly
2196   Thus according to my desire
In the month of August the eighth day
   The second fair surely shall be
       Held in the country for ever.
2200 And the third month September
Michael's feast, that shall be
   Held in the blessed parish of Noala,
And Meriasek ever
2204   In them right truly talked of.

Here the Duke of Cornwall shall parade, saying

I am Duke in all Cornwall :
   So was my father,
And a high lord in the country
2208   From Tamar to the end of the kingdom.
I am dwelling now, without a lie,
     Within the castle of Dynas
     Surely in Pidar,
2212 And in the high land
I have another castle,
Which is called Tyntagel :
     That is my chief dwelling-seat.

2216 It is said to me
     That there is opposite (?) Penwith
A man gracious right truly,
Over the sea thither he came.
2220   He is not far.
My steward, have you heard
Speak of him really?
     Tell me certainly.

         THE DUKE'S STEWARD.

2224 I have heard, mighty lord.
He is called Meriasek,
     A man gracious in his days.
By every one he is loved
2228 Likewise as is said
     Much good he has done in the country.

         THE DUKE'S CHAMBERLAIN.

Lord, I will say true
He has gone to another land
2232   Now it is a week past,

gans vn de*n* heb feladov
ny vue achy the kernov
 in neb le vythol guelys

DUX

2236 Praga ytheth mes an pov
dremas o in y dethyov
 ny glowys ken leferel
 ny govsy mas hones*ter*
2240 pur guir a fur a thadder
 lues re ruk y gormel

CAMERARIUS DUCIS

Tevdar pagan ongrassyas
in povma eff re dyrhays
2244 del glovsugh ha nynsyv pel
ny vyn gothe vn cristyan
in y oges pur certen
 marthys eff yv de*n* cruel
2248 m*er*yasek ganso lemen
 helhys vue in kerth heb fael   [*finit*

p. 89.   DUX CORNUBIE

Out mylw* war an ky plos
 prag na glowys helma kyns
2252 re*n* arluth the*n* beys am ros
me a ra pur cot y guyns
kyns ys dum*er*her the nos
 eff a deerbyn trestyns
2256 hag a guayn pur sempellos
 may kerna purguir y dyns

Bethugh p*ar*ys ov meyny
ny vanna alowe ky
2260 pur certe*n* achy thu*m* tyr
eff an p*re*veth hag in tyn
avodia sur mar ny vyn
 y woys a resek the*n* luyr

SENES[C]ALLUS DUCIS

2264 P*ar*ys on dywhy sur duk
mur a throk p*re*st eff re ruk
 a pan duthe in povma
in menek in lestevdar
2268 yma y pe*n*plas heb mar
 mur dotho ov resortya

By one man without fail
He has not been within Cornwall
    Seen in any place at all.

THE DUKE.

2236 Why has he gone out of the country?
He was an honest man in his days.
    I heard not other talk.
He spake not save decency.
2240 Right truly for much of his goodness
    Many have praised him.

THE DUKE'S CHAMBERLAIN.

Teudar, a graceless pagan,
In this country he has landed,
2244   As you heard, and it is not long ago.
He will not endure a Christian
In his neighbourhood, right certainly;
    A marvellous cruel man is he!
2248 Meriasek by him now
    Has been hunted away, without fail.

THE DUKE OF CORNWALL.

Out a thousand times on the dirty hound!
    Why have I not heard this before?
2252 By the Lord who gave me to the world,
    I will make his wind right short.
Before it is Wednesday at night
    He shall meet sadness,
2256 And shall gain a right simple loss,
    So that he may right truly gnash his teeth.

Be ye ready, my household.
I will not allow a hound
2260   Right certainly within my land.
He shall prove it, and severely.
If he does not go off
    His blood shall run to the floor.

THE DUKE'S STEWARD.

2264 Ready are we for you, sir Duke.
Much of evil now hath he done
    Since he came into this country.
In Meneage, in Les-Teader,
2268 Is his chief place without doubt.
    Many to him (are) resorting.

DUX CORNUBIAE

  Kyn geffo eff myllyov cans
  purguir ythons then mernans
2272   dre voth ihesu us avan
  me a vyn gothfes praga
  y tuthe sur then povma
   heb ov lessyans in certan
2276 ol warbarth duen alemma
   ov meny a luen golan
    Dux descendit cum xx^{ti} armatoribus
     [w^t stremers

p. 90.   DUX

  Leferugh ov arlythy
  pythyv guel thynny sensy
2280   the vetya gans an turant
  mar calla y tebel far
  drefen y voys sur heb mar
   erbyn fay crist dyspusant

SENESCALLUS

2284 Tregys vue in lestevdar
   honna yma in menek
  sav plas aral sur heb mar
   us then tebel genesek
2288   berth in porder
  honna veth gelwys goddren
  ena purguir an poddren
   thotho prest re ruk harber

DUX

2292 The soyth ny a vyn sensy
   in hanov crist us avan
  mar tryg in kernov defry
  ny a vet gans an belan
2296 ov baner dyspletyoghwy
   therago pur guir lemman
  del goth the arluth worthy
  me a vyn moys ahanan

        [ad tevdar

SECUNDUS NUNCIUS ad *Tevdarum*

2300 Heyl tevdar emperour a rays
  yma duk oma in vlays
   drehevys sur erthebyn

DUKE OF CORNWALL.

Though he may have thousands of hundreds,
Right truly they shall come to the death
2272   Through the will of Jesu who is above.
I will know why
He came surely to the country
    Without my license certainly.
2276 All together let us come hence,
    My household, with a full heart!

The Duke descends with twenty armed men
[with streamers.

THE DUKE.

Say, my lords,
What field is for us to hold
2280   To meet with the tyrant?
If I can, he will fare ill,
Because of his being surely, without doubt,
    Powerless against the faith of Christ.

STEWARD.

2284 He was dwelling in Les-Teader:
    This is in Meneage;
But another place surely without doubt
    The evil native has
2288   Within Powder,
This is called Godren:
There right truly the rotten fellow
    Has now made for himself a harbour.

THE DUKE.

2292 We will follow thee.
    In the name of Christ who is above.
If he dwells in Cornwall certainly
    We shall meet with the villain.
2296 My banner display ye
    Before me right truly now:
As becomes a worthy lord
    I will go hence.
                                        [To Teudar.

THE SECOND MESSENGER *to Teudar.*

2300 Hail, Teudar, Emperor of grace!
A Duke is here in the kingdom
    Risen surely against thee,

     ha ganso pur guir ost brays
1304 the vernans y fyn guelays
      bostya a ra in certeyn

    TEVDARUS IMPERATOR

    Out warnotho an falge plos
    me an deffy deth ha nos
1308 ree greff ovy erybyn
p. 91. y a gren age barwov
    tormentoris in arvov
     dugh in rag guyfen vyleyn

    PRIMUS TORTOR

      [*descendit ad teudar*[*um*]]

1312 Parys oll onn in arvov
   y a schakyage barvov
    neb a settya erthebyn
   mar a peth reys sensy guel
1316 me a leuer dyogel
    an iovle mur ny iust orthyn

    TEVDARUS

   The guel in hanov an iovle
    duen heb nefre omsone
2320 y an prenvyth by my sovle
    an duk hay dus rum ene
    kyns gase weyll
   yma parys dymmo lel
2324 pobyl omma dyogel
    moy certen es xv myl
      descendit cum xv armatoribus
       [with stremers

   Hic demon pompabit

p. 91a. PRIMUS DEMON

   Peys y say both fur and ner
   golsowugh orth iubyter
2328 agis tassens an berth north
   yma ov servons ov toys
   belsebuc ny a vyn moys
    thage gore in lel forth

And with him right truly a great host.
1304 Thy death he will see
He doth boast certainly.

TEUDAR THE EMPEROR.

Out on him, the false dirt!
I defy him day and night!
1308 Very strong am I against him.
They shall wag their beards.
Torturers in arms,
Come ye forward! Woe to him the villain!

FIRST TORTURER.

[*He goes down to Teudar.*

1312 Ready are we all in arms.
They shall shake their beards
Who set against thee.
If need be to hold a field,
1316 I say certainly
The great Devil will not joust against us.

TEUDAR.

To a field in the Devil's name!
Let us come without ever blessing ourselves!
1320 They shall pay for it, *par mon âme*,
The Duke and his folk, by my soul,
Before leaving work.
There is ready for me loyally
1324 People here clearly
More, certainly, than fifteen thousand.
He descends with fifteen armed men
[*with streamers.*

Here the Demon shall parade.

FIRST DEMON.

Peace I say both far and near.
Hearken ye to Jupiter
1328 Your holy father (?) from the north part!
My servants are coming.
Belsebuc, we will go
To put them on the right way.

II. BELSEBUK

2332 Mester henna yv grueys da
tevdar drok lor eff a ra
y confortya mar menyn
erybyn duen then tempel
2336 benytha ny welaff guel
es gul scherwynsy certyn

                      ad templum intret

TEVDARUS

Lowene dys du monfras   [*genuflectunt omnes*
me a vyn pesy the grays
2340 kyn moys the guell
byth ny garsen
gul da certen
na y predery dyogell

p. 91. b.   ### PRIMUS DEMON

2344 Tevdar wek manly omdok
ha byth na spar guthel drok
me ath venten
nynsa the ena the gol
2348 ragtho yma thymo tol
inweth rag the sovdrys ol
bethugh lowen

Sul voy ancov a rellogh
2352 the larchya preysys fethogh
kemendis wose helma

PRIMUS TORTOR

duen in kerth uskis lemen
ny reys dyn fors pendrellen
2356 mahum agen pev nefra

p. 91 *continued.*   ### SENESCALLUS

Ser duk me a weyl tevdar
ha parcel a throk coskar
pur thevrey orth y sewa
2360 covse ganso a vynnogh wy
ha govyn orto defry
in povma pendra wyla

BELSEBUC.

2332 Master, that is well done.
Teudar, evil enough he will do
    If we shall comfort him.
To meet him let us go to the temple.
2336 Never see I (aught) better
    Than doing evil certainly.

                Let him go into the temple.

TEUDAR.

Joy to thee, god Monfras!   [*They all kneel.*
I will beseech thy grace,
2340   Before going a-field.
Never would I love
To do good, certainly,
    Nor to think it, surely:

FIRST DEMON.

2344 Sweet Teudar, bear thyself like a man,
And never spare to do evil.
    I will support thee.
Thy soul will not go to loss,
2348 For it I have a hole,
Likewise for all thy soldiers.
    Be ye joyous!

The more deaths ye do.
2352 The largelier shall ye be praised,
    (And) commended, after that.

FIRST TORTURER.

Let us come away at once now.
We need not care why we should go.
2356   Mahound will own us ever.

THE STEWARD.

Sir Duke, I see Teudar
And a parcel of evil retinue,
    Very seriously, following him.
2360 Do you wish to speak with him
And to ask of him seriously
    What he seeks in this country?

DUX CORNUBIAE

	Manna purguir ov stywart
2364	kynthus inno tebel art
	byth ny vanna y thovtya
p. 92.	kynthusons ov thumwul creff
	me a dava age grueff
2368	in age meske gruaff rovtia

[ad stallum

	Ty turant a thyscregyans
	pendryv the kerth in povma
	tytel na chalyng dyblans
2372	aberth mam na tas oma
	purguir nyth us
	ty re wores mes an gluas
	meryasek neb o dremas
2376	acontis certen a zus

TEVDARUS

	Me ath wor gy mes an pov
	kyn moys avel meryasek
	mar corthyyth an plos myn gov
2380	neb a thuk peynis anwek
	sur in grovs pren
	a vethe gelwys ihesu
	rag vyngia purguir me yv
2384	war y servons eff certen
	devethys off ty myn reyv
	thage dyswul ol lemen

DUX

	Ny seff henna yth galloys
2388	ty falge ky omschumunys
	kynse me a scoyl the goys
	ha ty a veth devenys
	avel losov
2392	rum ena the guthel covle
	pagya mergh es by my sowle
	me a glowes in z° pov
	pendra deseff an map devle
2396	darvyngya war thuk kernov

p. 93.
TEVDARUS

Duk kernov hag oll y dus
indan ov threys me as glus
poren kepar ha treysy

THE DUKE OF CORNWALL.

  I will, right truly, my steward,
2364 Though in him is an evil art,
   Never will I fear him.
  Though they are making themselves strong
  I will handle their faces.
2368   In amongst them I will break.

  Thou unbelieving tyrant!
   Why is thy way in this country?
  Title nor claim, distinctly,
2372 On the side of father or mother here,
   Right truly, thou hast not.
  Thou hast put out of the kingdom
  Meriasek, who was an honest man
2376   Accounted certainly by folk.

TEUDAR.

  I will put thee out of the country,
   Before going, like Meriasek,
  If thou worshippest the dirty mouth of lies
2380 Who bore pains unsweet
   Surely on the cross-tree,
  And who was called Jesus.
  To take vengeance right truly am I
2384   On his servants certainly.
  I am come, thou luckless (?) mouth,
   To undo you all now.

THE DUKE.

  That stands not in thy power,
2388 Thou false, excommunicated hound!
  Sooner will I spill thy blood,
   And thou shalt be minced
    Like herbs,
2392 By my soul, to make broth.
  A girl's bastard thou wast, *par mon âme,*
   I have heard, in thy country.
  What does the Devil's son desire?
2396   To take vengeance on a Duke of Cornwall?

TEUDAR.

  Duke of Cornwall and all his folk,
  Under my feet I will crush them
   Just like grains of sand.

2400 kynnago ov poscessyon
bras in meske sur ov nascyon
me ren moghheys eredy
conquerrour off
2404 corff da in proff
dovtijs in meske arlythy

DUX

Ny sensevy ath creffder
ty turant vn faven guk
2408 der an golen me ath ver
mar nynseth in kerth war nuk
quik mes am grond
predery a raff heb fal
2412 in the pov ythesta gal
peys gevyans warna losal
bo voyd am syght a pur hond

Py fyn alyon
2416 war crustunyon
omma deseves settya
me a ra ath pen crehy
may teverre an brehy
2420 ha pesy gueff ov metya

p. 94.

TEWDARUS

By my fay an we* besen
a latha margh a calla
indelle ty gargesen
2424 drok thymo ty a russa
a mennen vy
purguir sevel in cosel
na vanna mes ty losel
2428 yma myterneth ryel
a thue thum gueres defry

DUX

The vyterneth schumunys
theth gueres bohes a veth
2432 galwy dis bras ha munys
hag ol the varogyen keth
hath arlythy
me agis gorte in plen
2436 the crist del off servont len
hag ol ov fobyl defry

* leg. wel?

    Though my property was not
     Large surely amongst my nation,
      I have greatened it already.
    A conqueror am I,
2404 A good body in proof,
     Feared amongst lords.

THE DUKE.

    I care not for thy might,
     Thou tyrant, one blind bean.
2408 Through the heart I will spit thee
     If thou go not away backwards
      Quick out of my ground.
    I do think without fail
2412 In thy country thou wast a rascal.
    Ask pardon of me, losel,
     Or get out of my sight, O very hound!

    How will an alien
2416 On Christians
     Here desire to set?
    I will make of thy head a hash,
    So that the juice (?) may drop,
2420   And thou wilt cry 'woe is me' to meet me.

TEUDAR.

    By my faith, and well besene,
     If I could kill a horse.
    So thou gudgeon,
2424   Ill to me thou wouldst do
     If I should like.
    Right truly, stand quiet
    I will not, but thou losel,
2428 There is a royal kingdom
     Will come to help me surely.

THE DUKE.

    Thy accursed kingdom
     To thee shall be little help.
2432 Call to thee great and small,
     And all thy caitiff knights,
      And thy lords.
    I will await you in the plain,
2436 As I am a loyal servant of Christ's,
     (I) and all my people, surely.

TEVDARUS

    Ty vyl pen pyst
    na gampol crist
2440   the ragovy
    ha mar a qureth
    ty a feth meth
        hath ost defry
2444 Plos marrek pour
      dar seposia
        prest a reta
    omma settya orth emperour

p. 95.   ### DUX

2448 Ea ty falge nygythys
    me ny won the voys genys
        in bysma the pastel dyr
    na deseff ty allyon plos
2452 in ov hertons deth na nos
        ny rovtyyth pel gothfeth guir

    Rag mellya gans tus vays
    del o meryasek henways
2456   mur ty a far the lakka
    by the dredful day off dome
    me a leuer dys ty grome
        mas pur sempel nyth sensa

TEVDARUS

2460 Ser duk ty a nagh the fay
    bo neyl presner thymmovy
        eseth kens haneth the nos
    mytern alwar ha pygys
2464 mytern margh ryel kefrys
    mytern casvelyn gelwys
        gans sokyr thym us ov tos

DUX

    Dens an rena pan vynnans
2468   omma y a veth bohays
    byth ny schappyons heb mernans
    re thu arluth mur a rays
    kynfy omma m[y]llyov cans
2472 ny a vyn ages gortays
    in hanov crist thyn yma wans
    orth escar crist batalyays

TEUDAR.

  Thou vile blockhead,
  Prate not of Christ
2440   Before me!
  And if thou dost
  Thou shalt have shame,
    And thy host surely.
2444 Very foul knight,
    Wilt thou think
    Readily
  Here to set (thyself) against an Emperor?

THE DUKE.

2448 Yea, thou false scoundrel,
  I know not that thou wast born.
    In this world to break up deer (?)
  Do not desire, thou dirty alien.
2452 In my heritage, day or night,
    Thou shalt not assemble longer, know for true.

  For meddling with good folk,
  As Meriasek was called,
2456   Thou shalt fare much the worse.
  By the dreadful day of doom
  I say to thee, thou groom,
    Good, very frankly, I hold thee not.

TEUDAR.

2460 Sir Duke, thou shalt deny thy faith,
  Or else a prisoner of mine
    Thou shalt be before this very night.
  King Alwar and Pygys,
2464 King Margh Ryel, also
  The king called Casvelyn
    With succour are coming to me.

THE DUKE.

  Let those come when they will,
2468   Here they shall be a small matter.
  Never will they escape without death,
    By God, great Lord of grace,
  Though there be here thousands of hundreds
    We will await you.
  In Christ's name we have a desire
    Against Christ's enemy to do battle.

p. 96.

TEVDARUS

  Cryst ha ty me a thefy
2476 hag omma ol agis fay
   atlyan kepar del ogh
  rag mennes thymo settia
  ov sovdrys gruegh heb lettya
2480   then crustunyon pennov trogh

DUX

  Dus rag mar quyk del vynny
  in hanov crist a vercy
   theth gortheby parys off
2484 ov sovdrys duen warnetha
  pur thefry kyns tremena
   ahanan y a perth coff

  gonnys] *Hic praeliabunt*

TEVDARUS

  Ov sovdrys dregh* thymo margh   [*horse aredy*
2488 na felle sur nynsus pargh†
   dare ov fobyl yv marov
  ha me tebelwolijs
  da ythomleth a feyys
2492   an duk yv corff heb parov

DUX

  Ho sovdoryon lemmen ho
  galles an turant then fo
   nynso abel thum perthy
2496 darum y bobyl yv marov
  gorthyans the crist caradov
   grontia dym an vyctory   [*ascendit*

p. 97.
  Peys warbarth myns os omma
2500 bevnans meryasek yma
   parte thyugh hythyv disquethys
  dugh an II. a dermen
  han remenant in certen
2504   dre gras du a veth guelys

  Evugh oll gans an guary
  ny a vyn agis pesy
   a luen golon

* The corrector appears to have made this *keregh* leg. *kyrgh* 'fetch thou.'
† MS. paragh.

TEUDAR.

Christ and thee I defy,
2476 And here all your faith,
    Castaways as you are!
For wishing to set on me,
My soldiers, without hindrance, make
2480   For the Christians broken heads.

THE DUKE.

Come on as quick as thou wilt!
In the name of Christ of mercy
    I am ready to answer thee.
2484 My soldiers, let us come upon them!
Right surely before passing away
    Of us they shall bear remembrance.

Guns.] *Here they shall fight.*

TEUDAR.

My soldiers, bring me a horse!   [*a horse ready.*
2488 No longer surely now is there sparing.
    Ruin! my people are dead,
And I ill-wounded.
Fighting well I have fled:
2492   The Duke is a person without peer.

THE DUKE.

Ho, soldiers, now ho!
The tyrant has gone to flight:
    He is now not able to bear me.
2496 Through me his people are dead.
Worship to loveable Christ
    For granting me the victory!   [*he goes up.*

Peace altogether all that are here!
2500 Meriasek's Life is
    In part to you set forth to-day.
Come ye on the second day in time,
And the remainder, certainly,
2504   Through God's grace shall be seen.

Drink ye all with the play,
We will beseech you
    With a full heart.

```
2508    wy agis beth gor ha gruek
        banneth crist ha meryasek
            banneth maria cambron
        pybugh menstrels colonnek
2512        may hyllyn donsia dyson
```

p. 98.

```
                    Celum
        Tortores            Silvester
    Infernum                    Magister
    Exulatores                Episcopus kernov
    Comes rohany    Capella   Dux Britonum .i. pater
                                  meresadoci
    Dux Cornubie              Rex Conanus
    
    Tevdarus Imperator        Constantinus
```

p. 99.

In secunda die Constantinus Imperator hic pompabit dicens

```
        Ithoff gelwys costentyn
            in rome chyff cyte an beys
        emperour curunys certyn
2516        ha der sylvester treylys
            the voys crystyen
        me a comond der ov gluas
            naha dewov nagyv vas
2520    ha gorthya crist luen a ras
            agen prennas in grovs pren
```

Hic comes Globus cecus incipit dicens

```
        A thu asoma grefijs
            rag na wela tra in beys
2524        pendra dale ol ov rechys
            ledyogh vy the veryasek
        me re glowes galosek
            y vose in y verclys
2528    thymo mar myn boys methek
            inta y feth rewardys
```

ARMIGER DUCIS GLOBI

```
        Bys dotho me agys led
        dre voth ihesu ny a sped
2532        ganso agen nygysyov
```

2508 Ye shall have, man and woman,
    The blessing of Christ and Mériasek,
        The blessing of Mary of Camborne.
    Pipe ye, hearty minstrels,
2512   That we may be able to dance forthwith.

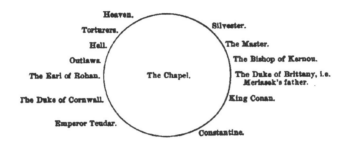

On the second day Emperor Constantine shall here parade, saying,

    I am called Constantine.
        In Rome chief city of the world
    Emperor crowned certainly,
2516   And by Silvester converted
        To be a Christian.
    I order throughout my kingdom
    Denial of gods that are not good
2520 And worship of Christ full of grace
        Who redeemed us on the cross-tree.

Here the blind Earl Globus begins, saying,

    O God, I am grieved
    For I see not aught on earth.
2524   What avails all my wealth?
    Lead ye me to Meriasek.
    I have heard that he
        Is mighty in his miracles.
2528 If he will be leech to me
        He shall be well rewarded.

A SQUIRE.

    Unto him I will lead you.
    Through Jesu's will we shall speed
2532   By him our errands.

duen scon inban then meneth
ha why covsugh arluth freth
dotho agis galarov

tranceat ad montem Mereadoci
[*And hys squyer ledys hym   and a staff yn hys handde*

COMES

p: 100.

2536 Arluth neff rum gueresa
ha yehes thym re grontya

MEREADOCUS

Arluth a ruk moyr ha tyr
pup vrol rum gueresa
2540 ha roy thym in forth a guir
ov bevnans oma gedya
ihesu arluth ortheff myr
hath lel gras dymo grontya
2544 ihesu pup vr ol ov desyr
yv in bysma the plesia

COMES

Meriasek lowena dys
densa ath conuersascon
2548 purguir ythoys acontys
hag in meske ol the nasconn
henwys oys pronter grassijs
the ryche ha bohosogyon
2552 parys certen ath guereys
the socra othomogyon

Me yv den dal nyth wela
kyn covseff orthys der reff
2556 the pesy me a vynsa
hag in ov gallus mar seff
the aquyttya

p. 101. mar mynnes gul dym guelas
2560 fout syght numbus ommeras
lemen mar qureth ov gueras
thys ny fyl peth an bysma

MERIADOCUS

A peth an beys num dur man
2564 the kyns sur na rych na guan
awos peth me ny socra
rag nynsyv mas tarosvan
ha pur sempel the cara

Let us come at once up to the mountain,
And you, strong lord, tell
  To him your ailments.
        Let him pass to Meriasek's mountain.
    [And his squire leads him. And a staff in his hand.

THE EARL.

2536 May Heaven's Lord help me,
And grant health to me!

MERIASEK.

May the Lord who made sea and land
  Always help me,
2540 And grant me in the way of truth
  To guide my life here.
Lord Jesu, look at me,
  And grant me thy loyal grace!
2544 Jesu, always my desire
  Is in this world to please thee.

THE EARL.

Meriasek, joy to thee!
  A good man of thy converse
2548 Right truly thou art accounted,
  And amongst all thy nation
Art named a gracious priest.
  To rich and poor,
2552 Ready surely with thy help
  To succour the needy.

I am a blind man that sees thee not.
Before I presume to speak to thee
2556 I would beseech thee,
  And if it shall stand in my power,
    Will repay thee,
If thou wilt make me see.
2560 In default of sight I am not able to help myself.
Now if thou canst help me
  Thou shalt not lack the wealth of this world.

MERIASEK.

Of the wealth of the world nought concerns me.
2564 Neither rich nor weak the sooner
  On account of wealth will I succour,
For it is nothing but a phantom,
  And it is very foolish to love it.

L 2

COMES

2568 Mur a varth yv genavy
na gerte rychyth an beys
bewe pel ny eltegy
heb pyth na denvyth genys
2572 der rychyth pur eredy
den a veth degemerys
in ban in mesk arlythy
ha ganse prest enorys

2576 .Govyn a myns a vynny
meryasek the ortheff vy
ha ny fellyth annotha
kyn teseryas punsov cans
2580 mar qureth dym gueles dyblans
gans our pur sur me ath pea

MERIADOCUS

Nynsyv the denvyth guertha
ov map grays du war an beys
2584 yma guel forth es honna
mar a pethy prederys

p. 102.   COMES

Ry peth dyso thym ny vern
vnw⁴ gueles a callen
2588 sensy quarel orth mytern
purdefry my ny dovtsen
na russen nes
guel vya gene the wyr
2592 prest gueles es x puns tyr
rag nefre kyn rollen des

MERIADOCUS

Oll the promes hath teryov
guethy lemen avel kyns
2596 me a vyn in ov dythyov
gul warlergh crist pen an syns

COMES

Me ath peys a luengolon
ty the vynnes ov sawya
2600 rag kerense an passconn
a thuk ihesu in bysma

THE EARL.

2568 Much wonder have I
 That thou lovest not the riches of the world.
Live long thou couldst not
 Without wealth, nor (could) any one born.
2572 Through riches right readily
 One will be accepted
Up amongst lords
 And by them quickly honoured.

2576 Ask all that thou wishest,
Meriasek, of me,
 And thou shalt not lack thereof.
Though thou shouldst desire an hundred pounds
2580 If thou makest me see distinctly
 With gold right surely I will pay thee.

MERIASEK.

It is not to any one to purchase.
 My son, God's grace on the world.
2584 There is a better way than this
 If it be considered.

THE EARL.

To give wealth to thee concerns me not.
 Once if I could see
2588 To hold a quarrel with a king
 Certainly I should not fear,
  Nor should I make alliance.
Better were it with me truly
2592 Now to see than though ten pounds (worth of) land
 For ever I should give to thee.

MERIASEK.

All thy promise and thy lands
 Keep them now as before.
2596 I will, in my days,
 Do according to Christ, the head of the saints.

THE EARL.

I beseech thee with a full heart
 That thou wouldst save me
2600 For love of the Passion
 Which Jesus bore in this world.

```
            scorgis gans an zethewon
              kentrewys treys ha dula
    2604  gans gu lym in tenewon
              del russons y y guana

          Der an golon
          y woys dyson
    2608    may tevera
          gueres den dal
          oma heb fal
              orth ihesu rag kerensa


                    MERIADOCUS

    2612  Orth ihesu rag kerense
              a qurelles opery kyns
              guereses ty a vye
              oll ath rychyth me a syns
    2616      nebes an fa                    [genuflectit
p. 103.       ihesu crist luen a vercy
              ihesu crist y syght grua dry
                  den denma del yth pess


                    COMES    [genuflectit

    2620  Ihesu arluth galosek
              rebo gorthys benytha
              han sans glorijs meryasek
              rum sawyas vy in torma
    2624  me a wyl lemen in tek
              bythqueth ny welys clerra
              del wothen letris ha lek
                  lel servont du yv helma


                    OBSESSUS

                  [yᵉ devyll aredy by hys syde

    2628  A gueresvy meryasek
              orth ihesu rag kerensa
              me yv vexijs anhethek
              gans tebel speris oma
    2632      numbus bewa
              eff am kemer gans schoris
              may wothaffsen boys leskis
                  le greff es perthy orta
```

Scourged by the Jews,
   Nailed, feet and two hands,
With a sharp spear (in) the side
   As they did pierce him

Through the heart,
His blood quickly
   That it might drop.
Heal a blind man
Here without fail
   For love towards Jesu!

MERIASEK.

For love towards Jesu
   If thou wouldst act before,
Cured thou wouldst be.
   All of thy riches I hold
     Less than a bean.   [*he kneels.*
Jesu Christ, full of mercy,
Jesu Christ, his sight bring
   To this man, as I beseech thee!

THE EARL   [*kneels.*

May Jesu, mighty Lord,
   Be worshipped ever,
And the glorious saint Meriasek,
   Who salved me this turn.
I see now beautifully,
   Never have I seen clearer.
As we know, lettered and lay,
   A loyal servant of God is this (man).

THE DEMONIAC

        [*the devil ready by his side.*

O help me, Meriasek,
   For love towards Jesu!
I am vexed (and) loathsome.
   By an evil spirit here
     I have not life.
He seizes me with shivering fits (?)
So that I would endure to be burnt:
   A lesser grief than to bear up against them.

SURDUS

2636 Me yv den na yl clowas
　　meryasek ty yv dremas
　　　　ov breys thym yma ov ton
　　y halses prest ov gueras
2640 rag kerense crist map ras
　　　　myr thynny bohosogyon　　　[genuflectit

MERIADOCUS

　　Ihesu crist der the vercy
　　　　mar sus drok sperys ogas
2644 ihesu gorre thy teythy
　　　　hag omma darber ʒehas
　　　　　　then ij denma
p. 104.　may fo guelys
2648 ov boys in beys
　　　　orth the servya

DEMON　　[vlulat en[er]goumenus

　　Out o' warnes meryasek
　　ty yv thymo molothek
2652　　orth ov domhel dres an pov
　　genes prest me numbus creys
　　wath me a ra moys deseys
　　　　rag atty dyso myngov

OBSESSUS

2656 The ihesu rebo grasseys
　　an drok sperys avodys
　　　　yma sur the ortheff vy
　　sav off numbus galarov
2660 meryasek in ov dythyov
　　　　sensys off mur dysogy　　　[ffinit

SURDUS

　　Ha my a clov
　　　　mar tha del reys
2664 in ov dethyov
　　　　ythoff sensys
　　　　　　the veryasek
　　dretho sawys
2668 ha gueresys
　　　　ython purdek　　　[ffinit

A DEAF MAN.

2636 I am one who cannot hear.
Meriasek, thou art a worthy man,
    My judgment to me is bearing
That thou couldst at once heal me.
2640 For love of Christ, son of grace,
    Look at us, poor (fellows).   [*He kneels.*

MERIASEK.

Jesu Christ, through thy mercy,
    If there be an evil spirit at hand
2644 Jesu, put him to his faculties,
    And here prepare healing
        For these two men.
So that it may be seen
2648 That I am on earth
    Serving thee.

THE DEMON   [*the demoniac howleth.*

Out, out on thee, Meriasek!
Thou art to me accursed
2652   Driving me through the country.
By thee now I have not strength,
Yet I will go, disease
    To sow for thee, thou mouth of lies.

THE DEMONIAC.

2656 To Jesu be thanks!
The evil spirit gone forth
    Is surely from me.
Whole am I, I have not ills.
2660 Meriasek, in my days
    I am greatly bound to thee.

THE DEAF MAN.

And I hear
    As well as need (be).
2664 In my days
    I am bound
        To Meriasek.
Through him healed
2668 And cured
    We are right fairly.

COMES GLOBUS

  Meryasek gorthys reby
  genes confortis onny
p. 105.   2672   ese in mur a ponfos
  ha dreys sur the lowena
  ny a beys rag venytha
    crist re sensa the gallos

MERIADOCUS

2676 Ov flehys wek eugh why dre
  ov banneth genogh neffre
    na letyogh vy am servys
  ha guetyogh the du grassee
2680 eff re ruk agis sawye
    adar my cresugh pup preys
          [*tranceunt omnes domum*

Hic Comes venetensis pompabit

  Me yv ȝurle in venetens
   arluth mur ov denyte
2684 then arluth du murworthyens
   ha grays thym ȝy ventine
   re tharbarre
  epscop an pov yv marov
2688 then colgy heb feladov
   me a vyn moys aleme
  reys yv thym meres hythov
   agen epscop thynny pyv a ve

ARMIGER COMITIS* VENETENSIS

2692 Ser arluth ny a genogh
  hebogh why sur na menogh
   ny sped mater in povma
  yma rych ha bohosek
2696 ov teserya meryasek
   epscop pur guir may fova   [*descendit*

p. 106.   ### COMES VENETENSIS
       [*ad decanum in collegio† in placea*

  Ser deyn lowene dywy
  ha the oll agys colgy
2700   me re duth sav guel aveys
  rag gothfes purthyogel
  pyv a veth epscop in lel
   omma lemen dewesys

   * MS. comes   † MS. colegia

EARL GLOBUS.

    Meriasek, worshipped be thou!
    By thee comforted are we
2672   Who were in much trouble,
    And brought surely to joy.
    We will pray for ever
        May Christ keep thy power!

MERIASEK.

2676 My sweet children, go ye home.
    My blessing with you ever!
        Do not hinder me in my service.
    And take care to give thanks to God.
2680 He hath healed you
        Through (?) me, believe ye always.
            [*All pass home.*

Here the Earl of Vannes shall parade.

    I am earl in Vannes.
        A lord, great my dignity.
2684 To the Lord God, great worship,
        And grace to me to maintain it.
        May he vouchsafe!
    The bishop of the country is dead:
2688 To the college without fail
        I will go hence.
    Needful is it for me to see to-day
        Our bishop for us who shall be.

A SQUIRE OF THE EARL OF VANNES.

2692 Sir lord, we will go with you.
    Without you surely not often
        Speeds a matter in this country.
    Rich and poor are
2696 Desiring Meriasek
        That he be bishop right truly [*he goes down.*

THE EARL OF VANNES
        [*to the dean in the college on the stage.*

    Sir Dean, joy to thee,
    And to all your college.
2700   I have come, saving better advice.
    To know right certainly
    Who shall be bishop loyally
        Here now chosen?

DECANUS [*in placea*

2704 Ser ȝurle ov arluth worthy
oma wolcum sur owhy
peys da on agis aveys
rag gothfos pur eredy
2708 pyv a vo epscop thynny
in guelle preys

COMES VENETENSIS

Yma oll an comen voys
gans meryasek ov cul noyys
2712 may fo epscop eredy
ha me ny won den byth wel
pyv a vyn ken leferel
gorthebugh omma dynny
[*Comes trancit domum*

CANONICUS

2716 Ny yv certen lowenek
rag cafus dyn meryasek
the voys revler
a thensa nynson tollys
2720 danvenogh rag y vollys
ov arluth ker

p. 107.   ### COMES VENETENSIS

Dus in rag ov maseger
ke thym the pap seluester
2724 lauer boys an guelhevyn
a vreten* orth y pesy
rag meryasek den worthy
epscop in venetensy
2728 y cafus prest y fensyn

NUNCIUS PRIMUS *ad comes* (sic) *venetensis*

Ser ȝurle ny vethugh tollys
the dre y troff y vollys
bys oma ny letya pel
2732 mones a raff
uskis ha schaff
genogh farwel

* MS. a vreter.

THE DEAN [*on the stage.*

2704   Sir Earl, my worthy lord,
     Here welcome surely are ye.
       Well satisfied shall we be with your advice
     To know right readily
2708   Who should be bishop for us
     In the shortest time.

THE EARL OF VANNES.

  All the common voice is
  With Meriasek making a noise
2712   That he be bishop readily,
  And I know not any one better.
  Whoso will say otherwise
     Answer ye here to us. [*the Earl goes home.*

THE CANON.

2716   We are certainly joyous
  To find for us Meriasek.
     To be ruler.
  In the goodman we are not deceived:
2720   Send ye for his bulls,
     My dear lord.

THE EARL OF VANNES.

  Come forward, my messenger!
  Go for me to Pope Silvester,
2724   Say that the chiefs
  Of Brittany are beseeching him
  For Meriasek, a worthy man.
  Bishop of Vannes,
2728   Have him at once we would.

FIRST MESSENGER *to the Earl of Vannes.*

  Sir Earl, you shall not be deceived,
  Home I will bring his bulls,
     Even here I will not delay longer.
2732   I will go
     Quickly and rapidly.
       To you farewell.

SILVESTER

  Gallus ha confort an tas
2736 rebo genen pup termen
   ihesu an map luen a ras
   sokyr ny mo ha meten
   an sperys sans benygas
2740 y gras genen may keffen
   maria mam ha guerhas
    the vercy du peys ragoen

   Mercy du prest yv parys
2744 the vap den mar an wyla
   nynsyv y voth boys kelys
   an peth a ruk the prenna
p. 108. insol bethugh glan zesseys
2748 avodyogh pegh in bysma
   ha rag an pehas us grueys
   kemerogh luen edrega
   ha bethugh war
2752 na dreylogh z° pegh na moy
   ha why a thue sur then ioy
    us in neff nangeves par

PRIMUS NUNCIUS   [ad silvestrem

   Sylvester gorthyans dywhy
2756 oma danvenys ovy
    a vreten* pur eredy
   rag weles sur arluth wek
   gallus may fo meryasek
2760   epscop sacrys purdefry
   in venetens† cyte dek
    helmyv both an arlythy

SILVESTER

   Wolcum ythos ov map wek
2764 den grassyes yv meryasek
    del glowys y acontia
   y vollys a veth screfys
   ha waree grueys dis parys
2768   may hylly prest lafuria

           [bollys aredy.

CARDINALE   [to ye masyger

   Yma an bollys parys
   maseger kemery dis
    der lescyens ov arluth da

* MS. vrereten   † MS. vetenens

SILVESTER.

 The might and the comfort of the Father
2736   Be with us always!
 Jesu, the Son full of grace
  Succour us evening (?) and morning!
 The holy blessed Spirit
2740   His grace with us that we may have,
 Mary, Mother and Virgin,
  To God's mercy pray for us.

 God's mercy is ever ready
2744   For the son of man if he seeks it.
 It is not His will that
  What he has redeemed should be lost.
 Up! be ye clean confessed,
2748   Avoid ye sin in this world,
 And for the sin that is done
  Take full repentance,
  And be ye wary,
2752 Turn unto sin no more,
 And ye shall surely come to the joy
  That is in heaven (and) that hath no equal.

FIRST MESSENGER   [*to Silvester.*

 Silvester, worship to you!
2756 Here am I sent
  From Brittany very readily
 To seek surely, sweet lord,
 Power that Meriasek be
2760   Consecrated bishop right earnestly
 In Vannes, a fair city.
  This is the will of the lords.

SILVESTER.

 Welcome art thou, sweet son!
2764 A gracious man is Meriasek,
  As I have heard him accounted.
 His bulls shall be written
 And anon made ready for thee
2768   So that thou mayst at once go onward.
          [*bulls ready.*

A CARDINAL   [*to the Messenger.*

 The bulls are ready.
 Messenger, take them to thee
  By licence of my good lord.

2772 yma notijs
sur ha covsis
mur thadder an keth denna

p. 109.   PRIMUS NUNCIUS

Ov arluth dywhy mur grays
2776 mar uskis why the vynnays
spedia sur ov negysyov
kumyas pesa
rag moys lema
2780 troha ham pov

SILVESTER

Banneth crist rebo genes
dynerugh arlythy an gluaes
thymo vy ha meryasek
2784 den grascyes ef a veth lel
byth nystufons guel bugel
in age oys gor na gruek

NUNCIUS [ad comitem venitensem

Heyl ser zurle in agis tour
2788 ov negesyov spedijs dour
the porpos yma gena
kemerugh thygh an bollys
meryasek pan gampollys
2792 an pap a ruk y presia

COMES VENETENSIS

Maseger wolcum ythos
lemmen ens tus then guelfos
the kerhes dyn meryasek
2796 dotho degogh lytherov
del ma guelheven an pov
orth y exaltya purdek

p. 110.   DECANUS

Arluth henna a veth grueys
2800 duen alemma gans mur greys
the veryasek
yma eff prest in guylfos
eff a thue mes a ponfos
2804 ganso mar plek

2772 There is noted
Surely and spoken
Much goodness of that same man.

FIRST MESSENGER.

My lord, to you much thanks,
2776 So quickly that thou wouldst
Speed surely my errands.
Leave I pray
To go hence
2780 To my province.

SILVESTER.

Christ's blessing be with thee!
Greet ye the lords of the country
For me, and Meriasek.
2784 A gracious man he will be loyally.
Never will they have a better shepherd
In their age, man nor woman.

THE MESSENGER [*to the Earl of Vannes.*

Hail, sir earl, in your tower!
2788 My errands sped vehemently
According to (your) purpose are by me.
Take to you the bulls:
When I spoke of Meriasek
2792 The Pope did praise him.

THE EARL OF VANNES.

Messenger, welcome art thou.
Now let folk go to the wilderness
To seek for us Meriasek.
2796 To him bear ye letters
As the chiefs of the country are
Exalting him right fairly.

THE DEAN.

Lord, that shall be done.
2800 Let us come hence with much might
To Meriasek.
He is at present in a wilderness.
He will come out of trouble
2804 If he pleases.

M

[*ad montem ad meriadocum*

Lowene dis meryasek
at oma dis lyther tek
 lemen redya
2808 an arlythy ol y myens
rag boys epscop venitens
 purguir orth the deseria

MERIADOCUS

Mur grays ol then arlythy
2812 ha thyugh a chenons worthy
 ny vannaff an dynyte
na benythe cafus cur
na charge vyth in bysma sur
2816 hedre vevhen benythe

CANONICUS

Meryasek nynsos den fur
bevnans ryel a feth sur
 pan veste epscop worthy
2820 iij cans puns gyllyth speyna
in blethen ha moy inta
the bollis parys yma
 nynseth in cost eredy

p. 111.   MERIADOCUS

2824 Vn conduconn sur owhy
kepar ha lues defry
 hythyv an dus sans eglos
pan lafuryens rag benefys
2828 ware y feth govynnys
 py lues puns a yl bos
 anethy grueys
ny remembrons y an charych
2832 a reys dethe ry har lych
 therag crist pan deer then vrueys

Myns angeves charge a cur
remembrogh* helma lemen
2836 eff a ree reken in sur
an enevov neb termen
 grugh attendia
mar peth prevys dyogel
2840 in gethna fovt in bugel
 go eff doys then keth chargna

* MS. remenbrogh.

[At the mountain to Meriasek.

    Joy to thee Meriasek!
    Lo, here for thee a fair letter
        Now to read.
2808 That the lords all
    To be bishop of Vannes
        Right truly are desiring thee.

MERIASEK.

    Much thanks to all the lords,
2812 And to you, O worthy canons!
        I wish not the dignity:
    Nor ever to have a cure,
    Or any charge in this world surely,
2816   While I am alive, ever.

A CANON.

    Meriasek, thou art not a wise man.
    A royal life thou shalt have surely
        When thou mayst be a worthy bishop.
2820 Three hundred pounds thou wilt be able to spend
    In a year, and more well.
    Thy bulls are prepared
        Thou wilt not go into cost readily.

MERIASEK.

2824 The same condition surely are ye
    Even as many certainly
        To-day of the folk of holy Church
    When they labour for a benefice
2828 Anon it will be asked
        How many pounds can be
            Made thereof?
    They remember not the charge
2832 Of the need to them to give a lengthy list
        Before Christ when they come to the Judgment.

    All that have charge of a cure,
        Remember ye this now,
2836 He will cause to reckon surely
        The souls every time:
            Consider ye:
    If there be proved certainly
2840 On that day fault in the Shepherd,
        Woe is him to come to that same charge.

The harhe a vo an rol
the pelle why a wor ol
    hy a veth prest ov redya
2844
nefre me ny fanna cur
marnes a vn ena sur
    du roy thym y lel revlya

DECANUS

2848 Ov breder duen ny the dre
ny vyn an den ma cole
    dotho orth neb a vyn da

        [*ad comes* (sic) *venetensis*

ser ʒurle ny vyn meryasek
2852 thynny ny bones tasek
    na cafus cur benytha

        [*ascendit et expectat ibidem*

p. 112: ### COMES VENETENSIS

Soweth prendreny dotha
mur a varth yv annotha
2856   vodya sur an dynyte
ny a vyn ompredery
forth rag y treyla defry
    ken plesijs me ny vethe

Hic pompabit episcopus kernov si placet

EPISCOPUS KERNOV

2860 Gelwys off epscop kernov
in breten heb feladov
    parlet worthy
the venitens* mannaff moys
2864 ena y fensen ov boys
    purguir gans an arlythy

CROSSER EPISCOPI KERNOV

Yma ena mur the gul
besy yv cafus cusul
2868   a tus fur a velogh why
pyv a vo epscop sacrys
meryasek yma notis
    boys dotho an ro defry

        [*finit*
        [*descendit*
        [*hic pompabit secundus episcopus*

* MS. vetinens

    The lengthier the roll shall be,
    The longer, you all know,
2844   It shall be ever a-reading.
    Never do I wish a cure
    Unless of one soul surely.
     God grant to me to rule it loyally!

      THE DEAN.

2848 My brethren, let us go home.
    This man will not hearken
     To one who wishes well to him.
         [To the Earl of Vannes.

    Sir earl, Meriasek will not
2852 To us be fatherly,
     Nor ever take a cure.
     [He goes up and waits in the same place.

     EARL OF VANNES.

    Alas, what shall we do to him?
    Much marvel is thereat
2856   To reject surely the dignity:
    We will bethink us
    Of a way to turn him really,
     Otherwise I shall not be pleased.

Here the bishop of Kernou shall parade if he likes.

     BISHOP OF KERNOU.

2860 I am called bishop of Kernou,
    In Brittany without fail
     A worthy prelate.
    To Vannes I will go;
2864 There I should like to be
     Right truly with the lords.

   THE BISHOP OF KERNOU'S CROZIER-BEARER.

    There is much to do there.
    Need is to take counsel
2868   Of wise folk, see ye?
    Who shall be bishop?
    Meriasek, it is noted
     That to him the gift is certainly.
          [He goes down.
     [Here a second bishop shall parade.

EPISCOPUS SECUNDUS

2872　Ov crosser duen alemma
　　　mur a weyl the gul yma
　　　　　war epscop venetensi
　　　meryasek yv dewesys
2876　sav eff ny vyn del glowys
　　　　　y receva eredy

p. 113.　　### SECUNDUS CROSSER

　　　Ser arluth by sen iowan
　　　my an kemer purlowan
2880　　mar mynner dym y profia
　　　hag a rose noblennov
　　　appen sur an colmennov
　　　　　ny vya reys ov dynnya　　　　　[*finit*
　　　　　　[*descendit secundus episcopus*
　　　　　　　[*descendit comes globus*

COMES GLOBUS

2884　Ser epscop kernov bon iour
　　　an cowethes peseff dour
　　　　　the venetens* moys a regh

EPISCOPUS KERNOV

　　　Wolcum ser zurle be thys day
2888　wolcum ser epscop worthy
　　　　　wolcum yv myns us genegh

SECUNDUS EPISCOPUS

　　　Ser zurle hag epscop kernov
　　　mur grays dyugh heb feladov
2892　　in vn forth kelmys onny
　　　in venetens
　　　yma dyblens
　　　　　mur the gul del glowys vy

COMES GLOBUS　　[*ad comitem venitensem*

2896　Ser zurle lowene dywhy
　　　ha reverens then hole colgy
　　　　　bras ha byen
　　　ny re duth oma adre
2900　in govenek exaltye
　　　　　meryasek in pur certen

* MS. venetenens.

SECOND BISHOP.

2872 My crozier-bearer, let us come hence:
Much of work to do there is
    On the bishop of Vannes.
Meriasek is chosen,
2876 But he will not, as I heard,
    Receive it readily.

SECOND CROZIER-BEARER.

Sir lord, by Saint Jovian,
I will take it right gladly,
2880   If it be wished for me to prove it.
And I would put nobles
At the end surely of the halters,
    It would not be needful to entice (?) me.

EARL GLOBUS.

Sir bishop of Kernou, *bonjour*.
2884 The company I beseech earnestly
    That ye will go to Vannes.

BISHOP OF KERNOU.

Welcome, sir Earl, by this day!
2888 Welcome, worthy sir bishop!
    Welcome are all that are with you.

SECOND BISHOP.

Sir Earl and bishop of Kernou,
Many thanks to you without fail.
2892   On one way are we bound.
In Vannes
There is clearly
    Much to do as I have heard.

EARL GLOBUS [*to the Earl of Vannes.*

2896 Sir Earl, joy to thee,
And reverence to the whole college,
    Great and small!
We have come here from home
2900 In the desire to exalt
    Meriasek very certainly.

p. 114.

    COMES VENETENSIS

  Wolcum ser zurle caradov
  wolcum owhy epscobov
2904   mur a anneys gyllys on
  meryasek yv dewesys
  the vones epscop sacrys
   sav eff ren nahas dyson

  [*descendunt omnes cum comes* (sic) *ventensis*

    EPISCOPUS KERNOW

2908 The dre mar tuth y vollys
  epscop eff a veth sacrys
   du dufen ken
  prag na vyn y kemeras
2912 dretho y hyl gul gueras
   ha les the ol y ehen

    SECUNDUS EPISCOPUS

  Dotho wath bethens covsys
  mar a kylle boys treylys
2916   then dynyte
  densa dy conuersasconn
  sur in mesk ol y nascon
   ny a wor guir y vose

    COMES GLOBUS

2920 Heb na herre lafarov
  ny a vyn heb feladov
   moys then teller may meve
  hag alena sur y dry
2924 den beneges ha worthy
   yv in meske age hense

p. 115.   EPISCOPUS KERNOV

  Henna ol ny a assent
  duen alemma verement
2928   brays ha byen
  tus hen guelhevyn an pov
  agen attent why a clov
   leyk ha lyen

    tranceat ad heremum [*in monte*

    SECUNDUS EPISCOPUS

2932 Oma yma meryasek
  ser zurle arluth galosek
   covsugh why dothe kynsa

THE EARL OF VANNES.

Welcome, loveable sir Earl!
Welcome are ye, bishops!
2904   Very ill at ease have we become.
Meriasek is chosen
To be consecrated bishop,
    But he refused us at once.

[All go down with the Earl of Vannes.

THE BISHOP OF KERNOU.

2908 If his bulls have come home
He will be consecrated bishop.
    God forbid (aught) else!
Why will he not take it?
2912 Thereby he might help
    And benefit all his race.

SECOND BISHOP.

To him again let it be spoken
If he can be turned
2916   To the dignity:
A good man of his converse
Surely amongst all his nation
    I know truly that he is.

EARL GLOBUS.

2920 Without any longer words
We will, without fail,
    Go to the place where he is,
And thence surely bring him.
2924 A man blessed and worthy
    He is amongst their chiefs.

THE BISHOP OF KERNOU.

To that we all assent:
Let us come hence, verily,
2928   Great and small,
Old folk, chiefs of the country,
Our attempt ye shall hear,
    Lay and learned.

Let him pass to the hermitage [on the mountain.

SECOND BISHOP.

2932 Here is Meriasek,
Sir Earl, mighty lord,
    Speak you to him first,

mar a mynna dre dec*ter*
2936 dones gene*n* heb awer
trueth yv y dystempra

COMES VENETENSIS [*ad meriadocum*

Lowene d*is* meryasek
o*mma* avel bohosek
2940 solla deth ty re vewas .
le*mmen* der the vvelder
exaltijs the reelder
ty yv dremas rag the voas

COMES GLOBUS

2944 De*n*sa ath co*n*ue*r*sasco*nn*
ty yv in meske the nascon
ha sevys an gois worthy
nytheseth purguir ragoys
2948 oma trege in ponfoys
rag henna dus gene*nn*y

p. 116. SECUNDUS EPISCOPUS

The vollys dufe the dre
in venetenes the sacre
2952 epscop gallus thyn yma
henna yv both oll an pov
ty a yl in the dethyov
purguir boys se*n*sis detha

MERIADOCUS

2956 Na govsugh an dynyte
rag kere*n*se cr*is*t avan
epscop ny vethe neffre
na cur ny vanna certan
2960 a vap de*n*vyth in bysme
mas ov ene ov honan
arlythy arlithy eugh dre
na letyogh ov devoco*nn*

EPISCOPUS KERNOW

2964 Na wele covs gere*nn*ov
hag orthe*n* guthel te*nn*ov
gans an pap pan yv ornys
mynny gy kyn na vynny
2968 ty a in kerth gene*n* ny
hag oma gays the cumyys

If he will through fairness
Come with us without grief.
 A pity it is to ruffle him.

THE EARL OF VANNES *to Meriasek*

Joy to thee, Meriasek
Here like a poor man
 For a long time thou hast lived.
Now through thy humility
Exalted to royalty
 Thou art for that thou art excellent.

EARL GLOBUS.

A good man of thy converse
Thou art among thy nation,
 And raised of the worthy blood.
Not, right truly, for thee is it meet
Here to dwell in trouble,
 Therefore come thou with us.

SECOND BISHOP.

Thy bulls have come home.
In Vannes to consecrate thee
 Bishop we have power.
That is the wish of all the country.
Thou mayest in thy days
 Right truly be bound to them.

MERIASEK.

Talk ye not of the dignity,
 For love of Christ above!
Bishop I would never be
 Nor, certainly, do I wish a cure
Of a son of any man in this world
 Save my own soul.
Lords, lords, go ye home,
 Hinder not my devotion!

THE BISHOP OF KERNOU.

Seek not to talk words
And against us to pull,
 When it is ordered by the Pope.
(Though) thou wilt, though thou wilt not
Thou shalt go away with us,
 And here leave thy height (?)

MERIADOCUS

[*meryasek yledyt*

Maria wyn gueres vy
maria the orthys gy
    erbyn ov both ledijs off
2972
maria mam ha guerhes
maria da y wothes
    an charg peys da my nynsoff

p. 117.
COMES VENETENSIS

2976 Meryasek nynsoys den fur
reys yv the ran cafus cur
    oma sur an enevov
le may fo bugel medel
2980 an lowern pur thyogel
    a leghya an dewysyov

Vnferheys kep*ar* del on
berth in eglos sent sampson
2984   bethens eff *consecratis*
gans worschyp ha revvte
nynsyv helme mas levte
    meryasek na veth *s*errys

MERIADOCUS

[*yn y' deyn ys church*

2988 Rag kerense an pasco*nn*
a thuk ihe*s*u ragon ny
kentrewys gans ʒethewon
    treys ha dule eredy
2992 guesk*is* gu in y golon
    may reses goys y guythy
cure*n* sp*er*n dre an grogon
an dryn a hethes defry
    thy ompenyon
1996
rag y gerense leme*n*
agys pesy me a vye*n*
epscop benytha na ven
3000   a thu orth an charg ny von

p. 118.
EPISCOPUS KERNOW

Na govs thyn geryov vfer
dus oma ese yth cheer
    guyske the dylles yth kerhyn
3004 gene*n* ty a veth taklays
del goth the epscop a rays
    tra ny fyl dyso certeyn

[*her meryasek weryth a gowne*

MERIASEK.
                              [*Meriasek led.*

    Blessed Mary, help me!
    Mary, from thee
2972   Against my will I am led.
    Mary, Mother and Virgin,
    Mary, well thou knowest
        With the charge well satisfied I am not.

THE EARL OF VANNES.

2976 Meriasek, thou art not a wise man.
    Need is for some to take the cure
        Here surely of the souls.
    In the place where there is a soft shepherd
2980 The fox, right certainly,
        Will lessen the sheep.

    One-minded as we are,
    Within the church of Saint Sampson
2984   Let him be consecrated
    With worship and sway.
    This is naught save loyalty,
        Meriasek, be not angered.

MERIASEK.
                              [*in the Dean's Church.*

2988 For love of the Passion
        Which Jesu bore for us,
    Nailed by the Jews
        Feet and hands,
2992 A lance thrust into his heart
        So that the blood of his veins ran,
    A crown of thorns through his skull,
        The thorns reached surely
2996   To his brains:
    For love of him now
    I will beseech thee
    That I be not a bishop.
3000   O God, of the charge I know not!

BISHOP OF KERNOU.

    Speak not to us vain words.
    Come thou here, sit in thy chair:
        Put on thy robe around thee:
3004 By us shalt thou be arrayed
    As becomes a bishop of grace.
        Aught will not fail thee certainly.
          [*Here Meriasek wears a gown.*

SECUNDUS EPISCOPUS

  Sens the vagyl in the leff
3008 in hanov crist us in neff
   ha maria guirhes pur
    [*bagyll of syluer & myter aredy*

  settyn muter war y ben
  ny a yll bones lowen
3012 y thoys then cur

EPISCOPUS KERNOW

  Lemmen gruen y venyga
  ihesu crist map maria
   reth gedya del vo plesijs
3016 lemen pen oys theth nasconn
  tus nobil installasconn
   deth gore yv devethys

COMES VENETENSIS

  Lemmen oll ny yv plesijs
3020 meryasek y voys sacrys
   epscop thynny
  pensevyk yv thy nasconn
  mentenour fay crustunyon
3024 socour the lues huny

p. 119   MERIADOCUS EPISCOPUS

  An dynnyte thymo vs reys
  ythevel gena y voys
   schame sur moy es honester
3028 peys da du thym dustuny
  nynsoff y cafus defry
   a ioy an bysme numduer

NUDUS INFIRMUS

  Du regys sawya tus vays
3032 rag kerense an pasconn
  a porthes crist map guirhays
  gueskis gu in y golon
  treys ha dule kentreweys
3036 berth in grovs inter ladron
  gans curen sperne curuneys
   may hethons thy ompynyon
   purguir an dreyn

SECOND BISHOP.

  Hold thy crozier in thy hand.
3008 In the name of Christ, who is in heaven,
   And Mary, a pure virgin,
    [*A crozier of silver and a mitre ready.*

  Let us set the mitre on his head.
  We may be glad
3012   Of his coming to the cure.

BISHOP OF KERNOU.

  Now let us bless him.
  May Jesu Christ, Son of Mary,
   Guide thee as he shall be pleased.
3016 Now thou art head to thy nation.
  Noble folk of (the) installation,
   An excellent day is come.

THE EARL OF VANNES.

  Now we are all well pleased
3020 That Meriasek is consecrated
   Bishop for us,
  Prince he is to his nation,
  Upholder of the Christians' faith,
3024   Succour to many a one.

MERIASEK THE BISHOP.

  The dignity that is given to me
  Seems to me to be
   A shame surely more than an honour.
3028 Well satisfied, God be my witness,
  I am not to have it really;
   For joy of this world I care not.

A NAKED SICK MAN.

  God save you, good people!
3032   For love of the Passion
  Which Christ, a Virgin's son, bore,
   A lance thrust into his heart,
  Feet and hands nailed
3036   On a cross between thieves,
  With a crown of thorns crowned,
   So that to his brains
    Right truly the thorns entered.

3040 lemen rag y gerense
regh thym queth rag ov huthe
me yv noth han guyns yv 3eyn

COMES VENETENSIS

A thermas cry war the gam
3044 nynsyv onest thys heb nam
dones the rag arlythy
ha ty noth the corff ol trogh
me ny welys na menogh
3048 moy podrek ay esely

NUDUS

A rag oll an golyov
a thuk crist cleth ha dyov
the vap den rag saluasconn
3052 ov corff vy yv antythy
pedrys squattis ov guythy
numcar neb lues map bron

p. 120. Menogh gans yrgh ha clehy
3056 me re vue in mes dre nos
rewys an doyr pur defry
ov golyov luen a plos
prest ov sclaldya*
3060 ny gar den ry thym guely
podrethek am esely
drefen purguir ov bosa

MERIADOCUS EPISCOPUS

Ty a feth purguir delles
3064 kynthellen vy prest inhoth
trueth mur yv the gueles
pedrys 3° kyk avel poth

NUDUS

Mur yv sur ov galarov
3068 ha feynt off heb feladov
mensen cafus dyweth tek
ny vyn mernans ov gueles
yma orth ov goheles
3072 drefen ov boys anhethek

MERIADOCUS EPISCOPUS

Ihesu re grontya 3ehes
thyso oma a dremaes
kefrys corff hag esely

* leg. scaldya?

3040 Now for love of him
Give ye me a garment to cover me,
I am naked and the wind is cold.

THE EARL OF VANNES.

O worthy man, cry on thy way,
3044 It is not honourable for thee without exception
To come before lords:
And thou naked (and) thy body all broken.
I have not seen often
3048 (One) more putrid in his limbs.

THE NAKED MAN.

O for all the wounds
Which Christ bore, left and right,
For salvation to the son of man!
3052 My body is powerless,
Rotten, stricken are my veins
Not any son of a breast loves me.

Often with hail and ice
3056 I have been out through night,
The ground frozen right earnestly.
My wounds full of filth
Always inflaming.
3060 No one likes to give me a bed,
Stinking in my limbs
Because, right truly, I am.

BISHOP MERIASEK.

Thou shalt right truly have raiment,
3064 Though I (myself) should now go nakedly.
Great pity it is to see thee,
Thy flesh putrid like rot.

THE NAKED MAN.

Great surely are my sorrows,
3068 And faint am I without fail,
I would fain have a fair end.
Death will not see me.
It is avoiding me
3072 Because of my being loathsome.

BISHOP MERIASEK.

May Jesu grant healing
To thee here, O worthy man,
Likewise body and limbs!

3076 rag dendel dyso kefyans
ihesu arluth a selwyans
sav an denma heb ely
kemmer queth dresos dyblans
3080 omconfortya may hylly

[a gown or mantell apon Nudus

NUDUS

Ihesu arluth galosek
ren tala dis meryasek
sav yv thymo pup esel
3084 war ov corff nynsus goly
an kyk poder eredy
sav ha dealer yv lel

p. 121.

COMES VENETENSIS

Gorthyans dyso meryasek
3088 ny wothyan mer galosek
the vote sur in bysma
worthy oys then dynyte
ny a vyn mones the dre
3092 pup ol ay du a lemma

[tranceat domum et cometis

MERIADOCUS EPISCOPUS

Banneth du genogh rebo
an dynnyte us dymmo
reys oma sur drethogh why
3096 me an grontse dyogel
lowenhe the den arel
du dustuny

tunc tranceant domum omnes

PRIMUS LAZARUS

Arluth an neff pendra raff
3100 rag certen my yv mar claff
ny gar map den ov gueles
del re glowys meryasek
a wereses tus bohosek
3104 panak vo age deses
mones dotho colonnek
mannaff the weles gueres

3076 For gaining to thee affection,
Jesu, lord of salvation,
   Heal this man without a salve!
Take raiment over thee clearly
3080   So that thou mayst comfort thyself.
    [*A gown or mantle upon the naked man.*

THE NAKED MAN.

May Jesu (the) mighty lord
Repay this to thee, Meriasek!
   Healed for me is every limb,
3084 On my body is not a wound,
The putrid flesh already
   Whole and diseaseless it is truly.

THE EARL OF VANNES.

Honour to thee, Meriasek!
3088 I knew not that thou wast
   So mighty surely in this world.
Worthy art thou of the dignity.
We will go home
3092   Every one on his side hence.
    [*Let him go home, and the Earl's (people).*

BISHOP MERIASEK.

God's blessing be with you!
The dignity that is to me
   Given here surely by you,
3096 I would grant it
Gladly to another man,
   God (be my) witness.

      Then let all go home.

FIRST LEPER.

Lord of the heaven, what shall I do?
3100 For certainly I am so sick
   No son of man loves to look on me.
As I have heard, Meriasek
Has healed poor folk,
3104   Whatever be their disease:
Go to him heartily
   I will to seek help.

SECUNDUS LAZARUS [*ad meriadocum*

       Meryasek dursona dys
3108 ny yv ij then debertheys
          ny reys thyugh y leferel
       rag kerense crist avan
       ny ages pesse certan
3112   gul gueres dyn dyogel

p. 122.   CAPELLANUS MERIADOCI

       Sevugh ues a denewen
       nynsyv purguir rag clevyen
          dones in fays arlythy
3116 thyugh cothe sevel abel
       ha gortes pur thyogel
          alusyen an den worthy   [*finit*

MERIADOCUS EPISCOPUS

       A na moy ov chaplen wek
3120 na repreff tus vohosek
          dymo a vo devethys
       parusse ovy dethy
       es then brasse arlythy
3124   us in gluascour thymo creys

       Clevyon pendra govsugh why
       us nygis dyugh ortheff vy
          leferugh in hanov du

PRIMUS LAZARUS

3128 Rag kerense arluth neff
       gueres dyn orth agen gref
          clevyon deberthys ny yv
       notyys yma
3132 the voys densa
          heweres prest orth tus du

MERIADOCUS EPISCOPUS [*genuflectit*

       Maria myternes neff
       peys gena the crist a rays
3136 maria orth age greff
       an othomogyan guerays
       maria del yth peseff
       sav an rema corff ha fays
3140 maria a wonetheff
       dywhy re wrontya ȝehays

SECOND LEPER [*to Meriasek.*

    Meriasek, a great blessing to thee!
3108 We are two separated men,
        Needs not to say it to you.
    For love of Christ above
    We would pray you certainly
3112   To heal us surely.

MERIASEK'S CHAPLAIN.

    Stand ye without on one side!
    It is not truly for lepers
        To come in the face of lords.
3116 You it behoves to stand afar
    And await certainly
        The worthy man's alms.

BISHOP MERIASEK.

    Ah no more, my sweet chaplain,
3120 Reprove poor folk
        That may be come to me.
    More ready am I for them
    Than for the greatest lords
3124   That are in the kingdom, believe me.

    Lepers, what say you?
    Have you an errand with me?
        Speak in God's name.

FIRST LEPER.

3128 For love of the lord of heaven
    Help us from our grief.
        Separated lepers are we.
    It is noted
3132 That thou art a good man,
        Helpful always towards God's folk.

BISHOP MERIASEK [*kneels.*

    Mary, Queen of heaven,
        Pray with me to Christ of grace,
3136 Mary, from their grief
        Help the needy ones.
    Mary, as I beseech thee,
        Heal these, body and face.
3140 May Mary, whom I serve,
        To you grant healing!

p. 123.
PRIMUS LAZARUS

 The ihesu rebo grasseys
 ov cow⁴ ty yv sawys
3144 cler ha tek knesen ha fays   [*finit*

SECUNDUS LAZARUS

 Indella ythoys thegy
 teka den nyth welys vy
  na clerra the ihesu grays
3148 meryasek reverons dywhy
  in guythres den benygays.   [*finit*

MERIADOCUS EPISCOPUS

 Ov flehys eugh why de dre
 ha thymmo na regh grasse
3152 mas only the crist avan
 cresugh helma ov flehas
 ihesu us ol ov queras
  ha creff ha guan   [*tranceat*

Hic pompabit Rex Massen

3156 Guelwys off mytern massen
  arluth bolde in ov dethyov
 then guylfoys in purcerten
 me a vyn mones deyow
3160 prest the helghys
 honter grua parys the kuen
 ham meyny oll in tyen
 kefrys lek ha mab lyen
3164 parusugh the voys gena

p. 124.
VENATORES REGIS

 Arluth ny a veth parys
 mylguen ha rethys* kefrys
  yma thym stoff annetha
3168 kyn settyen oma karov
 dystogh y fye marov
  cresugh henna   [*finit*

Hic filius Mulieris cuiusdam ut invenitur in miraculis
de beato mereadoco pompabit dicens

 The den yonk ythyv dufer
3172 bones in mesk arlythy
 ena eff a deske dadder
 ha manhot pur eredy
  may fo the guel

* MS. rechys

FIRST LEPER.

To Jesu be thanks!
My comrade, thou art healed,
3144   Clear and fair, skin and face.

SECOND LEPER.

So thou art, thou.
Fairer man I never saw thee,
3148   Nor clearer, to Jesu thanks!
Meriasek, reverence to you,
    In work a blessed man.

BISHOP MERIASEK.

My children, go ye home,
And give not thanks to me,
3152   But only to Christ above.
Believe ye this, my children,
That Jesu is all helping
    Both strong and weak.   [*Let him go off.*

Here King Massen shall parade.

3156 I am called King Massen,
    A lord bold in my days.
To the wilderness very certainly
    I will go on Thursday,
3160   Ready to hunt.
Hunter, make ready thy hounds,
And my household altogether,
As well layman as student,
3164   Prepare ye to go with me.

THE KING'S HUNTERS.

Lord, we shall be ready.
Greyhounds and nets likewise,
    I have wealth of them.
3168 If here we set on a hart,
Forthwith he would be dead,
    Believe ye this.

Here the son of a certain woman (as is found in 'the Miracles of Blessed Meriasek') shall parade, saying,

To a young man it is a duty
3172   To be amongst lords,
There he will learn goodness
    And manhood right readily
    So that he may be the better.

3176 me a vyn mones heb bern
lemen the corte an mytern
ov mam wek genogh farwel
[descendit

MULIER .i. MATER EIUS

Ov map banneth maria
3180 genes rebo
guel plesijs me a vya
so mot y go
ty the drega
3184 in tre oma genevy
maria mam a vercy
me a vyn moys the pesy
kekefrys thagen socra
ad ecclesiam tranceat

3188 Maria lowene dis
ha gorthyans bys venytha
maria wyn beth guereys
ha socour thym in bysma
p. 125. 3192 maria numbus flehys
marnes vn map thum cherya
maria wek myr thy leys
ol ov threst warnes yma

FILIUS [ad regem massen

3196 Heyl dyugh ov arluth mytern
thyugh oma y tuth heb bern
kepar del yv ov dute
mar mynnogh oma neb preys
3200 thymo comendya servys
awos arveth me an gruae

REX

Wolcum oys ov servont len
then guylfoys mones lemen
3204 ny a vyn sur g° sportya
kemerens pup y arvov
yma drok turant in pov
ny garsen orto metya
[descendit cum armatoribus

Hic Tyrannus pompabit dicens

3208 Me yv turant heb parov
in dan an hovle pensevyk
pan veua fol ha garov
nynsus in beys genesyk
3212 thym asetya

3176 I will go without grief
       Now to the court of the king.
              My sweet mother farewell to you!
                     [*He goes down.*

           THE WOMAN i.e. HIS MOTHER.
       My son, Mary's blessing
3180   Be with thee.
       Well pleased I should be,
           So mote I go,
           That thou shouldst dwell
3184   At home here with me.
       Mary, mother of mercy
       I will go to pray
           Likewise to succour us.
                     [*Let her go to the church.*
3188   Mary, joy to thee
           And worship for ever!
       Blessed Mary, be help
           And succour to me in this world
3192   Mary, I have not children
           Save only one son to cherish me.
       Sweet Mary, see to his benefit
           All my trust is in thee.

           THE SON [*to King Massen.*
3196   Hail to you, my lord king,
       To you here I have come without grief
           As is my duty.
       If you will, here, at any time
3200   To me entrust service
           For wages I will do it.

                   THE KING.
       Welcome are you, my leal servant.
       Go to the wilderness now
3204   We will surely to sport.
       Let every one take his arms,
       There is an evil tyrant in the country
           I should not like to meet with him.
                     [*He goes down with armed men.*

           Here the Tyrant shall parade, saying,

3208   I am a tyrant without equal,
           Prince under the sun.
       Though he be mad and rough
           There is none in the world born
3212   To set against me.

moys the[n] guelfos me a vyn
the sportya purguir lemyn
kefrys brosyen ha kemyn
3216   parusugh the voys gena

p. 126.   PRIMUS MILES TYRANNI

Ov arluth a fur galloys
parys rag moys then guelfoys
ny yv genogh alema
3220 agis greons yv lescijs
ha ny warbarth hernessijs
cansov in arvov oma   [finit

SECUNDUS MILES TYRANNI

Yma oma kuen munys
3224 v lon bowyn dufunys
y a depse in ij deth
lonk ylo ha lap keryn
scurel wyrly ky melyn
3228 blak bert labol ky degueth
    [finit. dessendat

REX

Nov honter quik myr adro
mar quelyth game ioy reth vo
dulle the kuen desempys
3232 me a weyll busch brays a dus
annethe yma thym schus
age bones ongrassyeys
    [ye hert aredy yn ye wode

SECUNDUS VENATOR REGIS

Hethov me a weyll carov
3236 pur* uskis y feth marov
awoys ovn a then genys
ser kyng na vethugh dyswar
yma an turant heb mar
3240 er agis pyn drehevys
yn pur certen

p. 127.   REX

Genen y feth gorthebys
gorten oma ov sovdrys
3244 ha warbarth omparusen
    [and ye hert yhontyd

* MS. parur

I will go to the wilderness
To sport right truly now :
Likewise great persons and common
3216   Prepare ye to go with me.

FIRST SOLDIER OF THE TYRANT.

My lord of great power,
Ready to go to the wilderness
    Are we with you hence.
3220 Your greyhounds are leashed
And we together harnessed
    Hundreds here in arms.

SECOND SOLDIER OF THE TYRANT.

Here are little hounds
3224 Five loins of beef minced
    They would eat in two days
Lonk ylo and *Lap Keryn*,
Scurel wyrly a yellow hound,
3228   Blackbird, *Labol* a workaday hound.
                    [*Let him go down.*

THE KING.

Now hunter, quick, look around !
If thou seest game joy mayst thou have.
    Let go thy hounds at once.
3232 I see a great flock of folk
Of them I have fear
    That they are graceless.
                  [*The hart ready in the wood.*

THE KING'S SECOND HUNTER.

Peace : I see a hart
3236 Right soon he will be dead.
    Notwithstanding fear of man born.
Sir king, be ye not unwary.
The tyrant is without doubt
3240   Against you arisen
    Very certainly.

THE KING.

By us he shall be answered.
Let us wait here, my soldiers,
3244   And together let us prepare ourselves.
                [*and the hart hunted.*

Hic tortores pompabunt

PRIMUS TORTOR

 Cowethe na vethen lent
 galles purguir an turent
  then guelfoys del glowys vy
3248 war y lergh guel yv mones
 ken sur ny a veth blamyes
  ha kerethys eredy

SECUNDUS TORTOR

 Thenny mar a cruk donfen
3252 agen part yv in certen
  warnotho sur attendia
 ethe adre me ny won
 agen mav plosek caugyan
3256   eff a alse aspya

TERTIUS TORTOR

 Danvenen ny agen mav
 guas pur uskis in meske ix
  the vothfes marseth adre
3260 ha dens eff thagen guarnya
 yma ov quan rewardya
  y servysy rum ene

PRIMUS TORTOR

 Hen na wer thyn bones lent
3264 ny yllyn pee agen rent
  the guel awos y wagis
 mar ny veth thyn arluth guel
 ny venen bones na pel
3268   by my sovle dotho pagys

p. 128.
SECUNDUS TORTOR

 Ty vav scherevwa* del oys
 myr an turant then guelfoys
  mar a mynna lafurya
3272 ha dus thagen guarnya ny
 may hyllen pur eredy
  moys ganso thy confortya

TERTIUS TORTOR

 Gueyt pel na veth heb doys dyn
3276 duen ny glebyn agen meyn
 lemen cowethe gentyl

* MS. stherevwa

Here the torturers shall parade.

FIRST TORTURER.

Comrades, we should not be slack:
The tyrant right truly has gone
  To the wilderness as I have heard.
3248 After him it is better to go,
Else surely we shall be blamed
  And chastised readily.

SECOND TORTURER.

To us if he hath sent
3252 Our part is certainly
  On him to attend.
(Whether) he has gone homewards I know not.
Our boy, dirty hog,
3256   He might spy.

THIRD TORTURER.

Let us send our boy,
A lad, very quickly, amongst nine,
  To know if he has gone home:
3260 And let him come to warn us.
He is rewarding poorly
  His servants, by my soul.

FIRST TORTURER.

This helps us not, to be slack,
3264 We cannot pay our rent
  The better because of his wages.
If he is not a better lord to us
We will not be any longer,
3268   By my soul, pages of his.

SECOND TORTURER.

Thou boy, most rascally as thou art,
See the tyrant, to the wilderness
  If he will go onwards,
3272 And come thou to us to warn us,
That we may right readily
  Go with him to comfort him.

THIRD TORTURER.

Beware, he will not be far without coming to us.
3276 Let us come, let us wet our mouths,
  Now, gentle comrades.

in kerth galles tobesy
molleth du war y vody
3280 scherevwa yv in meske myl

[*iij tortores tranceant in tento filius* (sic)
mulieris iuxta

CALO

Wel an negys a veth grueys
the lowenha *agis* breys
dretho na ve   [*descendat*
3284 ser turant agys pagys
sur ny vynnons fovt wagys
vn stap lafurye adre

TYRANNUS

Dar dufe hy the henna
3288 thage herhes marsama
me as pee indan one*n*
may teffons thymo pur schaff
martese*n* gans keher claff
3292 dethe a pup tenewen
dyso gy y comondyaff
wele dyn pob y welen

p. 129.   CALO

War ov forth hyr
3296 se*r* turant floyr
honnyv marthys cusel da
atta guelynny pa*r*ys
ba na sparyovgh bethens peys
3300 rag dysky dethe tou*n*tya

TYRANNUS   [*ad tentum tortores*

Hov ser*is* pyv us intre
nyth heb oy atte o*m*me
malbe yeman in harber
3304 py halles an rema moys
re vahom du a galloys
moghheys thymo ov awer

CALO

Me *agis* gor bys detha
3308 in tave*r*n sur ov eva
y mons pur ruth age myn

Away Tobias has gone,
God's curse on his body!
    Most rascally he is amongst a thousand.
     [*Let the three torturers pass into the tent of the Woman's Son hard by.*

THE DRUDGE.

So the errand shall be done
That your mind the gladder
    Thereby shall not be.   [*let him go down.*
Sir tyrant, your pages
Surely will not for want of wages
    One step go on from home.

THE TYRANT.

Harm! will it come to that?
To fetch them if I am,
    I will pay them under ash,
So that they may come to me very quickly
Perhaps with a sore stroke (?)
    To them on every side.
To thee I command
    See for us every one his rod.

THE DRUDGE.

On my long way,
Sir flower of tyrants,
    This is wondrous good counsel.
Behold rods ready
And spare ye not: let them be paid
    For teaching them to teaze.

TYRANT [*at the torturers' tent.*

How sirs, who is it that is at home?
A nest without an egg, lo here!
    .... servant in harbour.
Where could these have gone?
By Mahound, god of power,
    Greatened for me (is) my grief.

THE DRUDGE.

I will put you even to them.
In a tavern surely drinking
    Their mouths are very red.

arluth gesugh vy the govs
ornugh ragthe pob y bovs
3312 may fo claff age duklyn

clamat ille in alio tento

Hov mestresy us lemyk
me a leu*er* the plemyk
thywy nowothov nowyth
3316 guelheys yv ages nygys
by my fay y feth wag*is*
ha henna wy a clowyth
mars*us* dagre*n*
3320 dymo leme*n*
ystennogh oma an pyth

p. 130.   PRIMUS TORTOR

A wolc*um* the dre gargese*n*
pendra leu*er* an podren
3324 a reys dym mones dotho
dus nes hag assy an poyt
thysogy eff a cost groyt
kyns dybert so mot y go

SECUNDUS TORTOR

3328 By god ny re eves ree
yma bohes tus the pee
molleth du thage*n* mest*er*
raghyl yv in y pemont
3332 argya orto ny ammont
ythese*n* pel a theller

TERTIUS TORTOR

Ty vav prag na ruste dre
don age*n* wagys ome
3336 byth ny yllyn soweny
boys age*n* gober hep pee
ix nobyl a calame
a russe sokyr thynny

TYRANNUS

3340 Wel wel me a bee an scot
ha warbeyn kylly ov hot
by my sovle ny warth mas ran
lemme*n* tobesy gueras
bys may fons ov teharas
the gerthes gays an guelan

    Lord, allow ye me to speak,
    Order for them every one his bout
3312   That their buttocks may be sore.

    He shouts in another tent.

    How Masters, is there a sup?
    I will tell uprightly*
      To you new news.
3316   Your errand is shewn,
    By my faith there will be wages
      And that ye shall hear.
    If there be a drop
3320   For me now,
      Reach out here the thing.

     FIRST TORTURER.

    Ah, welcome home, gudgeon!
    What does the stinkard say?
3324   Is there need for me to go to him?
    Come nearer and try the pot:
    To thee it shall cost a groat
      Before parting, so mote I go.

     SECOND TORTURER.

3328   By God, we have drunk overmuch.
    There are few people to pay,
      God's curse to our master!
    A rascal is he in his payment.
3332   To argue with him avails not.
      We are far behind.

     THIRD TORTURER.

    Thou slave, why didst thou not
    Bring home our wages here?
3336   Never can we thrive
    That our hire is without being paid.
    Nine nobles on the calends of May
      Would have helped us.

     THE TYRANT.

3340   Well, well, I will pay the shot,
    And, on pain of losing my hood,
      By my soul, a good part will not laugh.
    Now, Tobias, help
3344   Till they be apologizing.
      Let the rod go along!

* lit. 'to plummet,' *d'aplomb, ad perpendiculum.*

Tyrannus et calo verberant tortores

p. 131.
PRIMUS TORTOR

Dar ena ythesogh why
molleth du the tobesy
    eff re ruk agen tolla
3348
a ser arluth faverugh ny
nebes esen ov teby
    y fethe hy in forma

SECUNDUS TORTOR

3352
Ser arluth na cronk na moy
trogh yv agen esely
    benithe ny vethen vays
myscheff war gorff tobesy
3356
eff revue treytour thynny
    gony ellas

TERTIUS TORTOR

Arluth gays thym ov bevnans
me a vyn pesy gevyans
3360
    boys mar thyek yth keuer
molleth du the corff ov mav
mar uskis ytheth y pav
    thyugh rag gul thynny bysmer

TYRANNUS

3364
Lemmen ythogh rewardis
ha mar tuff thagis kerheys
    arta sur why a far guel
dugh genevy desempys
3368
    alemma then guelfos snel

p. 132.
DEMON

Peys y hot both wylde and tame
y say monfras ys my name
benythe numbethe schame
3372
    awoys gul drok
yma thymo servysy
orth ov gorthya pur vesy
    in dyweth a thue ʒum lok

SECUNDUS DEMON

3376
Der the ingynnys hath hus
sotel oys ov tolla tus
    sav me yv gueyth

The tyrant and the drudge beat the torturers.

FIRST TORTURER.

Ruin! are ye there?
God's curse to Tobias:
 He has deceived us.
Ah, sir lord, favour us!
We were not thinking at all
 That it would be in this way.

SECOND TORTURER.

Sir lord, beat no more!
Broken are our limbs:
 Never shall we be well.
Mischief on Tobias' body!
He has been a traitor to us.
 Woe is us, alas!

THIRD TORTURER.

Lord, leave me my life!
I will beseech forgiveness
 For being so sluggish as regards thee.
God's curse to my slave's body!
So quickly went his foot
 To you to do us injury.

THE TYRANT.

Now you are rewarded!
And if I come to fetch you
 Again, surely you will fare better.
Come with me forthwith
 Hence to the wilderness, quickly.

DEMON.

Peace I order, both wild and tame.
I say Monfras is my name.
Never had I shame
 On account of doing evil.
I have servants
Worshipping me right busily:
 In the end they will come to my jail.

SECOND DEMON.

Through thy engines and thy magic
Subtle art thou, deceiving folk,
 But I am worse.

ov hanov yv schyrlywyt
3380 ahaneff neb a ra fyt
　　me an aquyt in gode feyth

PRIMUS DEMON

Duen ny lemmen then tempel
an turant a vyn cowel
3384 　gul sakyrfeys
may hallo guthel moy drok
myryn orto vn golok
　　kyn na vo hy rag y leys
　　　　　[descendat ad templum

TYRANNUS

3388 Seris dugh oll in tempel
nynsyv helma du sempel
　y terfen y enora
　　　　　[genuflectunt omnes
omma pen tarov schylwyn
3392 offrynnya sur me a vyn
　tan 3˚gy map ydama

p. 133.　　### PRIMUS TORTOR

Thum du ny vanna boys gorth
mahum kemer dys pen horth
3396 　gorovrys y gernygov
na gymer meth am present
lemen pan ywe messent
　me an set ryb the frygov

SECUNDUS TORTOR

3400 Thum du offrynnyaff pen margh
tan ha gore in the argh
　present worthy
yma orto skyrennov
3404 eff a dall denerennov*
　rag baban a welogh why

TERTIUS TORTOR

Thum du iovyn benygas
me a offren iij bran vrays
3408 　marthys rond age mellov
y a dall denerov vj
me as kerhes purguir de
　war geyn margh mes an hellov

* leg. deneren nov ?

My name is Shirlywit.
3380 With me whoso will match
    I will pay him off in good faith.

FIRST DEMON.

Let us come now to the temple.
The tyrant will completely
3384   Make sacrifice
So that he may do more evil.
Let us look at him one look,
    Though that be not for his advantage.

                      [*he descends to the temple.*

TYRANT.

3388 Sirs, come ye all into the temple!
This is not a foolish god:
    He deserves to be honoured.

                      [*All kneel.*

Here a white-naped bull's head
3392 Offer surely I will.
    Take, to thee a son am I.

FIRST TORTURER.

To my god I will not be adverse.
Mahound, take to thee a ram's head,
3396   Gilded his little horns.
Take no shame of my present,
Now since it is well-scented
    I will set it by thy nostrils.

SECOND TORTURER.

3400 To my god I offer a horse's head,
Take, and put in thy chest
    A worthy present.
There are on it frontals.
3404 It is worth nine pence
    For a bauble (?) you see.

THIRD TORTURER.

To my god, blessed Jove,
I will offer three ravens,
3408   Wondrous round are their limbs.
They are worth sixpence.
I fetched them right truly for him
    On a horse's back out of the marshes.

CALO

3412 Thum du iovyn in y fath
me a offren lawen cath
   ny yl boys guel legessa
me as droys a voruelys
3416 le may fue an iovle elys
   degens ytte om hascra
pen bogh ha gaver pelys
ov du lemen thyn grassa
      [*et cantant omnes*

p. 134.
DEMON

3420 Me agis son an barth cleth
drok hag anfusy inweth
   guetyogh vsia
ha pyle bohosogyan
3424 molothov kentrevogyan
   thywhy sowyny a ra

PRIMUS TORTOR

Nov lemen duen ygyn forth
agen tassens an barth north
3428   re roys thynny
purguir y venedycconn
ha pyle bohosogyon
   y commondias thyn defry

SECUNDUS TORTOR

3432 Yma debren thov ij vregh
mar bel bones heb gul pegh
   duen alema
mar sus treytour
3436 byth moy feytour
   a vynner the dalhenna

TERTIUS TORTOR

Ny reys thyn fors py thellen
rag bener re thewellen
3440   menogh y rer y pesy
gans agen kerens nessa
ha wath oll the lowenha
   pup vr oll y fethenny

THE DRUDGE.

3412 To my god, Jove, in his face
I will offer a tom-cat:
    There cannot be better to catch mice.
I have brought it from Morville
3416 A place where the devil has been anointed (?).
    Let him take, behold them in my bosom,
A buck's head and a skinned goat.
    My god, now thank us.
              [*And all the torturers sing.*

THE DEMON.

3420 I will sain you from the left side.
Evil and misfortune likewise
    Take care to use,
And to pillage poor men.
3424 Curses of neighbours
    Will make you thrive.

FIRST TORTURER.

Now at present let us come on our way.
Our holy father from the north part
    Has given to us
3428 Right truly his blessing,
And to pillage poor men
    Has commanded us really.

SECOND TORTURER.

3432 There is an itch to my two arms
So long to be without committing sin.
    Let us come hence.
If there be a traitor,
3436 Ever more a scoundrel,
    He would be laid hold of.

THIRD TORTURER.

Needs not for us to care where we go,
For never may we return!
    Often will he be besought
3440 By our nearest kinsmen,
And yet all the gladder
    Always we shall be.

SECUNDUS VENATOR REGIS

3444 Arluth me ages guarnyas
fetel ese turant brays
er agis pyn drehevys
attense enos in prays
3448 ha ganso ost brays ervys   [*finit*

p. 135.
REX

Pup ol tennens thy arvov
ny a grên agen barvov
mar ny omthegen the guel
3452 an turant yv ongrassyas
menogh y car ewyas
ha guerrya purthyogal

Sav bytegyns
3456 in spyt thy dyns
me an gorthyb gans reson
ha mar a myn
mellya certyn
3460 a wysk gu in y golon
    [*ad stallum w*ᵗ *ij stremeres*

TYRANNUS

Hov serrys pan a aray
leferugh thym wᵗout nay
pyv a ros dywhy lescyans
3464 rag dones in ov grond vy
the helghya best arlythy
gorthebugh war beyn mernans

REX

Ser turant ke war the gam
3468 bythqueth ny vue map the vam
genys wath then eretons
saff in neys na veth re tont
me yv prest arluth an gront
3472 nansyv blethynnyov vgons

p. 136.
TYRANNUS

Ser prence yv why us omma
guel vya dyugh omdenna
a dermen ha pesy grath
3476 mar a tuen ha debatya
mas an nyyl party omma
ov teberth purguir ny warth

SECOND KING'S HUNTSMAN.

3444   Lord, I have warned you
    How there was a great tyrant
      Risen against you.
    Behold him there in the meadow
3448   And with him a great host armed.

THE KING.

    Let every one draw to his arms.
    We will shake our beards
      If we do not bear ourselves the better.
3452   The tyrant is graceless.
    Often he likes moving
      And making war very certainly.

    But nevertheless
3456   In spite of his teeth
      I will answer him with reason,
    And if he will
    Meddle certainly
3460   Thrust a spear into his heart.
        [*To the stall with two streamers.*

THE TYRANT.

    How sirs, what an array!
    Tell ye to me without nay,
      Who has given to you license
3464   To come into my ground
    To hunt lords' beasts?
      Answer on pain of death.

THE KING.

    Sir tyrant, go thy way:
3468   Never has there been a son of thy mother
      Born yet to the heritage.
    Stand nearer, be not too lofty,
    I am now lord of the ground
3472   It is now twenty years.

TYRANT.

    Sir Prince, is it you that are here?
    Better were it for you to withdraw
      In time and to beseech grace.
3476   If we come and fight,
    Well one of the two parties here
      At parting truly will not laugh.

REX

  Nov by hym that iudas solde
3480 ny senseff ath geryov bolde
   vn faven kuk
  byth nynsoff the omager
  na der reson vyth danger
3484   dyso ny ruk

  Thymo quarel
  mar pottyth lel
   a falsury
3488 the aquyttya
  kyn moys lema
   me a ra gans lendury

TYRANNUS

  Ty falge horsen [n]am brag vy
3492 avond tellek theth cregy
   hath chettis plos
  me am beth goys the colon
  scollys omma war an ton
3496   kyns hy bos nos

p. 137.   ### REX

  Ny seff henna yth galloys
  ty nag ongrassyas del oys
   mentenour a thyscregyans
3500 ren arluth crist a vercy
  me nyth sense guel es ky
   denagh the tebelvryans

  Bo me a vyn
3504 scollya the lyn
   oma war ton
  byth na wyle
  neb ur braggye
3508   an crustunyon

TYRANNUS

  Fy dis hag oll theth nasconn
  fy mylwyth then crustunyon
   denagh the fay
3512 bo ty ha myns us genas
  a vyrwe omma re satnas
   der beyn ha mur anfusy

THE KING.

  Now by Him that Judas sold,
3480 I care not for thy bold words
    One blind bean.
  Never am I thy vassal,
  Nor through any reason lordship
3484   For thee have I made.

  On me a quarrel
  Of falsehood
    If thou really puttest,
3488 Repay thee,
  Before going hence,
    I will with usury.

THE TYRANT.

  Thou false whoreson, insult me not
3492 A halter with a hole (?) to hang thee
    And thy foul chits!
  I shall have blood of thy heart
  Spilt here on the meadow
3496   Before it be night.

THE KING.

  That stands not in thy power,
  Thou, ungracious as thou art!
    Upholder of unbelief!
3500 By the Lord Christ of mercy,
  I hold thee not better than a hound.
    Deny thine evil privilege,

  Or I will
3504 Spill thy blood
    Here on meadow.
  Never seek
  At any time to insult
3508   The Christians.

THE TYRANT.

  Fie on thee and all thy nation!
  Fie a thousand times on the Christians!
    Deny thy faith,
3512 Or thou and all that are with thee
  Shall die here, by Satan!
    Through pain and much misfortune.

REX

  Nefre ny nehyn an fay
3516 awos ovn ahanes gy
   nag ʒethov ongrassyas
  rag mentons fay crustunyon
  oma parys war an ton
3520 ny dovtya y voys treas

p.138.   ### TYRANNUS

  O! o! o!* bemont ectour
  ens lemen pup thy arvov
  an iovle agis acectour
3524 rebo pan vowhy marrov
  mar quregh fynsya
  sesyogh thymmo an prevyon
  falge plosethes crustunyon
3528 then dour gansa

REX

  Why a gren agis barvov
   treytours kyn gul indella
  yma parys tus arvov
3532 thagis gortheby oma
   dugh pan vynnogh
  sovdrys dehesugh detha
  the ʒethov sur obaya
3536 nefre ny vanna orthogh

         Hic praeliabunt

REX MASSEN

  Out gony reys yv feya
  bo neyl marov on oma
   intorma ny yv rewan
3540 yma ran sur kemerys
  gans an ʒethov ongrassys
  a thu fetel veth lemman   [*finit*
         [*tranceat domum*

TYRANNUS

  Wel far yov sovdrys ryel
3544 an remyv fyys abel
  us nag onen vyth sesijs

* The original scribe wrote *Out charlys* over which the corrector placed *O! o! o!*

THE KING.

  Never will we deny our faith
3516 For fear of thee,
    No! graceless Jew!
  To maintain the faith of Christians
  Here ready on the meadow
3520   I fear not that it should be tried.

THE TYRANT.

  Out, out, out, Beaumont, Hector,
   Let every one go now to his arms.
  The devil be your attendant
3524   When you are dead
    If you flinch (?).
  Seize for me the worms,
  False, foul Christians,
3528   To the ground with them!

THE KING.

  Ye shall shake your beards,
   Traitors, before doing so.
  Ready are armed people
3532   To answer you here
    Come when ye will.
  Soldiers, strike at them.
  A Jew obey surely
3536   Never will I for you.

        [*Here they shall fight.*

KING MASSEN.

  Out, woe is us, need is to flee!
  Or else dead are we here.
   This turn we are too weak.
3540 Some surely are taken
  By the graceless Jew.
   O God, how will it be now?

        [*Let him pass home.*

THE TYRANT.

  Well fare you, royal soldiers,
3544 These are fled afar.
   Is never a one seized?

TERTIUS MILES TYRANNI

Vs vn de*n* yonk at oma   [*capiat filius mulieris*
me re ruk sur y sesia
3548   ser turont gothfeth thym grays   [*finit*

p. 139.
TYRANNUS

Nov wel far the gentel knyght*
eff a pee purguir y wyght
    a our kyn boys dylyfrys
3552 hag a nagh pelle y fay
bo in p*re*son eredy
    pedry y ra in stockys

FILIUS

Henna yv an pyth na raff
3556 ihesu c*ri*st ny denahaff
    awoys a ylly dym gul
wath in dyspyt war the dyns
me a worth kep*ar* ha kyns
3560   neb a ruk an gol han sul

TYRANNUS

Wel wel mar nynseth ay nagh
in p*re*son ty a in bagh
    ho why geylers dugh omma
3564 gorugh helma in p*re*son
mar ny nagh c*ri*st map maryon
    ena pedry† eff a ra
        [*ascendit in curro‡ suo*

CARCERARIUS

Ser turant the voth y re*n*
3568 dus in rag oma ty the*n*
    in p*re*son the growetha   [*ad Filius*
ty re fue napyth redovnt   *mulieris*
moys the serry an turant
3572   leme*n* ty a oyl henna

p. 140.
GARCON

Ny a vyn y carhara
purguir na ala guaya
    na luff na troys
3576 gogy pan vus ov p*er*thy
oma ty a ra pedry
    ny feth na deves na boys

* MS. kynght   † MS. predry   ‡ MS. turro.

THIRD SOLDIER OF THE TYRANT.

    There is a young man, lo here!   [*let him take the*
    I have surely seized him.   *Woman's Son.*
3548   Sir tyrant, give thanks to me.

THE TYRANT.

    Now well fare thee, gentle knight.
    He shall pay right truly his weight
        Of gold before being delivered,
3552   And shall further deny his faith,
    Or in prison readily
        He shall rot in (the) stocks.

THE SON.

    That is the thing I will not do:
3556   Jesu Christ I will not deny
        Because of what thou mayst do to me.
    Still in spite of thy teeth
    I will worship even as before
3560   Him that made the holiday and the Sunday

THE TYRANT.

    Well, well, if thou wilt not go from refusing him
    Into prison thou shalt go in short.
        Ho ye gaolers, come here!
3564   Put ye this man into prison,
    If he denies not Christ, Son of Mary,
        There he shall rot.
                [*He goes up in his chariot.*

A GAOLER.

    Sir tyrant, thy will we shall do.
3568   Come forward here thou man,
        In prison to lie.
    Thou hast been somewhat (?) too lofty,   [*to the*
    To go to anger the tyrant.   *Woman's Son.*
3572   Now thou wilt bewail that.

A BOY.

    We will imprison him,
    Right truly so that move
        Can neither hand nor foot.
3576   Woe to thee when thou wast parting!
    Here thou shalt rot:
        Thou shalt have neither drink nor food.

PRIMUS NUNCIUS [ad matrem Filius
          Heyl dyso a venen tha
3580 me ath warn prest a vn dra
          the vap yma kemerys
          gans an turant ongrassyas
          me ny won ragtho ellas
3584   pendra veth grueys   [finit

               MULIER
          Ellas ov holen yv trogh
          ellas thym nynsese flogh
              mas eff na confort in beys
3588 maria gonys a raff
          thy fesy gans colen claff
              rag ov map me a vyn moys

[tranceat ad eclesiam beate marie. genuflectit
 et expectut ibidem

          Maria mam ha guerhes
3592 me a vyn the luenbesy
          maria ov map gueres
              ha restoria thymo vy
          maria me reth cervyes
3596   thum gallus bythqueth defry
          maria wyn rag ov les
              y colmennov grua terry
          maria mar a mynnes
3600   delyfrys bya surly

p. 141.   TYRANNUS
          Hov geylers golsovugh wy
              me a charg war beyn tenna *
          boys na dewes na regh ry
3604   then guas a ruk vy orna
          the preson pur eredy
              an vorov rum lel ena
          me a vyn prest y cregy
3608   y quartrona hay denna

          CARCERARIUS [ad tyrannum
          Arluth the voth a veth grueys
          eff nefre ny veth goleys
              me a wor the guir henna
3612 mar peth cregys an vorov
          vastya boys heb feladov
              ny venen adro dotha

              * MS. tenuna

MESSENGER [*to the Son's mother.*
Hail to thee, O good woman!
3580 I warn thee at once of one thing.
Thy son is taken
By the ungracious tyrant.
I know not for him, alas,
3584 What will be done.

THE WOMAN.
Alas, my heart is broken!
Alas, to me there is no child
But he, nor comfort in the world.
3588 Mary I do serve:
To beseech her with a sick heart
For my son, I will go.
[*Let her pass to the church of the Blessed Mary.
She kneels and waits in the same place.*

Mary, Mother and Maid,
3592 I will beseech thee fully,
Mary, help my son,
And restore him to me.
Mary, I have served thee
3596 According to my power ever earnestly,
Blessed Mary, for my good
Break his bonds.
Mary, if thou wouldst,
3600 He would be delivered surely.

TYRANT.
How gaolers, hearken ye!
I charge on pain of drawing,
Neither food nor drink give ye
3604 To the lad whom I ordered
To prison right readily.
To-morrow, by my loyal soul,
I will hang him,
3608 Quarter him, and draw him.

GAOLER [*to the tyrant.*
Lord, thy will shall be done.
He shall never be loosed,
I know that of a truth.
3612 If he be hung to-morrow,
Waste food without fail
I would not about him.

P

MULIER

  Maria me reth pesys
3616　 rag ov map sur lues guyth
  maria wath ny vynsys
   thymo vy gul confort vyth
  maria me a weyl neys
3620　 am creya vy fors ny reyth
  maria mercy mar suys
   in nos praga nam clowyth

  Maria nynsus nahen
3624　 ny ammont ov peiadov
  maria ov map certen
   yma in tyn colmennov
  maria creys thym lemen
3628　 rag ov flogh an caradov
  maria the vap byen
   gene dre ytha hythov

p. 142. Maria ater the vregh
3632　 dulle thym the vap ihesu
  awoys ovn peryl na pegh
   eff a dre gena hythyv
   dus dus a vaby
3636　 farwel genes maria
  ny vanna the annya
   oma na moy ov pesy

         tranceat domum [*cum ihesu*

  Ihesu crist lowene dys
3640　 purker ty a veth guythys [*cofyr aredy*
   avel ov flogh ov honyn
  hag in quethov fyn malys
   in ov cofyr sur gorys
3644　 oma alwethys certeyn
  lemen me yv lowenheys
   moys the powes me a vyn

   MARIA [*in celo dicit*

  Ihesus ov map caradov
3648　 myns us grueys heb feladov
   dalour y wothes certen
  ha pendra us in golon
  confort thum cervons dyson
3652　 boys y carsen

THE WOMAN.

  Mary, I have besought thee
3616   For my son surely many times.
  Mary, yet thou hast not willed
   To do me any comfort.
  Mary, I see again
3620   For my crying thou carest not,
  Mary, if there be mercy,
   Why dost thou not hear me to-night?

  Mary, it is not otherwise:
3624   My prayer avails not.
  Mary, my son certainly
   Is in strait bonds.
  Mary, believe me now,
3628   For my son, the loveable,
  Mary, thy little Son
   With me home shall go to-day.

  Mary, outside of thy arm,
3632   Let come to me thy son Jesu.
  Notwithstanding fear of peril or sin,
   He shall go home with me to-day.
    Come, come, O baby!
3636 Farewell to thee, Mary,
   I will not annoy thee
    Here praying more.

       [*Let her go home with Jesu.*

  Jesu Christ, joy to thee!
3640 Full dearly thou shalt be kept [*A coffer ready.*
   Like my own child,
  And swaddled in fine clothes,
  Put into my coffer
3644   Here locked surely.
  Now I am gladdened:
   I will go to rest.

MARY *says in heaven.*

  Jesus, my loveable Son,
3648 All that is done, without fail,
   Well enough thou knowest certainly,
  And what is in the heart.
  Comfort to my servants at once
3652   I should like to be.

IHESUS

  A vam grua del vy plesijs
  neb ath worth a veth esijs
    kyn fensi polge ov cortes
p. 143.   3656 theth servont myr
  grua the desyr
    ha both the vreyes

     [*descendit maria cum ij angelis
      ad carcerem*

MARIA

  A then yonk fetel esta
3660 mur yv the lavyr oma
   heb y dyndyl
  sav a vo in bevnans da
  grays du purguir the henna
3664   in dyweth certen ny fyl

FILIUS

  Ihesu arluth thum gueres
  byth ny alla omheres
    dyegrys off gans gvynder
3668 ny won rum caredevder
  pendra yv an golevder
    us adro thym heb awer

MARIA

  Omconfort drefe warvan
3672 kynthos gyllys feynt ha guan
    wath ty a veth confortys
  in nos na gymer dyglon
  me ath dylerff an preson
3676   oma y tuth rag the leys

p. 144.   ### FILIUS

  Grovs crist benedicite
  pyv re duth thymo ome
    han darasov ol degeys
3680 nos tevle ytho nam nygen
  ha lemen sur golvygyen
    adro thym yma cothys
  hag yma forme a vynen
3684   myternes pur in y greys

JESUS.

O mother, do as thou mayst be pleased.
Whoever worships thee shall be eased
    Though they be tarrying a moment.
3656 To thy servant look,
Do thy desire,
    And the will of thy mind.
        [*Mary descends with two angels
            to the prison.*

MARY.

O young man, how art thou?
3660 Great is thy labour here
    Without deserving it.
But he who shall be in the good life,
God's grace right truly to that (man)
3664   At the end certainly shall not fail.

THE SON.

Lord Jesu, to help me!
I cannot help myself.
    Blinded am I by whiteness.
3668 I know not, by my loveableness,
What is the radiance
    That is around me without grief.

MARY.

Comfort thyself, rise up!
3672 Though thou art become faint and weak
    Yet thou wilt be comforted.
To-night lose not heart: *
I will deliver thee from the prison.
3676   Here I have come for thy good.

THE SON.

O cross of Christ, benedicite!
Who has come to me here,
    And the doors all shut?
3680 A dark night now, to me not otherwise,
And now surely radiance
    Around me is fallen,
And there is a form of a woman,
3684   A queen, right in the midst of it.

* lit. 'take not unheart.'

MARIA

Dore in mes the garov
the orthys an carharov
   prest me a den
3688 ha dyso an darasow
vgoreff heb feladow
nynsus dyalwethy gov
   am guyth certen

3692 Lemen ov map ke theth vam
ha lafer dethy heb nam
   maria theth delyfrya
ha spesly lauer dethy
3696 drens hy ov map dymovy
ha gruens ov servia deyly
   arta awose helma

p. 145.

FILIUS MULIERIS

Maria gorthys reby
3700 maria guyff nynsen vy
   genes the vones ledijs
maria thyso mur grays
maria na ve the rays
3704   gon guyr y fyen dyswreys

MARIA

Ov banneth genes heb nam
ham banneth y roff theth vam
   lauer in delle dethy
3708 kyn thevely dethy pel
ov boys heb y clowes lel
   ny vennen y ankevy   [*finit*
                             [*tranceat maria ad celum*

CARCERARIUS

Out gony mata sa ban
3712 haneth oll an beys gans tan
yma purguir han presan
   ov colowhy
me a greys boys grueys forth lan
3716   ena defry

GARCON

An presnour in kerth galleys
han darasov oll degeys
   pyv an iovle revue oma

MARY.

Bring out thy legs:
From thee the fetters
    At once I will draw,
3688 And for thee the doors
Open without fail.
There are not false keys
    In my keeping certainly.

3692 Now, my son, go to thy mother,
And say to her without error
    That Mary delivered thee,
And specially say to her,
3696 Let her bring my Son to me,
And let her serve me daily
    Again after this.

THE WOMAN'S SON.

Mary, worshipped be thou!
3700 Mary, worthy I was not
    By thee to be guided.
Mary, to thee much thanks!
Mary, (if) thy grace were not
3704   I know truly I should be undone.

MARY.

My blessing (be) with thee, without exception,
And my blessing I give to thy mother:
    Say thus to her;
3708 Though it should seem that far from her
I am without hearing her loyally,
    I will not forget her.
        [*Let Mary pass to heaven.*

THE GAOLER.

Out, woe's us, mate, stand up!
3712 To-night all the world with fire
Is right truly, and the prison
    A-blazing.
I believe that a clear way is made
3716   There really.

THE BOY.

The prisoner has gone away,
And the doors all closed.
    Who the devil has been here?

3720 duen then turant leferyn
a molleth du in gegyn
  at oma sur drog athla

p. 146.   CARCERARIUS [*ad tyrannum*
   A ser turant gony gony
3724 an presner in kerth defry
   galles eff haneth in nos
golovder ganso revue
bythqueth moy ovn numdarfe   [*finit*
3728   re thu am ros

    TYRANNUS
Out govy harov harov
  py ma ov fresner feyys
why a feth purguir marov
3732   mara sywe dyenkys
rum lel ena
an horsens revue methov
ha re ases tus an pov
3736   me a wor thy delyvrya

    GARCON
Ay turant ke war the gam
molleth du the vap the vam
  yma ree ov leferel
3740 heb ty vyth nag ovlya
delyfrys der varia
  fetel ywa dyogel
hagis boys wy de vlamya
3744   war vohogo[g]yon cruel   [*finit*
         [*yerde aredy*

    TYRANNUS
Ay dar indelle vethy
  mal myscheff regis doga
ov sclandra mar mynnogh why
3748   ha leferel ov bosa
omma cruel
why an prev^t du in test
have that me agis lest
3752   rag desky drok thym covsel [*finit*
  verberat eos

3720 Let us come to the tyrant: let us say:
O God's curse in the kitchen,*
　　See here surely an evil outlaw.

THE GAOLER *to the tyrant.*

O sir tyrant, woe's us, woe's us!
3724 The prisoner away really
　　He has gone this very night
Radiance was with him,
Never had I greater fear,
3728 　　By God who made me!

THE TYRANT.

Out woe's me, haro, haro!
　　Where has my prisoner fled?
You shall be right truly dead
3732 　　If he has escaped
　　　By my loyal soul!
The whoresons were drunk,
And allowed the people of the country,
3736 　　I know, to deliver him.

THE BOY.

O tyrant, go on thy way!
God's curse to thy mother's son!
　　Some are saying,
3740 Without any oath or howling (?),
Delivered by Mary
　　As he is certainly,
And that you are to blame,
3744 　　To the poor men cruel.
　　　　　　　　　　　　[*a staff ready.*

THE TYRANT.

Ah, ruin, will they be so?
　　May ill mischief bear you off!
If you will slander me,
3748 　　And say that I am
　　　Here cruel,
You shall prove it, God in witness!
Have that! I will hinder you
3752 　　From teaching (folk) to speak ill of me.
　　　he beats them.

　　* lit. in the kitchen.

p. 147.
FILIUS

  Hebasca thywhy ov mam
   mur reverons the varia
  thynny prest y fye cam
3756 mar ny rellen y gorthya
   in guelhe preys
  hy re ruk ov delyfrya
  mes a preson mam kerra
3760 le may theua drokhendelys

MULIER

  Maria rebo* gorthys
  dasvewys yv ov sperys
   ov map the gueles oma
3764 fetel vusta delyfrys
  laver thymo me ath peys
   ov map kerra

FILIUS

  Maria thymo in nos
3768 purguir a thueth then preson
  gans golov ha mur a tros
   in coske bo dufen dyson
   ny won esen
3772 hy purguir am degolmas
  han dares dym egoras
  hag vfel am comondyas
   thum mam the dre may thellen

3776 Inmethy lauer theth vam
  me theth delyfrye heb nam
   sav thymo restoryans hy
  ov map henna nynsyv cam
3780 pan vsy y flogh dethy   [*finit*

p. 148.
MULIER

  The varya wyn mur grays
  a vyna hy the guerays
   in dyweth ny veth tollys
3784 y flogh me a gemerays
  the orth y yamach a rays
   drefen nages restorijs
   thymo gensy
3788 marthys claff o ov holon
  an flogh then ymach dyson
   me a vyn don eredy

* perhaps revo.

THE SON. [*he goes up to his mother*

Sweetness (?) to you, my mother,
　Much reverence to Mary!
For us ever it would be wrong
3756　　If we did not worship her
　　In best time.
She has delivered me
Out of prison, dearest mother,
3760　　A place where I was evilly handled.

THE WOMAN.

Mary be worshipped!
My spirit is revived
　To see my son here!
3764　How wast thou delivered!
Tell me, I beseech thee,
　My dearest son.

THE SON.

Mary to me at night
3768　　Right truly came to the prison
With light and much noise.
　Asleep or awake
　　I know not whether I was.
3772　She right truly unchained me,
And opened the door for me,
And gently bade me
　To go home to my mother.
3776　She said: 'tell thy mother
That I have delivered thee without exception,
　But to me let her restore
　My son: that is not wrong
3780　　Since she has her (own) son.'

THE WOMAN.

To blessed Mary much thanks!
If she will help thee,
　At the end thou wilt not be deceived.
3784　Her child I took
From her image of grace
　Because thou wert not restored
　　To me by her.
3788　Wondrous sick was my heart.
The child to the image at once
　I will bear readily,

        Ha mos quik bys in eglos
3792 oma atte guythys clos
          y aperia ny vynnys
        maria lowene dis
        maria dyso mur grays
3796   ov map dym dry pan vynsys
      [*descendit ad ecclesiam beate marie cum ihesu*

        Maria kemer the flogh
        maria re vuff relogh
          in the gever
3800 sav mercy y raff pesy
        hag onen ath servysy
          nefre bethe heb awer*
                [*finit tranceat domum*
                [*demens et paterfamilias paratus*

p. 149.   DEMENS   [*forling and suagynk*

        Out warnogh wy falge guesyon
3804   prag y russugh ov kelmy
        agis pennov myllusyon
        me a ra age therry

        PATERFAMILIAS

        Lauer purguir mar kyllyth
3808 henna lemen y fyllyth
          rag pur fast ythos chenys
        the veryasek me a vyn
        the wore purguir lemyn
3812   mar kyllyth bones sawys

        DEMENS

        Lauer thymo lagasek
        pendrama gans meryasek
          mar guir an iovle theth lesky

        PATERFAMILIAS

3816 Meryasek dyugh lowena
        den mes ay revle us gena
          ha tus re ruk ov heskey
        may rellen y dry oma
3820   the voys socrys genogh wy

  * Here the scribe writes *finit hec pagina*.

And go quick to the church.
3792 Lo here it is, wrapt close:
I would not open it.
Mary, joy to thee!
Mary, to thee much thanks,
3796 Since thou wouldst bring me my son.

[*She goes down with the image of Jesus to the church of blessed Mary.*

Mary, take thy child,
Mary, I have been overlax
Regarding thee.
3800 But mercy I beseech,
And one of thy servants
Ever I shall be without grief.

[*Let her go home.*
[*A madman and a head of a family ready.*

A MADMAN *hurling and swagging.* *

Out on you, ye false fellows!
3804 Why have you bound me?
Your lousy heads
I will break them.

HEAD OF A FAMILY.

Talk right truly if thou canst.
3808 That now thou shalt lack,
For right fast thou art chained.
To Meriasek I will
Put thee right truly now
3812 If thou canst be healed.

THE MADMAN.

Tell me, thou big-eyed,
What thing is with Meriasek?
So truly the devil burn thee!

THE HEAD OF A FAMILY.

3816 Meriasek, joy to thee!
A man out of his mind is with me,
And folk have advised me
That I should bring him here
3820 To be succoured by you.

* *Flirl*, to throw, to hurl. One that falls down with some violence and noise is said to come down with a swag. Kennett cited Halliwell, s. v. *swag*.

MERIADOCUS EPISCOPUS

  Ihesu arluth us avan
  re werese creff ha guan
   trewethek syght yv helma
3824 gueles den yonk tek certan
   cheynys in keth vanerma

p. 150.   DEMENS

  Awoys ov bones cheynys
  a tefes dym nebes neys
3828 me a pylse the pen blogh
  hag a russa
  dyso oma
   garrow pur trogh

   MERIADOCUS [*genuflectit*

3832 Ihesu arluth me ath peys
   gueres omma an denma
  ihesu crist arluth grassyeys
   thy skyans lemen drofa
3836 ihesu arluth map guerheys
   y envy gor the orta
  ihesu gront na ven nehys
   ha peys gene maria

3840 Gorta ty then dym omma
  in hanov map maria
   me a vyn the degelmy
  neb a yl hag a ylly
3844 ressawhyagy heb yly
   amen warbarth gruen pesy

     DEMENS

  The crist ihesus murworthyans
   ha thys meryasek nefra
3848 cryst thym re dros ov skyans
   drethos meryasek oma
  meryasek in ov bevnans
   me a vyn prest the servya
3852 meryasek dyso reverans
   sensys ovy theth gorthya   [*finit*

p. 151.   MERIADOCUS

  Thum oratry moys manna
  the besy war varia
3856 prest ov gueres

BISHOP MERIASEK.

May Jesu, lord that art above,
Aid strong and weak!
    A piteous sight is this.
3824 To see a young man, fair certainly,
    Chained in this same manner.

THE MADMAN.

Because of my being chained,
If thou wouldst come to me somewhat nearer,
3828   I would peel thy blockhead,
And I would make
For thee here
    Legs all broken.

MERIASEK [kneels.

3832 Jesu, Lord, I beseech thee
    Help here this man.
Jesu Christ, gracious Lord,
    To his wits now bring him.
3836 Jesu, Lord, son of a virgin,
    His enemy put from him!
Jesu, grant that I be not denied,
    And beseech with me, Mary.

3840 Wait, thou man, for me here:
In the name of Mary's Son
    I will unbind thee.
May he who can, and who will,
3844 Heal thee without salve!
    Amen together let us pray!

THE MADMAN.

To Christ Jesu, much honour,
    And to thee, Meriasek, ever!
3848 Christ has brought me my wits
    Through thee, Meriasek, here.
Meriasek, in my life
    I will always serve thee.
3852 Meriasek, to thee reverence!
    Bound am I to honour thee.   [he ends.

MERIASEK.

To my oratory I will go
To pray to Mary
3856   Always to help me,

·ha thum guythe pup seson
omma the orth temptasconn
   ha the orth pup drok covsy(s)
                [ad oratorium genuflectit

3860 Ihesus arluth luen a ras
        gorthyans dys ha lowena
     ihesu arluth in pup plas
        guyth ov ena heb mostya
3864   ham corff kefrys
     maria gvyn guyrhes pur
     maria beth ov socur
     maria a gara mur
3868   the du ker peys rag ov leys

           IHS.
     Ov eleth ker eugh then beys
     susten an neff bethens reys
        the veryasek
3872 megys y feth gans ov grays
     benyges yv in pup plays
        y oberov dym a plek

p. 152.   (MI)CHAEL
     Ihesu de voth a veth grueys
3876 dotho eff ythen uskys
     genen y feth confortis
        in forth wella
     dotho megyans
3880 degen dyblans
        the orth an formyer guella
                Descendunt [organs or syngyng

           GABRIEL
     Meryasek lowena dis
     crist ker regyn danvoneys
3884   oma prest theth confortya
     kyn theses ov thyr penys
     oma ty a veth megys
     gans boys eleth in torma

*Sumens cibum cum laudibus diuinis epulis
   quotidie sentit se refectum*

        MERIADOCUS [genuflectit
3888 Ihesu arluth nor ha neff
     pup vrol rebo* gorthys
     ihesu crist nynsefeth greff
     in bysma ath lel wonys

        * perhaps revo.

   And to keep me at every season
   Here from temptation,
     And from every evil thought.
         [He kneels at the oratory.

3860 Jesus, Lord, full of grace
    Worship to thee and joy
   Jesu, Lord in every place,
    Keep my soul without corruption,
3864   And my body likewise.
   Blessed Mary, pure virgin,
   Mary be my succour!
   Mary, whom I love much,
3868   To dear God pray on my behalf.

      JESUS.

   My angels dear, go ye to the world.
   Let the food of heaven be given
     To Meriasek.
3872 Nourished he shall be with my grace,
   Blessed he is in every place,
    His works are pleasing to me.

      MICHAEL.

   Jesus, thy will shall be done,
3876 To him we shall go quickly,
   By us he shall be comforted,
    The best way.
   Nourishment to him
3880 Let us bear clearly
    From the best Creator.
     They descend. [*Organs or singing.*

      GABRIEL.

   Meriasek, joy to thee!
   Dear Christ hath sent us
3884   Here now to comfort thee.
   Though thou art at three penances
   Here thou shalt be nourished
    With angels' food this turn.

Taking sustenance with praises of God, every day he feels
  himself recruited with sumptuous food.

    MERIASEK [*kneels.*

3888 Jesu, Lord of earth and heaven
    Always be worshipped,
   Jesu Christ, there will not be grief
    In this world from thy loyal service.

           Q

3892 ihesu dyso y crasseeff
gans boys neff pan of megys
ihesu arluth ny dovtyeff
kyn fen treddeth ov penys

p. 153. *Hic dux .i. primus Magus pompabit*

3896 Me yv arluth heb parov
duk inweth astronymer
the helghya heb feladov
the prince par del yv dufer
3900 moys me a vyn
ha geneff cowethe da
an epscop purguir a thuea
the certen plas er ov fyn

DUX .i. SECUNDUS MAGUS

3904 Besy yv thyn bones war
yma dragon vras heb mar
in caff oma rebon ny
mar a tuny er y fyn
3908 marov on bras ha byyn
da yv boys fur eredy

VENATOR [*ducibus magos*

Yma oma tus arvov
hag archers gans guaregov
3912 abel purguir dy latha
me thovtya gans ov huen
marnes y a vo ree luen
kyns es dybarth y squerdya

[*descendit cum armatores*

Hic episcopus poly pompabit

3916 Me yv epscop a theveys
ha parlet mur ov rasov
y tethewys nansyv meys
mones inhans then prasov
p. 154. 3920 erbyn duk magus a breys
den fur in y worthebov
ov crosyer ota parys
lemen thum gormennadov

CROSSER EPISCOPI POLI

3924 Me yv parys arluth da
sav guan revle yma oma
na yllyn lefya kyn moys

3892 Jesu, to thee I give thanks.
    Since by heaven's food I am fed,
Jesu, Lord, I fear not
    Though I be three days at penance.

Here a Duke, to wit, the first Magician, shall parade.

3896 I am a lord without peers,
    A duke, likewise an astronomer.
To hunt without fail
    As it is a duty for a prince
3900   I will go,
And with me comrades good.
The bishop right truly he will come
    To a certain place to meet me.

A DUKE, to wit, THE SECOND MAGICIAN.

3904 Need it is for us to be wary.
There is a great dragon without doubt
    In a cave here by us.
If we come against her
3908 Dead are we great and small.
    It is well to be wise readily.

HUNTSMAN [*to the Dukes the Magi.*

Here there are armed folk,
And archers with bows
3912   From afar right truly to slay her.
I fear not with my hounds,
Unless they shall be too full
    Before parting to tear her.

        [*he goes down with armed men.*

Here the bishop of Pola shall parade.

3916 I am a bishop exactly (?)
    And a prelate, great my graces.
I have promised, it is now a month,
    To go down to the meadows
3920 To meet Duke Magus of price,
    A man wise in his answers.
My crucifer, art thou ready
    Now according to my orders?

THE BISHOP OF POLA'S CRUCIFER.

3824 I am ready, good lord.
    But a bad rule is here
    That we may not dine before going.

gvak yv thym an pengasen
3928 a molleth du in gegen
schant yv an dewes han boys
Descendunt

EPISCOPUS POLI

Heyl dyugh duk nobil magus
me ham crosser presagus
3932 reduth dywy 3ᵉ sportya
na wethen ree then ternans
rag yma dragon dyblans
hag onen vras sur omma

PRIMUS DUX MAGUS

3936 Noov wolcum ffadyr byschyp
ny thue dragon me a dyp
oges thynny
mar thue in syght me an gor
3940 yma omma pobil lor
rag y latha eredy

[*her y dragon aredy in yᵉ place*

p. 155.
SECUNDUS DUX MAGUS

Na drestiyn ny the henna
arlythy duen alema
3944 attahy sur defethys
out drethy bethen marov
gans flam tan mes ay ganov
nys gorta myl den ervys

[*her a gonn yn y dragon ys movthe aredy & fyr*

PRIMUS DUX

3948 Hov dehesugh warnethy
nansus ran lenkis gonsy

[*sum of yᵉ sovdrys y sowlyd*

pythyv an iovle a reny
mahom reges ancumbra
3952 in agen meske ov scumbla
avel wy mark attahy

EPISCOPUS POLI

A gony gony fyen
ken marov bras ha byen
3956 re corff mahum on oma

    Empty have I the end of the paunch (?).
3928 O God's curse in the kitchen,
     Scant is the drink and the food.
          [They go down.

BISHOP OF POLA.

    Hail to you, noble Duke Magus!
    I and my crozier-bearer, Praesagus,
3932   Have come to you to sport.
    Let us not keep overmuch to the low land,
    For there is a dragon clearly,
     And a big one, surely here.

FIRST DUKE MAGUS.

3936 Now welcome, father bishop!
    The dragon will not come I think
     Near to us.
    If she come in sight, I know it,
3940 Here there are people enough
     To slay her readily.
    [Here the dragon ready in the open space

SECOND DUKE MAGUS.

    Let us not trust to that.
    Lords, let us come hence!
3944   Behold her surely unconquered!
    Out! by her we shall be dead
    With flame of fire out of her mouth.
     A thousand armed men abide her not.
  [Here a gun ready in the dragon's mouth and fire.

FIRST DUKE.

3948 How, strike at her!
    Now are some swallowed by her!
       [Some of the soldiers swallowed.

    What the devil shall we do?
    May Mahound cumber you!
3952 Amongst us dunging
     Like water, mark! behold her!

THE BISHOP OF POLA.

    Ah woe's us, woe's us! let us flee
    Else dead, great and small,
3956   By Mahound's body, we are here.

  duen then emperour costentyn
   ha dotho eff leveryn
    y vryans eff yv helma

    PRIMUS DUX [*ad constantinum*

3960 Heyl *ser* emperour costentyn
   ha warnes ny a cry out
   deswreys yv an pov lemyn
   ha d*er* the wryens heb dovt
3964   lues marov
p. 156. an dragon vrays us in caff
   vn d*en* the gerthes ay saff
    ny gas nan lathe heb wov

    EPISCOPUS POLI

3968 Bythqueth ny vue vays in pov
   aban vys crystyan heb wov
    molleth du war ath treylas
   ny glowys gans d*en* genys
3972 a worthya crist nygythys
    bythqueth the faria in fays

    CONSTANTINUS

   Arlythy eugh wy war gam
   crist ha maria y vam
3976   dua rag ag*en* gueras
   dus oma ov maseger
   ha kergh uskys sylvest*er*
    the covs gena a fur spas

    NUNCIUS [*ad constantinum*

3980 Costentyn arluth somper
   me a doro syluest*er*
    oma dywy an vorov
   ny goske welen indan droys
3984 na nefre ny debre boys
    er na govs*en* orth y ganov
          [*ad syluestrem*
   Siluest*er* lowena dys
   then emperour dones uskys
3988   reys yv thywy in certeyn
   rag ef a vyn covs orthys
    pu*r* wyr lemmyn   [*finit*

Let us come to the emperor Constantine,
And to him let us tell,
    His lordship is this.

FIRST DUKE *to Constantine*.

3960 Hail, sir emperor Constantine!
    And on thee we cry out.
Undone is the country now,
    And throughout thy lordship without doubt
3964   Many dead.
The great dragon that is in a cave
One man to go from his standing
    She will not let without killing him truly.

BISHOP OF POLA.

3968 Never has there been good in the country
Since thou becamest a christian without a lie.
    God's curse on him who converted thee!
I have not heard that any one born
3972 Who worshipt evil Christ
    Ever fared well.

CONSTANTINE.

Lords, go your way.
Christ and Mary his Mother
3976   Will come to help us.
Come here, my messenger,
And fetch quickly Silvester
    To speak with me for a short space.

MESSENGER *to Constantine*.

3980 Constantine, lord without equal,
I will bring Silvester
    Here to you to-morrow.
A rod shall not sleep under foot,
3984 Nor ever shall I eat food.
    Until I speak at his mouth.
                                  [*To Silvester.*

Silvester, joy to thee!
To the emperor to come forthwith
3988   Need is for you certainly,
For he will speak to thee
    Right truly now.

SILVESTER   [*descendit siluester*

      The constentyn me a due
3992 thy comondment benythe
          eff yv arluth mur y nel
                  [*ad constantinum*
      ser emperour dyugh lowene
      oma prest me re dufe
3996 ha ny vynnys lettya pel

IMPERATOR CONSTANTINUS

      Ima oma sur dragon
      ov latha pobil dyson
          heb numbyr sur del clowa
4000 tovlel a rons warnavy
      bones an causer defry
          begythys rag ov bosa
                  · [*descendit constantinus**

SYLUESTER

      Dre voth crist arluth avan
4004 an dragan me a ra guan
          dregen in pov na relle
      may welle myns us in rome
      ihesu crist a bev ry dome
4008 ha gul kepar del vynne

PRIMUS DUX *magus*

      Cans den lethys war ov feth
      nav re vue sur in vn geth
          prest gensy hy
4012 mar qureth y ouercummya
      the crist ny a vyn treyla
          var off ny yllyth defry

SYLVESTER

      Thum peiadov alema
4016   mones a vanna rygthy   [*genuflectit*

IHC.

      Pedyr lemen thymo kea
      the syluester eredy
      gueyt in tek y confortye
4020 ha gans henne y desky

* MS. constantinum.

SILVESTER. [*Silvester goes down.*

To Constantine I will come
3992 According to his command ever
He is lord: great his might.
[*To Constantine.*

Sir Emperor, joy to you!
Here at once I have come
3996 And I would not hinder long.

EMPEROR CONSTANTINE.

There is here surely a dragon.
Slaying people
Without number surely, as I hear,
4000 They do cast on me
That I am the causer really
For my being baptized.
[*Constantine goes down.*

SILVESTER.

Through the will of Lord Christ above
4004 The dragon I will pierce
So that she may not do hurt in the country.
So that all that are in Rome may see
Jesus Christ owns the (right of) giving doom,
4008 And doth as he will.

FIRST DUKE MAGUS.

A hundred men slain, on my faith,
Now were surely in one day
By her.
4012 If thou canst overcome her
To Christ we will turn.
I am aware that thou wilt not be able really.

SILVESTER.

According to my prayer hence
4016 I would go before her. [*he kneels.*

JESUS.

Peter, now for me go
To Silvester readily.
Take care fairly to comfort him,
4020 And therewithal to teach him.

                an dragon y ra fethe
                    der ov gallus defry*
                ytheseff orth y care
    4024   ny vanna y ankevy

PETRUS

            Arluth the voth me a ra
            syluester scon y guarnya
                an dragon nangeffo ovn
    4028   eff as led avel on doff
            ha der gallus du in proff
                as comond then dysert dovn

descendit petrus [solus ad syluestrem in placea

            Syluester wek beth lowen
    4032   crist a vyn orthys certen
                fethe purguir an dragon
            the ij chaplen kemery
            genes thegy eredy
    4036   ha gueres ad du dyson

SYLVESTER

            Arluth neff rum gueresa
            me ny won thum confortia
                pyv us oma devethys
    4040   mur yv gallus crist avan
            ha trestia a raff certan
                pup vr ol eff thum guereys

PETRUS

            Me yv the crist abostel
    4044   ha pedyr ov hanov lel
                na thovt dysset in matter†

159   Then dragonn covs in delma
            ihesu crist map maria
    4048   ha genys a lel werheys
            a fue marov in grovs pren
            hag anclethys in beth men
                then tresse deth dasserrys
    4052   assendijs then neff inban
            deth brus eff a thue certan
                thagen brusy kyk in kneys

* The scribe wrote *eredy* which the corrector has struck out substituting *defry*.
† At least three lines are here wanting.

> The dragon he will vanquish
>> Through my power readily.
> I am loving him,
4024 > I will not forget him.

PETER.

> Lord, thy will I shall do,
> (And) Silvester at once warn him
>> Of the dragon that he should not have fear.
4028 > He will lead her like a tame lamb,
> And through God's power in proof
>> Will command her to the deep desert.

Peter descends [alone to Silvester in the open space.

> Silvester sweet, be glad!
4032 > Christ will for thee certainly
>> Defeat right truly the dragon.
> Thy two chaplains, take them
> With thee to her readily,
4036 >> And help from thy God at once.

SILVESTER.

> Lord of heaven help me!
> I know not to comfort me
>> Who is come here.
4040 > Great is the power of Christ above,
> And I do trust certainly
>> That always he will help me.

PETER.

> I am an apostle of Christ's,
4044 > And Peter is my loyal name:
>> Fear not deceit in the matter.

> To the dragon speak thus:
> "Jesu Christ, son of Mary,
4048 >> And born of a loyal virgin,
> Has been dead on the crosstree,
> And buried in a tomb of stone,
>> On the third day he arose,
4052 > Ascended up to heaven.
> On Doomsday he will come certainly,
>> To judge us, flesh in skin.

in y hanov ty dragon
4056   in mes oma thymo duys

     Syne an grovs kymer genys
     ha ty as led del vynneys
             poren theth voth z° honen
4060 ihesu a vyn daguereys
             rag the voys y servont len

             SYLVESTER

     Benyges rebo an preys
     me a vyn mones uskys
4064   then dragon sur alemma   [descendit
     dugh gene ov dev chaplen
     syne an grovs theragon scoen
             degeugh aberth maria
                     [a crosse aredy ffor primus
                         capellanus seluestris

             PRIMUS CAPELLANUS SILVESTRIS

4068 Me a thek pur guir an grovs
     hav cowyth inweth heb flovs
             degens lantern gans golov
     dovn yv an caff may ma hy
4072 cans pas del glowys ha moy
             crist guyth ny orth tewolgow
                     [secundus capellanus beryth
                         y' lantern

). 160.   PRIMUS DUX .i. MAGUS

     Serys duen ny the veras
     pan dyweth an thragon vras
4076   a ra syluester lemen
     ny grese vy mas pystry
     y wore gul eredy
             thagen tolla pur certen

             SYLVESTER [genuflectit

4080 In hanov map maria
     ihesu crist ythyv henna
             a fue marov anclethyys
     dasserrys then tresse deth
4084 then neff assendias inweth

   In his name, thou dragon,
4056   Come out here to me."

   The sign of the cross take with thee
   And thou wilt lead her as thou wishest,
    Right according to thy own will.
4060 Jesu will help (thee) well,
    For that thou art his faithful servant.

SILVESTER.

   Blessed be the time!
   I will go forthwith
4064   To the dragon surely hence.
   Come with me, my two chaplains:
   The sign of the cross before us
    Bear ye on behalf of Mary.

      [*A cross ready for Silvester's
        first chaplain.*

SILVESTER'S FIRST CHAPLAIN.

4068 I will bear right truly the cross,
   And my comrade likewise, without flout,
    Let him bear the lantern with a light:
   Deep is the cave where she is,
4072 An hundred paces, as I have heard, and more.
    Christ keep us from darkness!

      [*The second chaplain bears
        the lantern.*

FIRST DUKE i.e. MAGUS.

   Sirs, let us come to see
   What end of the great dragon
4076   Silvester will make now.
   I believe that nought save magic
   He can do readily,
    To deceive us right certainly.

SILVESTER *kneels.*

4080 In the name of Mary's Son,
   Jesu Christ is that,
    Who has been dead, buried,
   Raised on the third day,
4084 To heaven he ascended likewise

an berth dyov the du tays
deth brus eff a thue purfeth
the vrusi an drok han mays

4088 In y hanov dus in mes
par del yv gorhemynnes
gans crist dymo in bysma
      [exiuit de spelunca

PRIMUS DUX .i. MAGUS

atta an dragon ov toys
4092 war theller guel yv dyn moys
o' marov ythoff omma
pur guir gans hy anel poys
benytha vays ny vetha
      [cadat in terrore monstri

SECUNDUS DUX .i. MAGUS

4096 Hy rum lathes gans hy gvyns
re vahum wek pen an sens
alemma numbus gvaya
govy na vuma war kyns
4100 hager dyweth yv helma   [finit
      [cadat in terrore monstri

SILVESTER

Gorta oma ty dragon
in hanov crist cuff colon
me a vyn the thalhenna
4104 hath ledya kepar hag on
der gallus du in delma

CONSTANTINUS

Syluester gorthys reby
ty re proves eredy
4108 boys crist pen an arlythy
thymo othem o hena
seris pendra govsughwy
den benyges yv helma

EPISCOPUS POLY

4112 Yma omma tus varov
mar kyllons heb feladov
thage bevnans bones dreys

On the right side of God (the) Father.
On Doomsday he will come perfect
To judge the bad and the good.

4088 In His name come forth,
Even as is commanded
By Christ to me in this world.
[She issued from the cave.

FIRST DUKE i.e. MAGUS.

Behold the dragon coming!
4092 Back it is better for us to go.
Out! I am dead here!
Right truly by her heavy breath.
Never shall I be well.
*[Let him fall down in fear of
the monster.*

SECOND DUKE i.e. MAGUS.

4096 She has killed me with her wind.
By sweet Mahound, the chief of the saints,
Hence I cannot move.
Woe's me, I was not wary before!
4100 An ugly end is this.
*[Let him fall down in fear of
the monster.*

SILVESTER.

Stay here, thou dragon!
In the name of Christ, the loveable heart,
I will lay hold of thee,
4104 And lead thee like a lamb,
Through God's power, so.

CONSTANTINE.

Silvester, praised be thou!
Thou hast proven readily
4108 That Christ is the head of the lords.
Need to me was that.
Sirs, what say you?
A blessed man is this.

BISHOP OF POLA.

4112 Here there are dead folk.
If they can, without fail,
To their life be brought,

   cavs thynny eff a vya
4116 in ihesu map marya
   the cresy byen ha brays

SILUESTER

   Ihesu arluth creff ha guan
   ihesu an dusma leman
4120 vsy war dor omgellys
   gront dethe sevel in yagh
   mar a syns fur y a nagh
   in vrna tebel wythreys*

      [*Surrexit ij^{us} ducibus et omnes*

PRIMUS DUX .i. MAGUS

4124 Syluester gorthys reby
   in crist me a vyn cresy
    du a vercy y vosa
p. 162. an dragon yv tebelvest
4128 me a vyn pesy baptist
   ha gorthya map maria   [*finit*

EPISCOPUS POLI

   Thum skyans pan oma dreys
   me a vyn boys begythys
4132 gorthya ihesu benitha
   an falge dragon tebel preff
   ny gara gueles y grueff
   desawer vest yv honna

SILVESTER

4136 Na berthuth ovn annethy
   dre gras ihesu us avan
   then dysert me as gor hy
   then le na relle dregan
4140 in hanov crist a vercy
   me ath worhemyn dragan
   then guylfos quik mathylly
   avoyd ʒ° orthef leman
4144 drok nefre gueyt na rylly
   the vest na den creff na guan
   na byth moy na ʒ°wylly
   war beyn ancov ty belan

   * MS. looks *voythreys*.

Cause to us it would be
4116   In Jesus, son of Mary,
         To believe, small and great.

SILVESTER.

Jesus, Lord of strong and weak,
Jesus, this folk now
4120   That are on earth overthrown,
Grant to them to stand up whole.
If they be wise, they will reject
   In that hour evil-doing.
         [*The two dukes arise and all.*

FIRST DUKE i.e. MAGUS.

4124 Silvester, worshipt be thou!
In Christ I will believe
   That he is God of mercy.
The dragon is an evil beast.
4128 I will beseech a baptizer,
   And worship Mary's Son.

BISHOP OF POLA.

To my wits since I am brought,
I will be baptized
4132   (And) worship Jesus always.
The false dragon, evil worm,
I like not to see her face.
   An unsavoury beast is that!

SILVESTER.

4136 Do not bear fear of her.
   Through grace of Jesus who is above,
To the desert I will put her,
   To the place where she cannot do evil.
4140 In the name of Christ of mercy
   I command thee, dragon,
That thou go quick to the wilderness.
   Out of the way from me now!
4144 Take care that thou never do evil
   To beast, nor man, strong nor weak,
That thou never more return
   On pain of death, thou villain.

R

EPISCOPUS POLY

4148 In kerth sur galles holma
oll rome yv sensys nefra
   the enora syluester
grua scon agen begythya
4152 opynguelys yv omma
   nagus du mas ihesu ker   [*finit* -
          [*holy water aredy*

p. 163.   ### SYLVESTER

Me agys beseth warbarth
oma lemen kyns dybarth
4156   in nomine patris et* filij
et spiritus sancti amen
lemen ov mebyen lyen
   ware thum palys duen ny   [*finit*

SECUNDUS CAPOLLANUS SILVESTER

4160 Parys on the voys genogh
ny a ra bohes venogh
syluester servys dywhy
gorthyans the crist in torma
4164 lues enaff sur oma
   drethogh sawys us defry   [*finit*

CONSTANTINUS

Gorthyans the crist a selwans
der syluester in torma
4168 pobyl rome orth ij vernans
delyfrys ythyns oma
kynsol a debel cregyans
lues den dreys in forth da
4172 ha ny ol guythys dyblans
orth an dragon preff an pla

Duen ny oll gans procession
thy curte syluester dysonn
4176   gruen y gora
dotho oll ython sensys
lues oma deworijs
gans an dragon ongrassijs
4180   na ve eff sur a vya   [*finit*
      [*ad palacium pape procesconant*

* MS. ef

BISHOP OF POLA.

4148 Away surely this is gone.
All Rome is bound ever
    To honour Silvester.
Forthwith do thou baptize us.
4152 Openly seen is here
    That there is no God save dear Jesus.
                  [*Holy water ready.*

SILVESTER.

I will baptize you together,
Here now before parting,
4156   In the name of the Father and the Son
And of the Holy Ghost, amen.
Now, my sons of learning,
    Anon to my palace let us come.

SILVESTER'S SECOND CHAPLAIN.

4160 Ready are we to go with thee.
We will often do a little,
    Silvester, of service to you.
Worship to Christ at this turn!
4164 Many souls surely here
    Through you are healed really.

CONSTANTINE.

Worship to Christ of salvation!
Through Silvester this turn
4168 Rome's people from two deaths
    Are here delivered,
First of all from evil belief
    Many a one brought on a good road,
4172 And we all clearly preserved
    From the dragon, the worm of the plague.

Let us all come with a procession.
To his court forthwith Silvester
4176   Let us put him.
To him we are all bound:
Many here devoured
    By the graceless dragon,
4180   Were he not, surely would have been.
                  [*They go in procession to the Pope's palace.*

p. 164.   LANGUIDUS vel CONTRACTUS

       A thu assoma grefijs
       mans ov esely a heys
           mas orth dev croyth ny gerthaff
4184 assoff guan hag anhethek
       kelmys off the vryasek
          sav ny von pur in metyaff

       Me re vue in mes dres nos
4188 mur ov anwys ham ponfos
          pan veth lues ov cosca
       in pollov prest omhelys
       ov ij lyn ham kyk squerdys
4192   sevel am saff ny alla

       Devethys ythoff then plays
       dorsona thys a thremays
          rag kerense ihesu wek
4196 lauer dym a then grassyes
          py caffsenua meryasek

        MERIADOCUS

       Ov covs genes at eva
       pendra vynta annotha
4200   lauer in scon
       me a garsa
       in norvysma
       pup vr socra
4204   bohogogyon

        CONTRACTUS

       Me yv cropyl podrethek
       devethys dys meryasek
          purothomek the du gras
p. 165. 4208 rag kerense an pasconn
       a porthes ihesu ragonn
          meryasek grua thym gueras

       Numbus esel nag yv mans
4212 ha pur vr* yma mernans
          in beys orth ov gohelas
       numbus kerthes mas sklynkya
       ny gar namur in bysma
4216   doys in ov syght nam guelas
       noth off avel best oma
          war lur ov pedrevanas   [*genuflectit*

        * leg. *pup ur* or *pur guir.*

A FEEBLE MAN, OR A CRIPPLE.

O God, I am grieved!
Maimed are my limbs for a long time:
  Except on two crutches I walk not.
I am weak and loathsome.
Bound am I to Meriasek,
  But I know not when I shall meet him.

I have been out during night.
Great my chilliness and my trouble
  When many are sleeping.
In pools quite overturned.
My two knees and my flesh torn.
  I cannot stand up.

I am come to the place.
A blessing to thee, O worthy sir!
  For love of sweet Jesus,
Tell me, O gracious man,
  Where I may find Meriasek.

MERIASEK.

Speaking with thee, behold him.
What thing wouldst thou of him?
  Say forthwith.
I should like
In this world
Always to succour
  Poor people.

THE CRIPPLE.

I am a rotten cripple
Come to thee, Meriasek,
  Right needy, thanks to God.
For love of the Passion
Which Jesus bore for us,
  Meriasek, help me!

I have not a limb that is not maimed,
And always death is shunning me
  In the world.
I cannot walk but slink.
Not much in this world loves
  To come into my sight or to see me.
Naked am I, like a beast here
  On the ground crawling.

MERIADOCUS

  Ihesu a ruk neff ha nor
4220 me a peys omma in clor
    re therbara dis ȝehes
  mones ha doys may hylly
  kepar del yl heb yly
4224 sawya oll the esely
    a pup galer ha cleves

  Ihesu yv agen savyur
  retrehava the war lur
4228   maria reth weresa
  ha re grontya
  y both mar pea
    ȝehes thyso in torma

CONTRACTUS

4232 Arluth assoff lowenheys
    grassaff ȝe crist a vercy
  ha thys meryasek kefrys
  restorijs ov esely
4236   yv thym heb wov
  kerthes me a yl
  lemen heb peryl
    yagh ha pur salov

p. 166.
MERIADOCUS EPISCOPUS

4240 The ihesu rebo grassees
  the guyske kymer dyfles
    lemen densa yth kerhen
  ha tan dis dewes ha boys
4244 grasse the crist a galloys
    eff yv the vethek certen

CONTRACTUS

  Ihesu avan
  map guerhes* splan
4248   thyugh ren tala
  meryasek wek
  then bohosek
    parys owhy the socra

MERIADOCUS   [in oratorio iacebat

4252 Dugh why thym ov bredereth
  corff ov arluth del deleth
    hythyv me re recevas

   * MS. grurhes.

MERIASEK.

 May Jesus, who made heaven and earth,
4220 I beseech here gently
  Provide healing for thee,
To go and come that thou mayst,
As he can without a salve
4224 Heal all thy limbs
  From every disease and illness.

Jesus is our Saviour.
May he raise thee up from the ground!
4228   May Mary help thee!
And grant,
If it be her will,
  Healing to thee at this turn!

THE CRIPPLE.

4232 Lord, I am rejoiced.
  I give thanks to Christ of mercy
And to thee, Meriasek, likewise.
  My limbs restored
4236   Are to me without a lie.
I can walk
Now without peril,
  Healed and quite whole.

BISHOP MERIASEK.

4240 To Jesus be thanks!
For clothing take raiment
  Now, good man, around thee,
And take thou to thee drink and food.
4244 Give thanks to Christ of power:
  He is thy leech certainly.

THE CRIPPLE.

May Jesus above,
Son of a bright virgin;
4248   Repay it to you!
Sweet Meriasek,
To the poor man
  Ready are you to give succour.

MERIASEK [*he was lying in the oratory.*

4252 Come ye to me, my brethren.
My Lord's Body as one ought,
  To-day I have received.

```
                    reys yv dyberth otyweth
        4256            kyn fo tek an gowethas
                    The ihesu rebo grasseys
                    gans mernans me yv tuchys
                        reys yv mones an bysma
        4260    bredereth vsyogh dader
                    han vohosogyen pub vr
                        bethugh sokyr an rena

                        DECANUS  [ad meriadocum
                    Arluth fetel vyth dynny
        4264    mar teberthyth eredy
                        meryasek the orthen
                    me a wor in guir heb mar
                    benytho arluth ath par
        4268        pur thefry nygynbethen

p. 167.                 · MERIADOCUS
                    Yma an preys ov nesse
                    the crist me a vyn grasse
                        thym y thadder in bysma
        4272    ʒesseys vnctis communijs*
                    off lemen the ihesu grays
                    the orth crist lel map guirhas
                    rag ov servesy in beas
        4276        war thu pesy me a ra            [genuflectit
                    Neb am gorth vy in bysma
                        ihesu arluth gront dethy
                    gallus boys ʒesseys oma
        4280    kyns es merwel eredy
                    corff crist inweth receva
                        vngijs gans henna defry
                    then vlas neff age ena
        4284        may thella purguir then ioy

                    In le may feua gorthys
                        ·peseff rag an keth rena
                    maystefons y luen ʒeheys
        4288        pesy warnaff a rella
                    ha sawys a pup cleveys
                        aberth an corff han ena
                    susten maystefons kefrys
        4292        ha lor pegans the vewa

                    In kernov me ambeth chy
                        ryb maria a cambron
                    thum wyles neb a thue dy
        4296        me as aquit purdyson
                        kyn fo ov corff in ken le
                * MS. seems connnijs
```

   Need is it to part at last,
4256   Though fair be the companionship.
   To Jesus be thanks!
   By death I am touched.
    Need is it to go from this world.
4260   Brethren, practise goodness,
   And the poor people always,
    Be ye the succour of those.

     THE DEAN to *Meriasek*.

   Lord, how will it be to us
4264   If thou departest already,
    Meriasek, from us?
   I know truly, without doubt,
   Never a lord equal to thee
4268   Certainly shall we have.

     MERIASEK.

   The time is drawing nigh.
   To Christ I will give thanks
    For his goodness to me in this world.
4272   Confessed, anointed, houseled
   Am I now, thanks to Jesu.
   From Christ, loyal son of a virgin,
   For my servants in the world,
4276   On God, I do pray.   [*he kneels*.
   Whoever shall honour me in this world,
    Jesu, Lord, grant to them
   Power of being confessed here
4280   Before dying readily,
   Christ's Body likewise to receive,
   Anointed therewith certainly,
   To heaven's kingdom that their soul
4284   May go right truly to the joy.

   In the place wherein I may be honoured
    I pray for those same
   That they may have full confession
4288   If they should pray to me,
   And be healed of every disease
    Within the body and the soul.
   Sustenance that they may have likewise.
4292   And enough pittance for living.

   In Cornwall I shall have a house
    By Mary of Camborne.
   To see me whoever comes thither
4296   I will absolve him at once,
     Though my body be in another place.

                    in keth plasna neb a beys
                    gans ihesu y feth clowys
     4300   hay petyconn colenwys
                        lafyll purguir mar pethe

p. 168.   Ov gol a veth suer
                    in mes metheven
     4304   an kynsa guener
                        rag nefre certen
                    ov banneth vy
                    gans banneth crist pen an sens
     4308   the kemmys ov gol a sens
                        y pese bys venary

                            CANONICUS

                    Meryasek fetel esogh
                    adar medelheys brays ogh*
     4312   bethugh a cher
                    ny a yl boys morethek†
                    war the lergh ha herethek
                        mar seth the orthen in suer

                            MERIADOCUS
     4316   Du guener crist ihesu ker
                    a ruk merwel ragon ny
                    maythoff lowen du guener
                        dascor ov ena defry
     4320   thum selwadour
                    ha du guener rag henna
                    bethens ov gol vy nefra
                        sensys gans ov flehys dour

     4324   Bredereth dugh nes omma
                    in tokyn a gerensa
                        amma thyugh ol me a vyn
                    in hanov map maria
     4328   in vvelder deberthyn

                    in manus tuas domine
                    spiritum meum commendo
                            Et sic emisit spiritum
                    [yᵉ holy goste aredy ffro hevyn to fett
                        yᵉ sowle and yᵉ sovle aredy

p. 169.   IHS.
                    Ov eleth nygyogh then nor
     4332   the kerhes thymo pur clour
                        oma eneff meryasek

    * MS. seems *adar medelhe ys braysogh*   † MS. seems *merethek*

In that same place whoever shall pray,
By Jesus he will be heard,
4300 And his petition fulfilled
If it be, truly, right lawful.

My festival shall be surely
In the month of June,
4304 The first Friday
For ever certainly.
My blessing,
With the blessing of Christ, the head of the saints,
4308 For as many as keep my festival
I beseech for ever.

A CANON.

Meriasek, how are you?
Alas! you are greatly weakened.
4312 Be you of cheer.
We may be mournful
After thee, and yearning,
If thou goest from us surely.

MERIASEK.

4316 On Friday, dear Christ Jesu,
Did die for us,
So that I may be glad on Friday
To yield up my soul
4320 To my Saviour.
And on Friday therefore
Be my festival ever
Held by my brave children.

4324 Brethren, draw nearer here.
In token of love
I will kiss you all
In the name of Mary's son.
4328 In humility let us part.

Into thy hands, O Lord,
I commend my spirit.

And so he sent forth his spirit.
[*The Holy Ghost ready from heaven
to fetch the soul, and the soul ready.*

JESUS.

My angels, fly to the earth,
4332 To fetch me very gently
Here Meriasek's soul.

myns a deserias gront*is*
yma dotho war an beys
    4336   y van*er* o da ha tek

MICHAEL

Ih*es*u eff re the*n*delas
in gluas neff bones treges
      ʒiso y fue *ser*vont lel
4340 the volnogeth
par del deleth
      ny a ra snell   [*finit*
      [y*e* holy goste aredy and y*e*
      soule aredy

GABRIEL

Meryasek beth lowe*n*
4344 myns a deserijs *cer*ten
      thys yv grontys
then neff ty a
the lowena
4348   rag trega in ioy a beys   [*finit*

EPISCOPUS KERNOV

Ov crossyer me re glowes
boys m*er*yasek yn newores*
      moys ʒy veres me a vyn
4352 mar sywe byv bo marov
y cowyth heb feladov
me a greys in ov dythyov
      ny wela sur in bretyn   [*descendit*

p. 170.   COMES VENETENSIS

4356 Morethek off rag vn dra
meryasek del glowa
      yma sur war y vasken
dugh gena ov marogyon
4360 thy wore in doyr dyson
      ny a vyn mones le*m*men   [*descendit*

SECUNDUS EPISCOPUS.

Yma sur an arlythy
the veryasek eredy
      ov moys thy wore in doyr
4364 du kem*er* w*t* ay ena
ny veth arel an p*ar*na
      in trogel in brete*n* suyr
        descendunt

* MS. ynne wores.

All he desired granted
Is to him in the world.
4336   His way of life was good and fair.

MICHAEL.

Jesu, he has deserved
To dwell in heaven's kingdom.
  To thee he has been a loyal servant.
4340 Thy will
Even as is meet
  We will do swiftly.
     [*The Holy Ghost ready and
      the soul ready.*

GABRIEL.

Meriasek, be glad.
4344 All that thou desiredst certainly
  To thee is granted.
To the heaven thou shalt go
To gladness
4348   To dwell in joy for ever.

BISHOP OF KERNOU.

My cross-bearer, I have heard
That Meriasek is *in extremis* (?).
  I will go to see him
4352 If he be alive or dead.
His comrade without fail
I believe in my days
  I shall not see in Brittany. [*he goes down.*

EARL OF VANNES.

4356 Mournful am I for one thing.
Meriasek, as I hear,
  Is surely on his bier.
Come with me, my knights,
4360 To put him into the ground at once
  We will go now. [*he goes down.*

SECOND BISHOP.

The lords are surely
To Meriasek readily
4364   Going, to put him into earth.
God, take care of his soul!
There will not be another like that
  In a body in Brittany surely. [*he goes down.*

COMES VENETENSIS.

4368 Lowena dyugh arlythy
meryasek an den worthy
del glowa yv tremenis
thy wore in doyr purguir
4372 del grese kelmys ogh suyr
ha ny kefrys

EPISCOPUS KERNOV

Ea ser ȝurle eredy
par del ove den worthy
4376 agen part yv
mones purguir gans reverans
thy wore in doyr dywans
eff o lel servont ihesu

p. 171.   [*descendit comes globus*

SECUNDUS EPISCOPUS

4380 Lowena dywhy ha ras
peys* da off an cowethas
in torma pur eredy
tremenys yv meryasek
4384 ihesu arluth galosek
thy ena re grontya ioy

GLOBUS COMES

Eff o purguir den worthy
ay genesygeth defry
4388 del wothen ol in breten
ha moy worthy y vryans
yv the kemendya dyblans
del welys vy experyans
4392 gonethys ganso certen

Dal y fueff lues blythen
methek vythol ny gefen
a alho gul dym gueres
4396 pan duthe prest dotho eff
der gallus crist mytern [n]eff
ov golek thym restoryes
ha gras the ihesu heb greff
4400 meryasek am sawyes

    * MS. seems poys

THE EARL OF VANNES.

4368 Joy to you, lords!
Meriasek the worthy man,
As I hear, is passed away.
To put him into earth right truly,
4372 As I believe, ye are surely bound
And we likewise.

BISHOP OF KERNOU.

Yea, sir earl, readily,
As I am a worthy man,
4376 Our part is
To go right truly with reverence
To put him into earth quickly.
He was a loyal servant of Jesus.

[Earl Globus goes down.

SECOND BISHOP.

4380 Joy to you and grace!
Well satisfied am I with the company.
At this time right readily.
Departed is Meriasek.
4384 May Jesus, mighty Lord,
Grant joy to his soul!

EARL GLOBUS.

He was right truly a worthy man
From his birth really,
4388 As we all know in Brittany,
And most worthy his privilege
Is to be commended clearly,
As I saw a proof
4392 Wrought by him certainly.

Blind was I many years:
Any leech I got not
Who could work me a cure.
4396 When I came here to him,
Through the might of Christ, king of heaven,
My sight he restored to me,
And, thanks to Jesus without grief,
4400 Meriasek healed me.

p. 172.

EPISCOPUS KERNOV

 Luyes den yma sensys
 the veryasek sur in beys
  neffre purguir ʒy gorthya
4404 rag me an creys sans in neff
 purthefry y vones eff
  warlergh y ober oma

COMES VENETENSIS   [ad decanu·

 Du re sawya an colgy
4408 ser deyn leferugh thynny
  yv meryasek tremenis
 notijs in pov sur yma
 boys y eneff an bysma
4412 del greseff the ioy gylles

DECANUS

 Arluth eff yv tremenys
 y eneff gans an drensys
  creseff y voys
4416 teka dyweth in bysma
 ny glowys den rum lovta
  ʒº guthel na yonk na loys

CANONICUS

 Y leferys offeren
4420 du guener vetten certen
  glorijs ha tek
 warlergh henna leferis
 gans ancov y voys tuchys
4424 grays the ihesu galosek

   [yᵉ processyon aredy
    ij sansours

p. 173.

DECANUS

 The orth crist y ruk pesy
 certen desyr eredy
  the kenever an gorthya
4428 thotho eff agen gelwys
 ha thynny a comondyas
  doys oll dotho the amma

THE BISHOP OF KERNOU.

 Many men are bound
 To Meriasek surely in the world
  Ever surely to worship him,
4404 For I believe, a saint in heaven
 Full surely that he is
  After his work here.

THE EARL OF VANNES *to the dean.*

 May God save the college!
4408 Sir Dean, say you to us
  Is Meriasek passed away?
 Noted in the country surely it is
 That his soul from this world,
4412   As I believe, has gone to joy.

THE DEAN.

 Lord, he has passed away.
 His soul with the Trinity
  I believe that it is.
4416 Fairer end in this world
 I have not heard, by my loyalty,
  That any one has made, young or gray.

THE CANON.

 He said mass
4420 On Friday morning certainly
  Glorious and fair,
 After that he said
 By death that he was touched.
4424   Thanks to mighty Jesus.

  [*The procession ready and two censers.*

THE DEAN.

 Of Christ he did beseech
 Certainly (the) desire readily
  For whoever should worship him.
4428 To him he called us,
 And us he commanded
  To come all to him to kiss him.

Y ij luff y trehevys
war guir thu mercy creyays
ha then neff eff a verays
    lowenek in syght thynny
an vers in manus tuas
ys leferis heb powas
    pan o hy due eredy
y eneff y tascoras
    then tays du luen a vercy

CANONICUS

Ny wòr mas ran pur thyson
in beys y conuersasconn
    kyn wyske pan tek aveys
in y nesse hevys ruen
pup deth y weska certen
    na noys vyth ny ree poweys
in hotheys na lyynnyov
marnes in cala garov
    hyr ny vethe y huenneys

DECANUS

Havel o ov corthy crist
prest orth sen iowen baptyst
    guyn na syder ny vsya
mylwyth in nos purcertyn
ythe the pen y ij lyn
    ihesu crist rag y worthya

Ha mylwᵗ purguir in geth
war ben y ij lyn purfeth
    y fynna moys awoys greff
may ruk y ij lyn hothfy
mar vras scantlor y hylly
    trewythyov kerthes ay saeff

CANONICUS

Neffrev pesy bo redya
in eglos eff a vetha
    marnes dadder ny govsy
megys vue gans boys eleth
ken ny grese in god feth
    y halse bewe defry   [finit

His two hands he upraised.
4432 On the true God he cried mercy,
And to the heaven he looked,
   Joyous in our sight.
The verse *In manus tuas*
4436 He said it without pausing.
   When it was ended readily,
His soul he resigned
   To the Father God full of mercy.

THE CANON.

4440 A good part, right surely, knows not
His converse in the world.
   Though he wore fair cloth outside
Next him a shirt of horsehair
4444 Every day he wore certainly.
   Any night he rested not
In blankets (?) nor sheets.
Unless in rough straw
4448   Long used not to be his slumber.

THE DEAN.

Like he was in worshipping Christ
Quite to Saint John Baptist.
   Wine nor cider he used not.
4452 A thousand times at night right certainly
He went on the end of his two knees,
   Jesus Christ, to worship him.

And a thousand times right truly in the day
4456 On the end of his two knees perfectly
   He would go on account of mortification.
So that his knees swelled
So great that hardly could he
4460   At times (?) walk from his standing.

THE CANON.

Always praying or reading
In church he used to be.
   Aught save goodness he said not.
4464 Nourished was he with angels' food,
Else I believe in good faith
   He could not have lived really.

COMES VENETENSIS

  Assyv helma mur a col
4468 in breten sur thynny oll
    mestresy mar sogh parys
  mones deglos ny a vyn
  thy anclethyes in certyn
4472   an corff uskys

p. 175.   ### DECANUS

  Pup travle oma yv parys
  an cur yma arays
    del goth erbyn den worthy
4476 an pov fast ymons ov toys
  kerys o gans yonk ha loys
    in bysma dres arlythy ;

COMES VENETENSIS

  I tendeles y cara
4480 lues den guan in bysma
    pur guir eff a confortyas
  dal ha bother evrethyon
  palgy ha dyvers clevyon
4484   ny wothen covs mar luas

DECANUS

  Duen in kerth in hanov du
  ha maria mam ihesu
    gueresugh orth an geler
4488 may hyllen moys in eglos
  cryst roy thynny deth ha nos
    gul oberov a thadder

COMES VENETENSIS

  Me a vyn don an neyll pen
4492 bythqueth ny gerys moy den
    me a greys in norvysma
  eff a thadder o lenwys
  ha benesygter kefrys
4496   genys vvue in termen da

p. 175.   ### GLOBUS COMES

  Me a thek an pen arall
  meryasek purguir heb fal
  am sawyas pan ena* dal

    *leg. ena, enua?

THE EARL OF VANNES.

 This is much of loss
4468 In Brittany surely to us all.
  Masters, if ye are ready
 We will go to the church
 To bury certainly
4472   The body quickly.

THE DEAN.

 Everything here is ready.
 The quire is arranged
  As behoves to meet a worthy man.
4476 The country folk are coming fast.
 Loved was he by young and gray
  In this world above lords.

THE EARL OF VANNES.

 He deserved to be loved.
4480 Many weak persons in this world
  Right truly he comforted.
 Blind and deaf, maimed men,
 Palsied people, and divers lepers,
4484   We cannot say how many.

THE DEAN.

 Let us come away in the name of God,
 And of Mary, Jesu's Mother:
  Help ye at the bier
4488 That we may go into the church,
 May Christ grant unto us day and night
  To do works of goodness!

THE EARL OF VANNES.

 I will carry one of the two ends.
4492 Never loved I any man more
  I believe, in this world.
 He was filled with goodness
 And blessedness likewise:
4496   Born was he at a good time.

EARL GLOBUS.

 I will bear the other end.
 Meriasek right truly without fail
  Healed me when I was blind.

4500	gorthyans dotho benitha	
	kepar del oma sensys	
	benytha in ov densys	
	thy enora	[*finit*

DECANUS

4504	Lemen canens an clergy
	in hanov du a vercy
	han duen uskis alema
	y tendelas
4508	boys enoras
	sur in povma

Hic cantant

SECUNDUS EPISCOPUS

	Lemen parusugh an beth	
	in hanov crist del deleth	
4512	may hallen y anclethyas	
	del yv dufer den worthy	
	in agen meske eredy	
	dadder the lues huny	
4516	eff a ruk ʒ° ihesu gras	[*finit*

p. 177.

NUDUS

	An beth genen ny yv grueys
	kepar del enua* sensys
	thy wonys in norvysma
4520	efrethek ha claff pan en
	eff an† sawys in certen
	may coth dymo y gara

CONTRACTUS

	An beth genen yv glanheys	
	arlythy del vugh plesijs	
4524	gruegh why lemen	
	du asson ny herethek	
	ov queles corff meryasek	
4528	ov mones in dor certen	[*finit*

EPISCOPUS KERNOV

Both du nynsus offendia
an corff in beth y wora
gruegh lemen in hanov du

* Perhaps *enna*. † leg. *am*?

4500 Worship to him always
　　　As I am bound
　　Always in my manhood
　　　To honour him.

THE DEAN.

4504 Now let the clergy sing
　　In the name of God of mercy,
　　　And let us come quickly hence:
　　He deserved
4508 To be honoured
　　　Surely in this country.

Here they sing.

SECOND BISHOP.

　　Now prepare ye the tomb
　　In Christ's name as is meet,
4512 　　That we may bury him,
　　As is the due of a worthy man.
　　Amongst us readily
　　Goodness to many a one
4516 　　He did, to Jesus thanks.

THE NAKED MAN.

　　The tomb by us is made.
　　As I was bound
　　　To serve him in this world,
4520 Maimed and leper when we were
　　He healed us certainly
　　　So that it behoves me to love him.

THE CRIPPLE.

　　The tomb by us is cleansed.
4524 Lords, as ye are pleased
　　　Do ye now.
　　Pardie, we are yearning
　　Seeing Meriasek's body
4528 　　Going into the earth.

BISHOP OF KERNOU.

　　God's will is not to be resisted.
　　The body in the grave
　　　Now put ye it in God's name,

4532 ha me an benedicconn
a ra oma purdyson
abarth ov arluth ihesu

COMES VENETENSIS

In beth me an gor lemmen
4536 gueres dym ser ȝurle y len
in hanov map maria
atta an corff y wroweth
kyn fo mar fur an roweth
4540 oll ny a thue the helma

p. 178.   ### EPISCOPUS KERNOV

Arluth neff ren benyga
ov flehys gruegh y gutha
in hanov du
4544 ha duen the dre alema
hereth us orth ov grefya
ha lues heboff oma
purguir hythyv   [*finit*

COMES VENETENSIS

4548 Pes in hanov du avan
mens us oma kuntullys
bevnans meryasek certan
genen revue dysquethys
4552 in keth dethyov ma dywy
trestia inno a rella
ha lel pesy warnotha
ihesu re grontias detha
4556 age desyr eredy

Dywhy banneth meryasek
ha maria cambron wek
banneth an abesteleth
4560 evugh oll gans an guary
ny a vyn agis pesy
kyns moys an plaeth

p. 179.   Pyboryon wethugh in scon
4564 ny a vyn ketep map bron
moys the donsya
eugh bo tregugh
wolcum vethugh
4568 kyn fewy sythen omma

Finitur per dominum HADTON anno domini M'v'iiij.

4532 And I the benediction
Will make here at once
On behalf of my Lord Jesus.

EARL OF VANNES.

Into the tomb I will put him now.
4536 Keep for me, sir Earl, his cloak
In the name of Mary's Son.
Behold the body lying.
Though so great be our sway,
4540 We shall all come to this.

BISHOP OF KERNOU.

May Heaven's Lord bless him!
My children, cover him
In God's name.
4544 And let us come home from hence,
Yearning is grieving me
And many besides me here
Right truly to-day.

EARL OF VANNES.

4548 Peace in the name of God above,
All that are here gathered!
Meriasek's Life certainly
By us hath been set forth.
4552 In these same days to you.
Whoever trust in him
And loyally pray to him
Jesu has granted to them
4556 Their desire readily.

To you the blessing of Meriasek,
And of sweet Mary of Camborne,
The blessing of the apostles!
4560 Drink ye all with the play
We will beseech you
Before going from the place.

Pipers, blow at once.
4564 We will, every son of the breast,
Go to dance.
Go ye or stay,
Welcome ye shall be,
4568 Though ye be a week here.

p. 180.

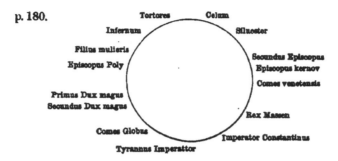

NOTES.

[*Notes by the Rev. Robert Williams of Rhydycroesau are marked thus*: (W.)]

7. *gwarthevyas* cognate with W. *gwarchad* 'a guarding' (W.): *th* may here be for *gh* as in *bothosek* 779, *berthuth* (for *berthugh*) 1376, 41 36. *latha* 1629, ar*th*elath Cr. But I would rather compare W. *gwarthaf* 'summit,' and perhaps the Latin *vertex* (vertices principiorum).

16. *perhennek* = W. *perchenog* 'possessor,' 'owner,' Br. *perchen*.

20. *angeffa* 3d sg. 2dy pres. of the irregular verb *cafus* 'to have,' 426, 1053, *cawas* 85. 255.

The other forms of this verb which occur in the foregoing drama are these :—

Present sg. 1. *ambus* 301. 494. 1367. *ambus vy* 1385. 2008. *numbus* 356. 566. 2560. 2632. 3192. 4098.
2. *kyn feste* 2046.
3. *angeves* 2834. *nangeves* 1937. 2754.

Secondary present Sg. 1. *ambeua* 1686. *maymbeua* 47. *ambethe* 1055, *numbeths* 3371. *numdarfe* 3727, *numdarfa* 1477. 1808. Sg. 2. *kyn feste* 2046. Sg. 3. *angeffa* 20, *nangeffa* 159. Pl. *astefe* 1935.

Preterite Sg. *ambusvy* 1726. *me rumbus* 1580. *ty re fue* 3570.

Future Sg. 1. *me am beth* 681. 1889. 3494. 4293. *ty a feth* 409. 2442. *a feth* 2818. *y feth* 304. 1218. 1466. *ny feth* 3578. *eff an goveth* 2090, *angeveth* 1001. *nyngeveth* 1124. Pl. *nygynbethen* 4268. *wy agis beth* 2508. *why agys beth* 1305. *y astevyth* 765, *y asteveth* 1199. *nygisbeth* 1770.

Conj. and Opt. *rethvo* 3230 [better *rethfo* O. 2265]. *kyn fy* 2018. *mengeffo* 1248. *kyngeffo* 2270. *rengeffo* 1022. 1277. *nangeffo* 4027. Pl. *maystefons* 4287. 4291. *nystufons* 2785.

22. *helma, helme* (ex *hen-lemma* 'this-in this place'? Rhys), a masc. and neut. demonstrative of constant occurrence in this play (see 135. 723. 742. 838. 999. 1010. 1054. 1073. 1129. 1269. 1455. 1522. 1641. 1923. 2012. 2023. 2080. 2190. 2251. 2627. 2762. 2835. 3153. 3389. 3564. 3698. 3823. 3959. 4100. 4111. 4467. 4540). The feminine is *holma* 1072, 1090, 4148 (=*hon-lem-ma*?).

25. 2025. 2034. 3879: *megyans* (if the g be soft)=W. *mawsiant*, if hard, (as in *megys* 3872, 3886) cf. W. *magu*, Br. *maga*.

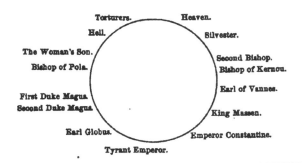

```
        Torturers.          Heaven.
     Hell.                    Silvester.
The Woman's Son.
  Bishop of Pola.              Second Bishop.
                               Bishop of Kernou.
 First Duke Magus.             Earl of Vannes.
 Second Duke Magus.
                               King Massen.
     Earl Globus.          Emperor Constantine.
          Tyrant Emperor.
```

27. *attendie, attendya* 848, 867, 1632, 1913 'attendere.'
30. *evnadow* for *yeunadow*, a derivative from *yeuni* 'to desire'. As to the forms in *adow* ex *atvo*—see Z². 832–3. and add *usadow* 35.
32. *colonnek* = W. *calonog* 'hearty,' 'valiant' 641. 672. 2719. 2944. 3132.
40. 641. 672. *densa* from *den-da* 'a good man' (W.)
61. *martege* (Br. *martese* 'forte' 'forsan,' Z². 726) for the usual *martesen*.
64. *mannafi, mannavy* 2123. *clowevy* 1957. *bethevy* 2130. *sensevy* 2406. *ovy* 3122. 3853 (=*ove* 4375), *nynsen-vy* 3700. cf. W. *a-garafi* Z². 506.
65. *leuf* from A.S. *leóf*, Eng. *lief*, Goth. *liubs*.
79. *dyvyn* W. *dyfyn* 'citation.'
80. *tos* borrowed from Eng. *tot* 'a small cup.'
96. *dyth* 'dictum,' Eng. *ditt, dite*.
98. *gobrow* pl. of *gobr* 'reward' (W.)
103. *yn-newer* W. *yn-hwyr* (W.) But cf. W. *dewaint* 'midnight'.
104. *lyfye, lyvya* 113, *lyfya* 270, Br. *lein*.
117. i.e. I make my livelihood by the profit on the boys' food (W.)
121. *worth un pris* 'for a while' (W.), or perhaps 'at one time'.
132. *dhe udhyll*, the infinitive of the verb meaning *facere*. Other forms are:—Infinitive *guthel* 639, 691, 2345, *gul* 378 (*dyswul* 1169, *umwul* 2366), *ou cuthel* 785, *ou cul* 688. Pres. Sg. *gruaff* 503, 1830, *y raff* 537, *y raf* 143. *gureth* 69. *mar qureth* 904, 1218. *a reth* 937. *me ath ra* 300, *ny ra* 425, *ny an grua* 964. *me an grua-e* 3201. (*om*)*grua* 477. Pl. *ny ren* 1124, *pendra reny* 958, *a reny* 3950. *ny regh* 1747 *a regh* 1912 *mar quregh* 3525. *a rons* 4000, *mar crons* 2085. Conjunctive Sg. *na rylly* 110. 4144. Pl. *a rellogh* 2351. Imperative Sg. *gura* 136. 1004. *grua* 637. 901. *gruens* 1202. 3697. Pl. *gruen* 3013. 3845, *gruegh* 372. 497. *grugh* 2838. *grueghwy* 1093. *na reugh* 108. Secondary present Sg. *na ren* 1198. *may ren* 1794. *me ren* 2402. *may rellen* 1777. 3819, *ny rellen* 3756, *pendrellen* 1065. *mar ny reva* 334. *am gruelle* 1488. *na relle* 4005. *na rella* 615. *a relle* 1474. First Preterite Sg. *ny ruk* 1987, 3484. *del russys, na russys* 1707 *pendrussis* 379. *na ruste* 3334. *gruk* 365. 475. 871. *a ruk* 949, *reruk* 1094, 2156. *y ruk* 2229, *mar a cruk* 32 and perhaps *am ros* 3728, if we have here the Bret. *e grez* Z². 594 (but see note on 472).

Pl. *a russyn* 2097. *ny russugh* 1531. *y russugh* 3804. *del russons* 26.

Secondary preterite: *na russen* 2590. *ny an grussa* 1763. *a russe* 1648, 3339 *a russa* 111. 2424. *ny russe* 2053.

Passive: *y rer* (= *y wrer* O. 1936) 3440. Participle *gwrys* 17, *grueys* 423. 436. 2767. *deworeys* 3962.

137. *sanseleth* = W. *santolaeth*, Br. *santelaez* Z². 847. cf. *skyentoleth* 157.
138. *gon* W. *gwnn*, Ir. *find*:—

Infinitive *gothfos* 1987, *gothvos* 28, *gothvas* 104, *gothfes* 828, 2273, *aswonfos* 1983.

Pres. Sg. *gon*, 138, *ny won* 101, 1483, 1487. *a won vy* 1478. *aswen* 73 *y wothes* 2974, 3649. *a wor* 38, 2843, *a wour* 1931, *a wore* 19, *ny wor* 4440. Pl. *y wothen* 309, *ny wothen* 1036, *del wothen* 2626. *a wothogh* 1439. *mar cothens* 1382. Secondary pres. *ny wothyan* 3088. Form compounded with the verb subst. *a cothfes* (si scires) 867. Imperative Sg. *gothfeth* 935, 2453, 3548. Pl. *gothvethugh* 1913.

139. *dus* (misprinted *due*) 2d sg. imperative of *dôs*.

Other forms of this irregular verb are:—

Infinitive *doys* 796, 824, *y thoys* 3012. *ou tos* 2466, *ou toys* 4476, *dones* 2436, 3045. Pres. sg. *mar tuff* 3365. *a due* 1296, 3991, *a thue* 907, 2024. 2429. *ny dhus* 250, *ny thus* 891, *mar a tue* 1106. *a thus-a* 3902. *dua* 3976. Pl. *mar a tuen* 3476, *mara tuny* 3907. Conj. sg. *kyn teffo* 251; *na thefo* 415, *may teffo* 1274, 1712. Pl. *may teffons* 1738. 3290. Imperative sg. *dus* 139. 596. 1083, 3002. *duys* 4056. *dens* 2467, 3260. Pl. *duen* 798, 1201, *duen ny* 1027. *dugh* 952, 1171, 1346. *dens* 1538. Secondary Present. *pan deffen* 906. *a teffes* 3837. First Preterite, sg. *y tuth* 3197, 3676, *pan duthe* 4396. *me re deth* 234. *y tuth* 1727, 2148. *mar tuth* 746. 2908. *a thuth* 1787, *a thueth* 2219; 3768. *re duth* 2700, 2899; *deve* 944. *dufe* 2095, 2950, 3287, *dufa* 1086: *re dufe* 1432. 3995. *redufa* 623, 650, *pan duthe* 2666, *y tuthe* 2274. Pl. *duthen* 1981. Passive pres. sg. *deer* 2833. Part. pret. *dus* 1869. *devethys* 625, 1091.

149. *cowgegyow* (both *gs* soft) pl. of *cowses* Br. *coudet, caoudet* (internum) Z². 108, *drok-cowsys* 3859.

151. *clour* 1312, *in clor* 4220, *pur clour* 4332. Br. *clouar, clouer* translated by 'doux.'

156. *drefa* = *drefs* 1450, for *dreheva* 'raise' (W.).

167. *newyth, henys* derivatives from *naw (= novus) and *hen* (= sen-ex).

184. *arlud flour* (flos dominorum): here *arlud* is in the gen. pl. so in *an werhes flour*, 631, *mester flor* 1076, *turant floyr* 3296. *doctour flour* 1391, *epscop flour* 1434, *empour flour* 1600.

186. *par*. cf. Quant deus out fait Adam et Eve sue *per, Vie de Seint Auban*, ed. Atkinson.

192. *moy gracyus*, cf. *moy worthy* 4389.

198. *bedneth* (also in 224, 225) for *benneth* 202. *mestrigy* (*g* soft) = magistratio. so *deulugy* 2096.

203. *benegycter* = *benesygter* 4495, so *tecter* 2935, *honester* 3027, *glander* 533. *eselder* 1166. *golouder* 2101 = *goleuder* 3669. *creffder* 2406, *welder* 2941, *reelder* 2942. *guynder* 3667, *caradeuder* 3668. More in Z². 829.

213. *re-woloways*: cf. W. *golewo* ' to light,' ' to illuminate.'
230. 4526. *du* an interjection as W. *myn Duw* (W.).
236. *kes-talkye*. Here as in *kes-colon* 1756, we have the W. *cyd*.
247. 2268. 2286. *plass, plas*=W. *plas* 'palatium.' In 4298 *plas* is= 'place.'
251. *kynteffou*=*kyn*+*deffo*+*ou* 'my.'
293. *nywy*: cf. perhaps W. *nyw* ' vivacity.'
296. *omgersyogh* from *omgesuryogh*: cf. W. *ymgysuro*: so *omry* 326, 2122. *omgrua* 477. *omguythe* 533. *omprevy* 1194. *ombrene* 1252. *omguytha* 1339=*omguythe* 1347. *omgolhugh* 1642, *omgemer* 1882. *omsone* 2319. *omdok* 2344. *omleth* 2491. *omheres* 3666. *ommeras* (ex *omwheras*) 2560. *ompredery* 2857. *omconfort* 3071. *omconfortya* 3080. *omgellys* 4120. *omparusen* 3244. *omthegen* 3451. *omdenna* 3474. *omgu*[*e*]*ythe* 1989.
309. *gras y wothen* ' we give (lit. know) thanks :' cf. *gothfeth thym grays* 3548.
311. *greffe* a mutation of *creffe, creffa* 321, the compar. of *creff*.
313. 357. 4539 *roweth* ' sway,' *royauté*?
327. 334. 341. 371. 396 *domethy, ty a dhommeth* 329. Br. *dimiziff* ' soy marier:' Cath. *dimezabl* ' nubilis,' ib., *dimezer* ' espouseur,' *dimezez* ' a bachelor,' ib. Root *vad* with the compound prefix *dom* (*dim*) =Ir. *timm* (*do*+*imm*).
379. *pendrussis* for *pe*+*an*+*tra*+*grassis*, as *pendrellen* 1065. 2355, for *pe*+*an*+*tra*+*grellen*.
387. 1100. 1954. 1984. *nessevyn* formed from the old superlative *nessav* (Ir. *nessam* ' proximus') as *guelhevyn* (optimates) 2724, 2928= *guelheven* 2791, from the old superlative *guelhav* (optimus).
406. 1655. *am govys vy. govys*=O. Ir. *fobith* Z². 659.
433. *degemorys, degemerys* 2573. cf. W. *dygymeryd* ' to accept.'
439. 830 *devethyans* lit. a coming: cogn. with the participle *devethys*.
440. 3919 *in hans* from *in-nans* as *in hoth* 3064 from *in-noth* 1933.
468. *trou* Fr. *trou*: *nasweth*=W. *nodwydd*, Ir. *snáthat*.
472. 521. *ry*: other forms of this irregular verb are:—
Present Sg. *rof* 150. 217. *reyth* 3620. *res* 1694. 2836. Pl. *regh*. Conjunctive Sg. *roy* 532. 2540. 2847. Imperative Sg. *roy* 549. 4489. Pl. *regh* 536. 1667. 3041. 3151. Secondary present Sg. *rollen* 2593. First Preterite Sg. *a reys* 1753. *a ros* 3463. *re ros* 1930. *am ros* 2252, and perhaps in 3728 *re roys* 3428. Secondary Pret. Sg. *rosen* 1687. *a rose* 2881. Part. pass. *reys* 3095.
481. *lee*=W. *lleiđu*. The original guttural is kept in *a leghya* 2981.
516. 1345. 4158. *mebyen lyen* pl. of *mablyen* 3163=Ir. *macc légind*.
541. *podrethek* 10.=W. *pydredig*.
542. *in gron*. cf. W. *cron* ' round,' ' circular.' Ir. *cruind*.
543. *schanlour*, better *scant-lor* 3459. *schant* 3929. *ascant* 658.
544. *kynweres*=*kyn* + *gueres* Z². 901.
566. 590 *numbus* ' I have not'=*nymbus* O. 356.
576. 1179. 1749. 3271. *lafurya,*=*lafuria* 1388, 2768. *lafurye* 3286. *lafuryys* 1567, *lafuryans* 480 : cf. the English phrase ' to labour on the way '=to go onward.
579. *sansesou* pl. of *sanses* fem. of *sans*. So *arlothes* 237, *kentrevoges* 1551, *mowes* 1646. *myternes* 3684.

587. 4194 *dorsona, dursona*, compounded with the prep. *dar* and *sona* W. *swyno* to preserve, to charm, signare, to *sain*.
605. 610. *go-ny* formed like *go-vy* 793, *gogy* 3576, *go-ef* 1895 : *go*=*vae* Ir. *fě*, in the phrase *fě amai*.
607. *yeys* a verb formed from the participle *yesseys* 2162, 2747. 4272. 4279.=A.S. *gesed* 'confessed,' p. part. p. of *gesecgan*.
650. *dressen*=*dres + an*.
659. 1338. 1347. 3655. *polge*, pulsus (venarum) : here as in *falge* 987. 1161. 1721. 2045. 2306. 2448. 3803. *felge* 1273. *calge* 2046, *s* has become soft *g*.
661. *corff* = W. *cwrw*, Ir. *coirm*, Z.² 821.
662. *effsen* (so *mensen* 1042, 1368. 2067. *rosen* 1657. *carsen* 1990. *godhaffsen* 2634) 1 sg. 2dy present of *eva* 'bibere.' Note the sharpening of the *v* before *s*.
668. *dovyr*=*dovr* 673, W. *dwfr*, O. Ir. *dobar*. *a wur* (leg. *vur*) *speys*. W. *byr* brevis, so 1012, 1741.
681. *schorys* re-occurs in line 2633. I think now it must mean 'shivers,' 'shivering-fits;' Mr. Williams would regard it as the English word *scores* 'marks,' and compare the Welsh name for the plague *haint y nodau* 'the disease of the marks.'
709. *omglowough* cf. W. *ymglywed* 'to feel oneself.'
719. *adar*, W. *adrawdd* 'say' (W.) But v. note on 4311.
746. *mar tuth an nur* perhaps 'if the hour (*an n-ur*) has come.' cf. *ty an n-oyll* 929.
757. *asogh* 1237. *assus* 'est' *asson* sumus 1120.
760. *regniis*, like *tregys*, 816, has an active meaning.
759. *me a veth* lit. 'I shall be', future for present as in 681 and elsewhere.
764. *penag*=*panak* 3104.
778. 953. 3287. 3346. 3745. *dar* seems an interjection or imprecation, W. *dera* 'fiend.' In 953. 2445. *dar* seems a preposition.
792. *y meth-e* here the *e* is a suffixed pron. of 3d sg. m. See Z². 606.
806. *dethe cloweys* lit. 'hearing to them' (W.), *clowes* 3709, *clowas* 2636.
847. *breys* 'womb' seems borrowed from Eng. *breast*.
850. *genegygva*, like *genesygeth* 4387 a deriv. from *genesek, genesyk* 3211.
864. 1019. 1478 *malbe dam*, an imprecation which I cannot explain.
867. *a cothfes y attendya*: cf. the imperative *gothvethugh y attendya* 1913.
892. *vyketh* = vyth-keth, *bythqueth*.
897. *peb les* perhaps 'of every court' (Ir. *lis*).
903. 24 39 *campol* p. part. p. *campollys* 2204. sg. pret. *campollys* 2791. Engl. *cample*, 'to talk, contend or argue.' Halliwell, *camble* 'to prate saucily,' ib.
908. *ruthy* W. *rhwyddad*, or compare (with Mr. Williams) *ryth* or *wryth* sorrow?
929. *ty an noyll* cf. *ty a oyl* 3572.
938. *sevuruth*=severitas?
957. should have been printed *y bescherev your patis*, which is wholly English ('I beshrew your pates') : cf. line 1451.
984. *besyon* from *vision(em)*, as *belan* from Pr. *vilan*.
997. *vij*... to be read *syth*
1006. *den varijs* cf. W. *bâr* 'fury'. But why the *v* in the Cornish?
1035. 1749. 2788. 2885. *dour* an adverb (in 4323, an adjective)=O. W. *deurr* (gl. acri) now *dewr*.

1047. *druss* for *drus* = W. *drud* : the *s* is inserted to make a rhyme with *mes*. So *grass* 669, *plass* 635 so *pur-goeth* 1979. *taem* 2093. *fael* 2249 *ragoen* 2742 *gluaes* 2782, *vyen* 2998, *dremaes* 3074, *scoen* 4066. So *suyr* 1924. *luyr* 2263, *duys* 405 6, *voas* 2943, *beas* 4275. In *turent* 3246 *s* is written for *s*. *fuir* 905.

1048. 3467. *ke war the gam*: so *a war agys cam* 2022, *eugh wy war gam*, 3974 so *cry war the gam* 3043

1060. *ny warth mas-ran* ' a good part (of the torturers) will not laugh.' The same phrase re-occurs 3342. *mas ran* 4440.

1075. *mach*=*mates*: for the change of *ts* to *ch* cf. *lych* (for *lits, list*) 2832.

1077. *damach* from *damage* as *ymach* 1805 3789 (*yamach* 3785) from *image*, *lyche* 240 from *liege*, *maryach* 332, *charych* 2831 from *marriage*, *charge*, with the sharpening of the final characteristic of Cornish: cf. *caff* 3906 from *cave*, *manhot* 3174, *gront* 3471.

1081. *hevelsa* 3d pl. *havalsens* 1206.

1090. *holmyu*=*holma*+*yu*: so *helmyu* 1522, 2762=*helma*+*yu*.

1100. *mar a s-aff*. note this form of *aff* 'eo' 'ibo' with prosthetic *s*. The other forms of this irregular verb found in the present drama are as follows:—

Infinitive *mos* 665, *mois* 130, *moys* 4364, *mones* 173, 3159, *myns* 1989.

Pres. & Fut. Sg. *marasaff* 1100. *nynseth* 2409. 2823. 3561. *marseth* 4315. *eseth* 2462. *a* 853, 1029, 3634, *ty a* 2968, *ny a* 801, *yth a* 1192, 1214, 3630, *pyth a* 369, *nynsa* 2347. Pl. *ythen* 3876, *marsegh* 588 *ythegh* 1521. Conjunctive: Sg. *pyth-ylly* 1103, *mathylly* 4142. Imperative: Sg. *a* 2022, *ke* 139, 3467, 3737, *kea* 1417. *kegy* 35. *kedhegy* 58. *ens* 1541, 2794, 3522. Pl. *eugh* 113, 965, 1354. *ens* 373. Secondary Present, Sg. *ellen* 1257. *maythellen* 985. 3775. *kynthellen vy* 3064 *ethe* 1588. *ythe* 4453. *maythella* 4284. Pl. *pythellen* 3438. *pythellens* 374. First Preterite: Sg. *ytheth* 2236, 3362 *pytheth* 448. *ytheth-a* 1028.

1110. 1124. *dregyn*=*dregen* 4005, *dregan* 4139 pl. of *drok ?*

1115. *levays* 3d sg. pres. of *levasy* (W.)

1127. *guelfos* (*guylfoys* 1132)=*guils-bos* (W.)

1187. *debron*=*debrén* 3432 = M. Br. *debruan* 'prurigo', in late Cornish *debarn*.

1253. 1896. 4186 *pur* 'when' (*pa-ur*)=Br. *peûr* 'quand'.

1257. *fors ny raff*,—English 'I do not force' i.e. I care not: *nynsus forse* 1440—Eng. *no force* 'no matter', *fors ny reyth* 3620 force thou givest not *i.e.* (thou carest not) cf. *they give no force* 'they care not', Halliwell. *ny reys dyn fors* 2355.

1264. 1835. *usons*. This new and obscure form belongs to the verb substantive. The other forms occurring in this play are as follows:—

1. Root I: Pres. Sg. *off* 577, *ythof* 6, *ythoff* 984, *maythoff* 1311. *nynsoff* 2975, 3482. *assoff* 509, 4184, *ovy* 2308, 3122, 3853. *maythovy* 2158, *oma* 4501. *ythoma* 1359, *maythoma* 1943, *ythama* 794, *ydama* 3393, *asoma* 2522, *assoma* 4181, *marsama* 3288. *os* 137, 203, *oys* 299, 462, *ythoys* 1854, 3012. *nynsos* 1996, 3016, *nynsoys* 2976, *nynsesos* 848. *ots* 2114, *ota* 1841, *nagote* 377. *yw* 1, *yu* 17, *ew* 307. *assyu* 4467,

marsyu 14, 2120 (= Br. *mardeu*), *nynsyu* 98, 360, 1438, *nansyu* 682, *kynthyu* 1145: with suffixed pron. *marsew-e* 1041. *yw-a* 1415, *yw-e* 3398. Pl. *on* 257, 1091, 2312, *onny* 2671, 2892. *asson* 1120, 4526, *ython* 1174, 1308, 1529. *nynson* 2719. *ough* 233, *ogh* 240, 241. *asogh* 1237, *ythogh* 1769, *maythogh* 288, *kynthogh* 492, *owhy* 2705, 2824. *yns* 3187, *ythyns*, 4169, *marsyns* 1806, *marasyns* 4122, *nynsyns* 2045. Secondary Pres. Sg. *esen* 3771, *nynsen* 3700, *enua* 4518. *maytheua* 3760, *pan eua* 4499, *es* 3786, *kyntheste* 1853. *ythesta* 2412. *o* 447, 450, *nynso* 1801, 2495, *marso* 874. *kynnago* 2400, *ove* 4375. Pl. *esen* 2145, 3350, *ens* 579, 916, 1280, 1791, 1800, *pythens* 2157.

Obscure to me are Sg. *ytheseff* 834, 4023=*ythese* 1387, 1963. *kyntheses* 3888, *fetel esta* 3659. *nynsese* 3586. *nynsusy* 1019, 1403. *pan usy* 3780. Pl. *ythesen* 3333. *esogh*, 4310. *usons* 1264, 1335, *kynthusons* 2366. Secondary present *ese* 872, 2672, *ythese* 862.

2. Root ĀS? Sg. 3. *us* 229, 238, 655. *nynsus* 366, 380, *nynsues*, 291, *kynthus* 1453, 2364, *nansus* 3949, *marsus* 1203, 1373, *marsuys* 3621, *pendrus* 1412, *namsus* 1554, *asus* 635, *assus* 757. *nynses* 180, *kynses* 908.

3. Root MAG. Pres. Sg. *yma* 8, *ima* 900, 2036, *ymae* 1978, *may-me-ve* 2922. Pl. *ymons* 1954, 1985, 1986, 3309, 4476. Secondary present (?) *y myens* 2808.

4. Root BU (Skr. *bhu*). Infinitive *bos* 26, *boys* 522, *boas* 2943, *bones* 352, 401: with possessive pronouns: *ou bosa*, 3062, *the vote* 3089, *the vota* 571, *y voss* 2052, *y vosa* 4126. Future Sg. *ny vedhaf* 109, *y fethaff* (misprinted *y sethaff*) 1101, *bethe* 3802, *ny vetha* 4095, *bethevy* 2130. *betheth* 531, *y fetheth* 1242, *mar a pethy* 2585, *vyth* 1073, 4263, *a vyth* 37, 89, *a veth* 331, 368, *ny veth*, 774, 811, *nynse feth* 3890, *mar peth* 422, 1607, *mara peth* 2315, *y feth* 725, 1298: with suffixed pron. *ny veth-e* 769, 810, *na vethe* 771, *a vetha* 1636, *a vethe* 1925, *mar pethe* 4301. Pl. *bethen* 1341, 3945, *ny vethen* 3354, *mar pethen* 420. *y fethenny* 3443. *bethugh* 1460, *vethugh* 4567, *ny vethugh* 1492, 2729, *y fethugh*, 1513, *fethogh* 2352.

Conjunctive Sg. *pan vy* 139 *reby*, 672, 2670, *may fy* 1823. *bo* (used as a disjunctive conjunction) 373, *may fo* 16, 761, 895, *na vo* 91, 1277, *a vo* 127, 1122. *kyn fo* 439, 1255, *kyn fo ve* 976, *na vova* 2064, *rebo* 556, 624, *pan vo* 1215, *py fo* 1880. Pl. *may fegh* 2162, *pan vegh* 1520, *pan vowhy* 3524, *kyn fewy* 4568, *may fons* 3344. Imperative Sg. *beth* 905, 3866. *bethens* 972, 1517, etc. *bethyns* 818. Pl. *na vethen* 3245. *bethugh* 292, 611. *na vethugh* 3238, *bethens* 274, 1614, 1637, 3299. Secondary Present Sg. *hedre ven* 55, 354, *na ven* 1135, 2999, 3838, *pan ven* 525, *kyn fen* 3895, *may fena* 4285, *y fethen* 1731, *mar pethen* 2159, *ny vethe* 2958, *kyn fes* 861, *may festa* 1710, 1717, *pan vesta* 1719, *pan veste* 2819, *pan ve* 80, *na ve* 1863, *ny ve* 204, *a pe* 1762, *mar pe* 614, *a vethe* 2151, 2382, *a vetha* 4462, *ny vethe* 4448: with suffixed pron. *pan veua* 3210, *na veva* 152, 2116, *appeua* 686. Pl. *pan venny* 68, *kyn feny* 892, *del vugh* 4524, *pan vegh* 1520, and perhaps *a pegh* 1496, *mara pewy* 194, *na vewy* 119, 322, *a vewhy* 1494 (these may be conjunctives). *kyn fens* 1540 : with suffixed pron. *kyn fens-i* 3655. First preterite Sg. *na vuff* 795, *re vuff* 3798, *y fuuff* 4393, *y fuff* 2154, *y fuff* 4393, *y fuff* 2154, *na vu ma* 4099, *na vef* 102, *pan vus* 3576, *aban vys* 3969. *y fus* 338, *nyn fus* 1855, *fetel vusta* 3764. *bus* 792, *rebus* 1304, 1490. *vus* 2249, *vvus* 4496. *ny vue* 2234, *del fue* 397, *a fue* 564, 887, *a fua* 1775, *y fue* 859, *may fue* 3416, Pl. *pan vuen* 605. Secondary Preterite Sg. *me a vyen* 2998, *y fyen* 3704. *bya* 3600, *vys* 1656, *ny vys* 663 *ny vya* 2883, *y fye* 1654, 3169, *a fya* 1497, *a vya* 1504, 1665 : with suffixed pron. *y vysa* 21, *mara peya* 186. Pl. *y fyen* 311, 317. *y fyen ny* 2170.

1268. *respela* : cf. *pelys* 3418, *pyle* 3430. *pylse* 3828, W. *pilio*.
1288. *grueys is=gurys* D. 1790 (W.)
1307. *hensy*, this is very obscure : cf. W. *hynhad*? Eng. *hent* furrow?
1311. *amuwys* Fr. ému.
1312. *gefugh* may be 2d pl. imper. of *cafus*, the infection of *c* being caused by a particle understood. If we read *gesugh* 'beseech ye,' cf. Ir. *guidid*?
1356. *lovrygyon* a deriv. from *lovr*, Ir. *lobar*.
1368. *stak*=Br. *stâg* 'attache', 'lien.'
1390. *strechya* Eng. *stretch* 'to walk in a dignified manner,' Halliwell.
1393, 2030 *trettya* from Eng. *tread*?
1408. 1469. *mayl* (i.e. *mâl*) is apparently an imprecation : cf. *malbe dam*.
1410. 1417. *preytha=preys + da*.
1412. *pendrus=pe + an + tra + us*: so *pendryu* 2015.
1413. *claff deberthys*. pl. *clevyon d.* 3130 : cf. *ÿ then debertheys* 3108. A leper in Welsh is *claf gwahanol* (*gwahan* 'separate') : *gwahanglaf* 'leprous' (W.).
1419. *gasel* a mutation of *casel*=W. *cesail*, Br. *kazel* (W.).
1420. 2241 *gormel* W. *gorfoli* 'to flatter.' But why is the *m* uninfected?
1421. 1427. *connek* a deriv. from *conn*=Ir. *conn* sense, reason, Glück 69.
1423. *tarthennou* : W. *dyrthon* (W.): cf. *les-derth* (gl. febrifugia) Vocab.
1433. *an gannas*=W. *y gennad* (W.).
1463. *stoff* here and in 1869 (cf. 1873) seems to means *cash*. In 3167 it means 'wealth' or 'store.'
1487. *methegyeth* a deriv. from *methek*=medicus.
1516. 1546. 4374 *ea* (a dissyllable), Lat. *eja*?
1518. *ysawys*=Eng. *y-saved*, as *yssys*=ge-sed.
1526. *dufunugh*, *dyvune* 1785, *dufen* 3770, from the prefix *de* and the root *svap*.
1528. *gal*=W. *gwael* 'vile' (W.).
1530, 1800 *cress*, a corruption of *cresa(f)*.
1537. *blythy* pl. of *blyth*=W. *blwydd* 'year.'
1552, 1555. *trussogh*, Eng. *truss* 'to pack up,' 'to make ready.'
1554. *namsus* probably a scribe's mistake for *nansus* : but Lhuyd has *nam* 'now.'
1556. *dewogys* (the *g* soft) p. part. pass. of *dewosa* 1575, *dewose* 1584, 1619. 3d sg. *dewoys* 1652. Br. *diwada* 'saigner.' From *de-* and *goys*, *gos*, O. Corn. *guit* (gl. sanguis), W. *gwaed*.
1565. *wegennou* for *whegennou*, a deriv. from *whek*.
1581. *malbew*, *malbe* 3303 seems an imprecation like *malbe dam*.
1589. *ievuje=ievody* of the Oxford plays 'je vous dis.'

T

1590. in the MS. rag astevery ancoel.
1604. *sul, sul voy* 2351. W. *sawl*.
1609. *ou thola* = *outh ola*. So *ou thumwul* 2366=*outh umwul*.
1644, 1652 *knak*=W. *cnec*.
1692. 1705 *gruegh, greegh* (?) 1776 connected with W. *gwrachell* 'a puny dwarf,' *gwrachen* 'a crabbed dwarf' *gwrachan* 'a little creature.'
1760. *a wetsa* cf. W. *gweddu* (W.).
1768. *drokcoleth* from *drok-goleth*. So *drok-cousys* 3859.
1811. *alwethou* pl. of *alweth*, Br. *alchouez*.
1824. *luyst* from *lust* with *y* inserted for sake of rhyme with *crist*.
1827. *omdhevas*=W. *amddifad*, Br. *emzivad*.
1853. 2630. 3072. 4184 *anhethek*. It is not easy to fix the meaning of this adjective. W. *annhuddawg* 'uncovered' and *anheddog* (unpacific) would suit phonetically, but the meanings are inappropriate. Br. *hêtuz* 'souhaitable' is perhaps cognate.
1878. 2747. *in sol* a corruption of *in sevel* (W.).
1926. 4367. *trogel* 'body' O. Ir. *troicit*.
1968. *hevys ruen*=W. *hefys rhawn*.
1971. *goverou* pl. of *gover* O. Corn. *guuer* (gl. rivus).
1989. *myns* ex *mynd*, W. *myned* 'to go.' *omguythe* better *omguethe* 'to make oneself worse' (*gueyth* 3378): cf. W. *gwaethu* 'to grow worse.'
2015. 2099 *pendryu*=*pe* + *an* + *tra*+*yu*.
2054. *annye, annya* 3637, *ynnio* to urge (W.). Is it not rather from the English *annoy*?
2069. 2194 *gortheren*=Br. *gourélin*.
2073. 2197. *est*=Br. *éost, est*, W. *awst*, all from (mensis) *Augusti* with loss of vowel-flanked *g*.
2076. 2200 *gwyn-gala*=Br. *gwengôlô*.
2078. *neffrea*: here *a* is added for sake of rhyme.
2099. *fesky*, W. *ffysgio* 'to hasten.'
2100. *terlemel*=*lemmel* 'to leap,' with the prefix *ter* (=Ir. *tair* ex *do-air*) Z². 906.
2106. *tanges* (*g* soft)=W. *tandod*.
2145. *dethwyth*=W. *dyddwaith*.
2243. *dyrhays* a mutation of *tyrâs*, cf. W. *tirio* 'to land.' (W.)
2270. *myllyou cans*=*m[y]llyou cans* 2471.
2287. *genesek*=Br. *ginidik* 'natif,' *genesyk* 3211.
2313. *schakyage*=*schakya*+*age*.
2328. 3427. *tassens*, the translation is a guess.
2368, 4134. *grueff* (*e* inserted for rhyme) from Eng. *groffe* 'face.'
2379. 2655. *myngou* seems a nickname for Christ.
2390. *devenys*=*dufunys* 3224 p. part. p. of a verb=W. *difynio*.
2396. *darvyngya* perhaps 'through (*dar*) taking of vengeance.'
2399. *treythy* perhaps connected with W. *traeth* 'sand.'
2409. *nuk* Fr. *nuque*? *war nuk* 'backwards'? see Z². 698, 697 as to using names of parts of the body to form prepositions.
2418. *crehy*, W. *orech* 'a crash' (W.).
2419. *brehy* is obscure, Nhg. *brühe* broth?
2423. *gargasen, gargesen* 3322=Br. *gargaden*.
2450. *pastel, pastell* Br. Cath. *pastel* 'morceau,' 'panneau,' *pastellaff* 'frusta facere.' With *genys the pastel dyr* ('born to a morsel of land') cf. *genys then eretons* 3469.

2453. *routyyth* for *reoutyyth* (cf. *reoute* 2985)? or cf. M. Eng. *rout* 'to assemble' Stratmann.
2477. *atlyan* pl. of *atal* offcast.
2489. *darne*, 2496 *darnn*, W. *darn* a piece, Br. *darn* partie, portion.
2555. *reff* = W. *rhyf* 'presumption' i.e. 'before I presume to speak to thee' (W.).
2590. *nes*, Br. *nesaat* 'faire alliance.'
2613. *opery* seems = *obery* (as *capel* 467 = *cabel*), but the meaning of the line is not clear.
2616. *nebes an fa* = *nebesa* (Br. *nebeutoch* 'moins') + *un fa*.
2644. *teythy* = W. *teithi* (W.): in *antythy* 3052 we have a cognate adjective with the negative *an-*.
2652. *oudomhel*: either this is for *outh om(w)hel* (cf. *umhelaf*, Cr. *ommelys* p. 203, *umhelys* p. 244, W. *ymchelwyd*), or *domw(h)el* is compounded, like *dometky* (see note on 327) with *dom-* = *do* + *om*.
2655. *atty* for *otty* Z². 606.
2681. *adar* seems = *ater* infra 3631.
2730. *y troff* ex *yth* + *droff* 'affero.'
    Infinitive *dry* 3819, *ou try* 673, *thy threy* 1008. Pres. Sg. *y troff* 2730, *a doro* 3981. Imperative Sg. *dore* 508, 3685., *dro-fa* 3835. *drens* 3696. Pl. *dregh* 2487, *drewhy* 1290. First Pret. Sg. *dros* 873, *redros* 3848, *droys* 3415. Part. pass. *dreys* 2673, 4114, 4130.
2738. *mo ka meten*: the *mo* seems opposed to *meten*, and is perhaps akin to W. *much* 'gloom.'
2832. *har* (compar. *harhe* 2842) for *her* (compar. *herre* 2920). W. *hir*. Ir. *sir*.
2833. *deer* lit. venitur.
2852. *tasek* = Br. *tadek* 'paternel.'
2833. *dynnya*: W. *denu* 'to entice' (W.).
2900. *govenek* cf. O. Ir. *fomenaid*, *fomentar* Z². 998, root MEN.
2969. *cumyys* Br. *kombout*, *kombot* 'étage'? Or is it W. *cymes* 'sufficiency' (W.)?
2985. *revute* for *reoute*.
3018. *gore* W. *goreu* 'best.'
3052. *antythy* see 2644.
3066. *poth* is perhaps the W. *pwd* 'rot in sheep.'
3086. *dealer* = *de* + *galer* 4225 = Ir. *galar*.
3104. *panak* = *penak*.
3113. *ues* i.e. *ves* for *aves*?
3133. *heweres* = *he* + *gueres*: *he-* or *hy-* (*hebasca*, 3753, *hyblyth* 'flexibilis') W. *he-*, *hy-*, Br. *ho- he-*, Z². 93, is Ir. *su*, Gr. εὐ, Skr. *su-*.
3144. *knesen*, *kneys* 4054 = Ir. *cnes*.
3171. 3899. *dufer* from *devoir*. In 4513 it means 'due.'
3201. *arveth* = *arfeth* D. 2262.
3224. *bowyn* = (caro) bovina.
3231. 3632. *dulle* 'let go' = *dul* (Ir. *dul* to go?) + *le* (Goth. *letan*?)
3232. *busch* Eng. *bush* 'a flock of sheep.'
3235. *hethou* W. *heddwch*: the final guttural lost.
3253. *kerethys* Ir. *cairigthe*.
3259. *indan onen* i.e. with an ashen stick (W.)
3291. *keher* W. *cur* 'ache' (W.).
3300. *tountya* Eng. *taunt* 'to tease,' Halliwell.

3312. *du-klyn=duo-clunes.*
3313. *lemyk,* W. *llymaid* (W.), a diminutive of some word=Ir. *loimm* 'a sup.'
3314. *plemyk* a dimin. of some word=W. *plwm* 'plumbum.'
3331. *raghyl* I conjecture to be the Eng. *rascal.* Mr. Williams would read *rag hyl* and regard *hyl* as a mutation of *cyl*=W. *cul* 'narrow.'
3338. *calame*=Br. *kala-mae* 'le premier jour de Mai.'
3341. *hot* A.S. *hôd,* or is it 'head,' A.S. *heáfud ?*
3344. *teharas* a mutation of *deharas,* W. *diheurau* (W.).
3360. *thyek* for *dhyek, dioc* (gl. piger). *di + oc=ὀκύς.*
3368. *snel, snell* 4342 Nhg. *schnell.*
3375. *lok* 'lock' was any close place of confinement,' Halliwell.
3391. *schylwyn* W. *ysgilwyn* 'whitenaped' (W.).
3396. *gorourys* p. part. p. of a verb=W. *goreuro.*
3397. *gernygou* a mutation of *kernygow* pl. of *kernyk* 'corniculum.'
3403. *skyrennou* pl. of *skyrenn*=O. W. *scirenn* (gl. stella 'splint' Ducange) now *ysgyren.*
3413. *lawen-cath* cf. W. *cath llawn-duf.*
3414. *legessa*=W. *llygota,* a denominative from *llygoden* Ir. *luch* f. gen. sg. *luchod,* acc. pl. *luchtha* a t-stem.
3427. *an barth north,* cf. 'make their last head like Satan in the North,' Tennyson.
3453. *ewyas,* cf. W. *euain* 'to move' (W.).
3470. *tont* Eng. *taunt* 'lofty,' 'loftily-masted,' Halliwell. *re-dount* 3570.
3482. *omager* Eng. *homager* 'vassal.'
3483. *danger* Eng. *dangere,* the power which the feudal lord possessed over his vassals. Halliwell.
3490. *lendury* a deriv. from a word=Eng. *lent* 'a loan:' cf. *falsury* from *fals.*
3492. *avond,* like W. *afwyn,* borrowed from *habéna* (W.) *tellek* 'perforatus' i.e. formed into a noose (W.) (from *tol*).
3517. *nag yedhou* : observe the *g* of *nag* kept before the semivowel.
3523. *acectour* 'assectator.'
3524. *remyu*=*re-ma-yu.*
3564. *in bagh* 'in a little.'
3570. *re fue* (if not a mistake for *re vue*) means *habuisti* ; see R. 2628. *napyth* for *nep-pyth* : *redount* from *re+tount.*
3631. *ater* (*adar* 2681) is perhaps W. *eithyr,* Ir. *echtar,* Lat. *extra.*
3645. *me yu lowenheys,* as to this mode of expressing the passive see Z². 540, and cf. 4258, 3640, 3654, 3673, 4232, 4251, 4518.
3667. *dyegrys* as if *deoculatus* : *egr=*oculus?
3674. *dyglon*=*dy-calon.*
3677. *grous* a mutation of *crous,* the interjection *a* being understood.
3681. *golvygyen* W. *goleuad* illumination (W.).
3721. *a molleth du in gegyn*=*a m. d. in gegen* 3928.
3727. *num-dar-fe* (=*num-darfa* 1477, 1808), note this instance of the prep. *dar* compounded with the verb subst. and cf. W. *dar-oed* Z². 573.
3751. *lest*=W. *llest* to hinder (W.).
3753. *hebasca,* cf. M. Br. *habasq* 'facilis,' 'suavis,' Cath.
3805. *myllusyon* pl. of *myllus* an adj. formed from *myl* 'beast.' Ir. *mīl* (*étaig*) 'louse.'
3817. *mes ay reule,* cf. Lat. *delirus* 'deviating from the straight line.'

3835. *dro-fa* 'bring him': *dro* 2d sg. imper. of *drey* and *fa* the suffixed pron. of the 3d sg. masc. So the suffixed pron. of 2d sg. *ressawhya-gy*=(*reth-sawya-gy*) 3844, 3d pl. *kemer-y* 4034.
3902. *a thuea*: the final *a* is added for rhyme's sake.
3927. *pen-gasen* W. *cest* paunch?
3933. *ternans* (perhaps *teruans*?) lit. land of (the) valley.
3936. *byschyp* from *bishop* with progressive assimilation.
3952. *scumbla*, Eng. *scumber* ' to dung.' Halliwell.
3953. *wy* a mutation of *gwy* 'water.'
3959. *vryans* (*wryens* 3963) a mutation of *bryans*=W. *braint*, O. W. *bryeint* ' privilegium ' Z². 845.
3983. *ny goske welen indan droys*, a proverbial expression, I suppose, like ' no grass grows under his feet.'
4060. *daguereys* for *dag+guereys*. Or is it for *dhe guereys* 'to help thee '?
4094. *anel*=W. *anal*, *anadl*, Ir. *anál*.
4188. *anwys*=W. *annwyd*.
4197. *caffsenna* from *caffsen-va*: cf. *may fe-ua* 4285.
4214. *sklynkya* cf. *sclaldya*, *sclandra*.
4218. *pedrevanas* cf. *pedrevan* ' lizard, elf, newt.'
4227. *retrehava*=*reth*+*drehava*.
4255. *otyweth* (W. or *diwedd*)=*wotyweth*.
4303. *metheven* W. *mehefin*.
4311. *adar* : is this *a dar* (778) or=*ater* 3631, and used here (and in 789) as an intensive? (' very greatly weakened you are ').
4314. 4526. *herethek*, W. *hiraethog*, derived from *hereth* 4545.
4358. *vasken* a mutation of *basken*, Br. *bazkañv*, *bazkaoñ*.
4380. *ras* = W. *rhad*, Ir. *rath* ' grace, favour.' This is not here, at all events, a mutation of *gras*=gratia.
4446. *hotheys* seems to mean ' coverings ' ' housings ' (W. *hws*), with *th* for *s* as often in auslaut (*plath*, *fath*, *rychyth* 429).
4448. *huenneys*=W. *hunedd* ' somnolence ' (W.).
4458. *hothfy*=W. *choyddo*.
4460. *trewythyou* for *trevythyou* pl. of *treveth* O. 799, or should we read *tre vythyou* ' between times '? (W.).
4461. *neffreu*=*neffre+ou*.
4470. *deglos*=*de-eglos*.
4473. *travls*=W. *traul* 'cost,' 'charge' (W.), or a mistake for *tra*? cf. 268.
4491. *don* to bear. Other forms of this verb are as follow:—
Infinitive *don* 4491. *ou ton* 2638. Present. Sg. *a thek* 1812, 4068. 4997. Pl. *degen* 3880. (*om*)*thegen* 3451. Conjunctive Sg. *doga* 3746. Imperative Sg. *dok-hy* 1419, (*om*)*dok* 2344. *degens* 3417. 4070. Pl. *degogh* 2796. *degeugh* 4067. First Preterite Sg. *a thuk* 451. 790. 1239. 2380.
4538. *an corff y wroweth* lit. ' the body, its lying ' (*groweth*).
4546. *heboff* ' without me,' *hebogh* ' without you ' 2693.

[278]

CORRIGENDA.

A. in the text.

Line 139. *for* due *read* dus
429. *for* fyghythrychyth *read* fyghyth rychyth
956. *for* besche reb *read* bescherev
1101. *for* ysethaff *read* yfethaff
1590. *for* ragas, ancoel *read* rag as, an coel
1858. *for* ingrassaff *read* in grassaff
2489. *for* dare *read* darne (the e over the n).
2496. *for* darum *read* darnn (the n perhaps a mere flourish).
2654. *for* moys *read* moy
3149 *dele the point.*
p. 30, note, *add* altered into lemyn
p. 66, after line 1172, *for* w *read* w⁶

B. in the translation.

Line 7. *after* warden *insert* [?] 119. *for* be not *read* you should not be 223. *after* Conan *insert* surely 247. 2286. 2286. *for* place *read* palace 292. *for* lord *read* king 304. *for* will be *read* thou shalt have 309. *for* I *read* we 322. *for* be not you *read* you should not be 420, 422. *before* be *insert* shall 426. *for* find *read* have 565. *after* world *insert a full stop* 566. *for* had *read* have not 579. *for* are *read* were 641, 672 *for* Kind (sir) *read* Good man 681. *for* marks *read* shivering fits 746 *mar tuth an nur* is perhaps 'if the hour (*an n-ur*) has come' 790. *for* died *read* bore death 856. *for* Went *read* Came 867. *for* Thou oughtest to *read* If thou couldst 916 *for* are *read* were 929 *for* catch *read* bewail 953. *for* regard *read* give heed 957. 958, 959 *read*

I beshrew your pates!
What thing shall we do through napping?
Ah, you hear me not calling?

966 *for* Cambrea *read* Carnbrea 1001. *after* Christian *insert* have 1020. *for* have *read* get 1025. *for* sitting *read* has gone 1027 *for* go *read* come 1035 *for* country quite *read* country's land [?] 1044. *read* I would not again 1060. *for* not a laugh but a cry *read* a good part will not laugh 1061. *omit* to 1072. *for* rock *read* Rock. 1115. *for* has ventured *read* ventures 1253. *for* Hast thou really *read* When hast thou 1280. *for* are *read* were, 1312 *for* clear *read* gentle 1477. *for* has not happened to me *read* I had not 1530. *omit* should 1531. *for* would not have *read* have not 1589 *for* for thee *read* children 1590 *read* For the omen (?) has lessened them 1594. *for* This *read* There 1607. *for* needs *read* need shall be 1636 *for* Whether *read* If 1694. *for* shall *read* He shall 1698 *after* For *insert* that 1719. *for* shalt *read* mayst 1800 *for* believed *read* believe 1812 *for* bore *read* who bears 1813 *for* were *read* have been 1855 *for* There has *read* Thou hast 1858 *add* for it 1896. *for* . . . *read* When 1898 *for* sin, *read* evil? 1963 *for* have been *read* am 2044 *for* have I loved *read* used I to love 2051. *for* If he were not *read* Were it not that he was 2053. *for* work *read* have wrought 2076. 2200. *before* month *insert* in the 2217 *for* opposite to *read* hundred

(Br. *kevren*). 2335 *for* go *read* come   2351. *dele the point.*   2386 *for* you *read* them   2449. *after* born *dele the point*   2450 *for* to break up deer *read* a morsel of land   2462 *for* be *read* go   2489. *for* Ruin! *read* Part of   2495. *for* is now *read* was   2496. *for* Through me *read* Part of   2585 if *bethy* be, as I now think, for *bethyth*, translate 'if thou wilt be wise'   2654. *for* go, *read* cause more   2655. *for* To sow for thee, thou, *read* For lo (there is) to thee a   2681. *for* Through *read* Without   2763. *before* sweet *insert* my   2785. *for* will *read* would   2836. *for* cause to reckon *read* give an account   2837. *for* The *read* Of the   2839. *after* there *insert* shall   3117 *before* certainly *insert* very   3245. *for* we should *read* let us   3287. *for* will *read* has   3415 *read* Morvelys   3632. *for* come *read* go   3721. *omit the asterisk and the note*   3770 *add* quietly   3992 *after* ever *add a point.*

FURTHER CORRIGENDA.

A. in the text.

Line 792. *for* y *read* y[n]
2261. *for* preveth *read* pre[n]veth
2576. *for* Govyn a *read* Govyna
3043. *for* cry *read* qy
3750. *for* prev' *read* pre[n]v'
3936. *for* Noov *read* Now

B. in the translation.

Line 9. *for* A *read* One   47. *for* live made *read* have grace   210. *after* goodness *insert* ever   509. *for* Sad *read* How sad   541, 542. *read* In my limbs rotten. I have become as a globe.   678. *for* thing is it? *read* shall I do?   727. *for* thing is this? *read* shall I do?   757. *for* there are many weak men *read* how many weak men there are   802. *for* this *read* that   854. *for* seest *read* hast seen   975. *read* Pay off the whoreson sadly   979. *for* go *read* come   1120. *read* To thee how we are bound   1237. *for* you are so foolish *read* how foolish you are   1307. *for* ways *read* old house   1403. *for* point *read* condition   1517. *for* them *read* those   1624. *for* would *read* do   1651. *for* their throats *read* its throat   1652. *for* them *read* it   1704. *for* of taking *read* thou hadst   1753. *for* he has *read* has been   1760. *for* deservest *read* shouldst take care   1853. *for* loathsome *read* foul   1911. *for* commandments *read* commandment   1997. *read* I am saying it   2261. *for* prove *read* pay for   2355. *read* We care not what we should do   2522. *read* O God, how I am grieved!   2630. *read* I am foully vexed   2644. *for* faculties *read* journeys (W. *teithian*)   2780. *for* To *read* Towards them and   2832. *for* Of the need *read* Which was given   2869. *after* be *insert* consecrated   2919. *for* I *read* We   2925. *for* chiefs *read* old houses   3010. *for* the *read* a   3043. *for* cry *read* go   3065. *omit* thee   3072. *for* loathsome *read* foul   3170. *for* this *read* that   3291. *for* a sore stroke *read* sore flesh (Br. *caher*)   3396. *for* Gilded *read* I have gilded   3438. *read* We care not where we go   3689. *for* Open *read* I will open   3750. *for* prove *read* pay for   3792. *for* wrapt *read* kept   3923. *for* orders *read* order   4036. *read* And God will help thee at once   4058. *for* wishest *read* mayst wish   4181. *before* I *insert* how   4184. *read* How weak I am and foul!   4232. *before* I *insert* how   4403. *for* surely *read* right truly   4467. *for* This *read* How this   4526. *before* we *insert* how   4528. *for* the earth *read* earth certainly!   4530. *for* in the grave *read* into the tomb

C. in the notes.

p. 266, l. 23 from bottom, *for* '2. *kyn feste*' *read* '2. *nyth us* 2373.'
p. 267, note on l. 104, *for* '*lein*' *read* 'M. Bret. *leiff* "prandium"'
p. 270, note on l. 757, *for* 'est,' 'sumus' *read* 'ut est,' 'ut sumus'
p. 270, note on l. 938, *for* sevuruth *read* sevureth
p. 276, note on l. 3396, *for* 'p. part. p.' *read* '1 sg. pret. act.'

BEUNANS MERIASEK.
THE LIFE OF SAINT MERIASEK.
A CORNISH DRAMA.
(London, Trübner & Co. 1872).

FURTHER CORRIGENDA AND ADDENDA.

A. in the Text.

Line 293	*for* kyff nywy	*read* kyffnywy
,, 685	*for* a sevya	*read* asevya
,, 792	*for* y methe	*read* y[n]methe
,, 1075	*for* tru mach	*read* trumach
,, 1590	*for* ragas tevery ancoel	*read* rag asteve ry an coel
,, 1855	*for* nyn fus	*read* nynsus
,, 1901	*for* inagefery	*read* mage sery
,, 2261	*for* preveth	*read* pre[n]veth
,, 2576	*for* Govyn a	*read* Govyna
,, 2655	*for* myngou	*read* myn gou
,, 3166	*for* rethys	*read* rechys *and cancel the note.*
,, 3263	*for* Hen na	*read* Henna
,, 3331	*for* raghyl	*read* ragh yl
,, 3740	*for* nag ovlya	*read* na govlya
,, 3750	*for* prevyth	*read* pre[n]vyth
,, 3890	*for* nynsefeth	*read* nynseseth
,, 3936	*for* Noov	*read* Now
,, 4007	*for* ry dome	*read* rydome
,, 4060	*for* daguereys	*read* da guereys

B. in the Translation.

Line 9 *for* A *read* One 27 *for* attend *read* understand 41 *for* wondrous kind *read* a wondrous good man 47 *for* live made *read* have grace 68 *after* be *insert* surely 73 *for* I know not *read* Nor know I 109 *after* be *insert* the 145 *for* temptations *read* temptation 151 *for* humble and pure *read* humbly and gently 205 *after* thee *insert* right 210 *after* goodness *insert* always 230 *for* that *read* how 264 *before* truly *insert* right 293 *for* shall have gaiety (?) *read* the guests 323 *for* all *read* here 341 *for* to marry *read* of marrying 348 *read* That I will not, through Jesus' grace, 367 *for* To teach thee *read* That thou hast learned 374 *for* not *read* never 377 *for* Thou *read* That thou 380 *for* not *read* nought at all 381 *for* learnest aught *read* hast learned 385 *for* Lands, houses *read* The lands, the houses 381 *for* a *read* the 389 *after* of *insert* the 397 *read* As hath been a multitude of men worthy 398 *for* them God was *read* their God 424 *omit* well 443 *after* me *insert* aught 471 *for* the rich busy man *read* rich man heedfully 477 *after* caused *insert* that 479 *for* To go *read* Has gone 481 *read* The less ever 483 *for* it *read* him 487 *for* Thou *read* That thou 503 *for* commend *read* entrust 509 *for* Sad *read* How sad 541 *for* My *read* In my 542 *for* Become in a heap *read* I have become as a globe 566 *read* Sorrow I have not 589 *for* now *read* certainly 612 *for* save *read* help 668 *for* great abundance *read* a short time 678 *for* thing is it *read* shall I do? 681 *read* By it I have shivering-fits 685 *read* God! how I should have a desire 727 *for* thing is this? *read* shall I do? 757 *read* Pardie, how many weak men there are 802 *for* this *read* that 848 *for* considering *read* understanding 854 *for* seest *read* hast seen 867 *read* If thou couldst understand it 937 *for* you do *read* Thou dost 948 *for* hard grace *read* sore disgrace 952 *for* us *read* me 973 *after* him *insert* diligently 975 *read* Pay off the whoreson sadly. 979 *for* go *read* come

1001 *omit* it 1004 *for* will assuage *read* do thou assuage 1005 *for* the *read* my 1038 *for* not seen *read* sought 1060 *read* Before parting only some will laugh 1075 *for* true mates *read* a passage 1120 *read* To thee how we are bound 1 1148 *for* ever *read* to (the) end 1149 *after* God *insert* will 1163 *for* no longer *read* somewhat long 1164, 1165 *for* it *read* them 1198 *for* We would *read* That we may 1227 *read* Will requite you 1237 *for* you are (so) foolish *read* how foolish you are 1269 *after* look *insert* at him 1275 *for* ascend *read* fall 1307 *for* ways (?) *read* old house 1349 *for* with *read* by 1352 *for* dragged *read* broken 1355 *for* remember *read* squat over 1369 *for* I would not be *read* that I be not 1387 *for* was *read* am 1402 *for* has happened to *read* aileth 1303 *for* point *read* condition 1412 *read* What are (the) ailments? 1414 *for* or sea *read* any more 1425 *after* got *insert* surely 1438 *for* conceal *read* call it 1480 *for* Ever *read* To the end 1482 *for* rise *read* thrive 1517 *for* them *read* those 1519 *for* a *read* one 1532 *read* Nor for you was this usual. 1536 *for* at home *read* within 1537 *omit* Up to 1562 *for* this *read* that 1567 *for* Laboured *read* Laborious 1568 *add* been. 1590 *read* For they had the gift of the loss 1603 *after* may *insert* thus 1624 *for* would *read* do 1632 *for* consider *read* understand 1651 *for* their throats *read* its throat 1652 *for* them *read* it 1668 *for* or *read* and 1686 *for* that *read* if 1704 *for* of taking *read* thou tookest 1719 *for* shalt *read* mayst 1746 *add* surely 1753 *for* he has *read* has been 1760 *for* deservest *read* shouldst take care 1762 *read* And if thy belief were good 1763 *for* cause *read* do 1766 *for* Incline *read* Bow down 1771 *add* surely 1782 *after* slay *insert* at once 1786 *read* But one night that I was awake 1820 *for* A *read* For one 1853 *for* loathsome *read* foul 1855 *read* There is not a fairer 1868 *for* has fallen to me *read* have I had 1898 *for* her *read* his 1901 *read* As greedily as a hog 1911 *for* commandments *read* commandment 1913 *read* See that you understand it 1921 *read* The time will come that Christ Jesus 1946 *for* our *read* the 1951 *after* friends *insert* right 1988 *omit the point* 1989, 1990 *read* So far as I could keep myself, Nor would I ever like (to do so) 1994 *for* simply *read* weakly 1997 *for* shall be to say *read* am saying.

2031 *for* Never *read* It will never 2038 *for* somewhat the world *read* the world's wealth 2042 *for* Wealth of the world *read* The world's wealth 2046 *for* hast *read* mayst have 2102 *for* Is it not now *read* It is nothing but 2145 *after* a *insert* certain 2158 *for* without *read* dismayed 2169 *for* thee *read* you 2191 *for* third fair *read* three fairs 2192 *for* it *read* them 2220 *read* It is not long (ago).

2240 *omit* his 2256 *for* simple *read* weak 2257 *for* gnash *read* shake 2261 *for* prove *read* pay *for* 2268 2286 *for* place *read* palace 2274 *for* the *read* this 2308 *for* Very *read* Too 2355 *read* We care not what we should do 2379 *for* mouth of lies *read* false mouth 2385 *for* luckless (?) *read* too false 2438 *for* blockhead *read* brayed head 2444 *for* Very *read* Poor 2453 *for* longer *read* long 2459 *read* Nothing but very weak I hold thee. 2505 *for* play *read* players 2522 *read* O God, how grieved I am ! 2523 *after* For *insert* that *and dele the point* 2535 *for* ailments *read* griefs 2555 *for* Before *read* Though *and after* thee *insert a point* 2558 *for* repay *read* requite 2664 *after* weak *insert* surely 2567 *for* foolish *read* weak 2630 *for* vexed (and) loathsome *read* foully vexed 2644 *for* faculties *read* journeys 2659 *for* ills *read* sorrows 2731 *for* longer *read* long 2739 *read* The blessed Holy Ghost 2780 *for* To *read* Towards them and 2832 *read* Which was given to them to give a strict list 2837 *for* The *read* Of the 2838 *read* Do understand 2842 *for* lengthier *read* stricter 2869 *after* be *insert* consecrated 2874 *for* the *read* a 2919 *for* I *read* We 2925 *for* chiefs *read* old houses 2969 *for* leave thy height (?) *read* take thy leave 2991 *add* readily 2994 *for* his *read* the.

3010 *for* the *read* a 3026 *for* to me *read* with me 3030 *after* For *insert* the 3036 *for* a *read* the 3039 *for* entered *read* might enter 3055 *for* hail *read* snow 3065 *omit* thee 3072 *for* loathsome *read* foul 3096 *add* certainly 3097 *for* Gladly *read* Most gladly 3114 *after* not *insert* right 3170 *for* this *read* that 3181 *for* Well *read* Better 3202 *for* are you *read* art thou 3208 *for* equal *read* peers 3254 *for* homewards *read* from home 3259 *before* home *insert* from 3267 *for* any longer *read* long· 3291 *for* a sore stroke (?) *read* sore flesh 3320 *for* For *read* To 3331 *for* A rascal *read* For ill 3263 *read* That ails us (his) being slack 3342 *for* a good part will not *read* only some will 3350 *read* Little were we thinking 3381 *for* pay him off *read* requite him 3389 *for* foolish *read* weak 3387 *for* that *read* it 3436 *for·* scoundrel *read* feigner 3438 *read* We care not where we go 3477 *for* Well *read* Only 3478 *after* parting *insert* right *and omit* not 3488 *for* Repay *read* Requite 3490 *for* usury *read* loyalty 3515 *for* our *read* the 3517 *for* No ! *read* Nor (any) 3527 *for* foul *read* foulness of 3643 *after* Put *insert* surely 3644 *for* surely *read* certainly 3662 *for* the *read* a 3689 *for* Open *read* I will open 3708 *for* that far from her *read* to her that long 3728 *for* made me *read* gave me (to the world) 3740 *for* howling(?) *read* perjury 3744 *omit* the 3750 *for* prove *read* pay *for* 3792 *for* teaching (folk) *read* learning 3792 *for* wrapt *read* kept 3814 *for* thing is *read* shall I do 3843 *for* will *read* could 3863 *for* corruption *read* defilement 3890 *read* Jesu Christ, grief has not gone 3923 *for* orders *read* order 3937 *for* The *read* A 3953 *for* water *read* an egg 3979 *for* for *read* in

4007 *for* (the right of) giving doom *read* sovranty 4011 *read* At once by her 4046 *for* 4036 *for* help from thy God *read* God will help thee 4058 *for* wishest *read* mayst wish 4060 *for* (thee) well *read* thee 4066 *add* forthwith 4070 *for* the *read* a 4099 *before* I *insert* that 4160 *for* thee *read* you 4181 *before* I *insert* how 4184 *read* How weak I am and foul ! 4225 *for* disease *read* grief 4232 *read* Lord how rejoiced I am ! 4268 *for* Certainly *read* Right certainly 4296 *for* absolve *read* requite 4301 *for* truly, right *read* right truly, 4338 *for* dwell *read* be dwelling 4348 *for* for ever *read* that abideth 4357 *after* not *insert* surely 4367 in the stage direction, *for* he goes *read* they go 4403 *for* surely *read* right truly 4405 *for* surely *read* certainly 4440 *read* Only some right surely know 4442, 4444 *for* wore *read* used to wear 4467 *for* This *read* How this 4526 *before* we *insert* how 4528 *for* the earth *read* earth certainly 4530 *for* in the grave *read* into the tomb.

C. in the Notes.

Note on 20 line 7 for *kyn feste* 2046 read *nythus* 2373.
,, 18 transpose *nygisbeth* 1770 to the beginning of the line.
,, line 32 For *641 etc. read* a deriv. from *calon.*
,, 40 After 673 *insert* 2719, 2944, 3132, 2232.
,, 293 Read *kyffnywy* = *convivae* (Ebel), Br. *couui* Cath.
,, 379 for *grassis* read *grussis.*
,, 472 line 5 dele *a reys* 1753, and in line 8, after 2881, *insert* Secondary pres. pass. *reys* 1753, 2355, 3438.
,, 481 for *lleidu* read *llai*
,, 757 to be omitted.
,, 892 for vyth-keth read *vythqueth* O. 616, 1991, D. 1251.
,, 938 for *sevuruth* read *sevureth*
,, 1075 read *trumach* = *trumeth* O. 1650, W. *tramwyaeth* ' a traversing.'
,, 1253 for (*pa-ur*) read *py ur* (qua hora) D 506, M. Br. *pe-eur* 'quando' Cath. now
,, 1247 line 2 *for* 1440 *read* 1540 *nynsus fors* O.2801, *na fors* D. 2758, and add to the note *ny reys thyn fors* 3428.

Page 272, line 20, for *asus* read *mar a sus.*
,, ,, ,, 27, for 2052 read 2051.
,, ,, ,, 30, dele *nynsefeth* 3820.

Note on 1307, read *hensy*, pl. *hense* 2925, is compounded of *hen* 'old' and *ty* ' house' pl. *te*, W. *ty* pl. *tai*, O.Ir. *teg* n. pl. *tige.*
,, 1853 *anhethek* is for *annethek* (see note on 440) : cf. Br. *annezer* ' crasse.'
,, 1989 to be omitted.
,, 2644 for ' in *antythy*' &c. read ' Rather cf. W. *teithiau,* pl. of *taith*, Ir. *techt*.'
,, 2652 *omit from* either *down to* or
,, 2832 read *har* (comp. *harhe* 2842,) from AS. *heard*, as *harlyth* O.2512, *hardlych* R.2597, from AS. *heardlice.*
,, 2962 read ' *cumyys* a by-form of *cummyas* (congé) Ebel. With *gays the cummys* cf. *gase farwel* 1286.
,, 3052 *antythy* = W. *annheithi* (*an* + *teithi*) 'without qualities,' Pughe.
,, 3231 3632 *dulle* (let go) for *dylle* : cf. W. *dyllwng.*
,, 3253 *read* 3250.
,, 3291 *add* Rather Br. *caher* ' char sans gresse' Cath.
,, 3314 for ' some word' read *plom* and add Br. *plom.*

Page 276 line 34, for 3524 *read* 3544.
Note on 4060 *omit for dag + guereys.* Or is it

Note on 4446 *in hotheys* seems *in notheys*, (cf. note on 440), and *notheys* is the pl. of *noth* = W. *nwydd* "stuff."

ADDITIONAL NOTES.

3. *gulas-cur*, = *gulas-cor* 170, *gulas* = W. *gwlâd* and *cor* = W. *cordd* tribus, circulus, Z. 1062. So *coscor* (*cosker* 1282) = W. *cosgordd*. Other compounds in this play are :—

I. Substantives with substantives : *genegyg-va* 850, *clogh-prennyer* 923, 1241, *guyl-foys* 1132, *guel-fos*, 1964, *myl-gy* 1281 pl. *mylguen* 3166, *our-lyn* 1965 (W. *eurlin*), *uhel-arluth* 2207, *pen-treg-se* 2215, *pen-plas* 2268, *pen-sevyk* 489.3022, 3209 (W. *pendefig*), *crous-pren* 2521. Perhaps also *ar-luth* (W. *arglwydd*) 278.

II. Substantives with adjectives : *den-sa* (*den* + *da*) 40, *pen-noth* 440, *prey-tha* (*pryt* + *da*) 1410, 1417, *schyl-wyn* 3391. Perhaps also *Mon-fras* 3370.

III. Verbs with substantives : *brath-ky* 1216, *mygh-tern* 179.

IV. Adjectives with substantives : *leun-vanneth* 211, 217 (*banneth*), *luen-golon* 297, 545 (*colon*), *luen-edrega* 2750. *mur-rays* 319, *mur-worthyens* 2684, 3846 (*gorthyans*), *mur-galloys* 3217, *mur-reverons* 3754. *plos-lustis* 427, *plos-marrek* 2444, *plos-myn* 2379, *guir-thu* 4432 (*du*), *guir-sans* 2125, *gou-ly*(a) 3740, *guan-cusel* 1594, *guan-reule* 3925, *marthys-cusel* 3297, *pur-lues* 2144, *pur-oges-car* 1939, *pur-hond* 2414, *bur-speys* *bur-spas*, 668, 1012, 3979, *bur-termyn* 1741, *brays-lafarou* 1597, *purpur-pannou* 1966, *plosek-caugyan* 3255, *lel-cregyans* 1319, *lel-gras* 2543, *-crystyan* 1001, *-servont* 2627, *-woonys* 3891 (*gonys*), *-werkeys* 4048 (*gwerkes*), *-ena* 3606, *hen-sy* 1307 (*ty*), *sans-eglos* 1320, 1876. *drok-pobyll* 1325, *-turant* 3206, *-sperys* 2657, *coleth* 1768 (*guleth*), *-coskar* 2358, *drog-athla* 3722, *falge-negethys* 777, *-teudar* 987, *-cregyans* 1161, *-horsen* 3491, *-dewou* 1721, *-plosethes* 3527, *-guesyon* 3803, *-dragon* 4133, *guyn-gala* 2076 (*cala*), *tebel-wythreys* 4123 (*guythres*), *-vest* 4127 (*best*), *-el* 969, *-dorne* 1284 (*torn*), *-genesek* 2287, *-cregyans* 4170, *-art* 2364, *-speris* 2631, *-vryans* 3502 (*bryans*), *-preff* 4133, *har-dygrath* 948, *har-lych* 2832, *desawer-vest* 4135 (*best*), *cuff-colyn* 1804, *hager-gas* 2143 (*cas*).

V. Adjectives with adjectives : *pur-wyr* 6, 9 (*guyr*), *pur-dek* 94 (*tek*), *-thyogel* 964 (*dyogel*), *-thyblans* (*dyblans*), *-thevry* 1948 (*devry*), *-lan* 1795 (*glan*), *-goeth* 1979 (*coth*), and many other compounds with *pur* : *marthys-claff* 3788.

VI. Adjectives with verbs : *guan-rewardya* 3261, *leuf-kara* 65, *luen-besy* 3592 (*pesy*), *lel-servye* 2050, *lel-reulya* 2847, *tebel-far* 2281.

VII. Adjectives with participles : *pur-gerys* 398 (*kerys*), *drok-hendelys* 3760, *glan-yesseys* 2162, 2747, *tebel-wolijs* 2490 (*golijs*), *opyn-guelys* 4152.

Note on 7, 4, after 'summit' insert *a-wartha* 390.

Note on 20, l.9. after '1686' insert [*am beff* Cr. 1018, *am bef* Cr. 1979]. l. 12. add *asteve* 1590.

21. *y vye-a* an error for *y fye-a*. So *yth vryongen* 780, *reth-vo* 3230, for *yth fryongen, reth-fo*. Conversely *na fue* 842 for *na vue*, *a fue* 887, 1813, 4082, 4049, *a fua* 1775 for *a vue*, *a fya* 1497 for *a vya*, *a feth* 3731 for *a veth*, *a fur-rays* 319, for *a vur-rays*.

22. add 'which occurs also in Cr. 1084.'

27. *add* 'to understand' (*entendre*). So in Cr. 1568 (may hallan ve attendya pan vanar lon ythewa 'that I may be able to understand

what mannner of beast it is', and in R. 447 (ty a yl y *attendye* bos guyr ow cous 'thou canst understand that my speech is true'). The p. part. p. occurs in P. 202. 4 (rag nago crist *attendys* 'for Christ was not understood').

62. *benneth varya*, like *carek veryasek* 1072, *fynten woys* P. 224, 2. *myl woly* R. 998, *myl vap mam* O. 324, *cleze dan* Cr. 965, *golvan ge* Wms, *Lex Cornubrit.* s. v. *ce*, is an example of the infection of the initial of a noun governed by a feminine noun. So in modern Welsh: *nodwydd ddur, y seren foreu.*

104. add M. Br. *leiffaff* 'prandere' from *leiff* 'prandium.'

136. *blonogeth* by metathesis from *bolungeth* = Lat. *voluntat(em)*. Metathesis of the liquids, especially *r*, is frequent in this play: *der* 172, *omgersyogh* 296, *parlet* 515, *ov tereval* 602, *grueys* 1288, *gruegh* 1692, *abreth* 209, *kerna* 2257, *scherwynsy* 2337, *dermas* 3043, *sakyrfeys* 3384, respectively for *dre, omgesryogh, prelat, drehevel, gureys, guregh, aberth, krenna, schrewynsy, dremas, sakryfeys*. So in the Vocab. we have *grueg* for *gurec*, and even in Old-Welsh *gruiam, credam* for *guriam, cerdam.*

140. *esyes* = *esijs* 3654, p. part p. of *esya* 1422.

151. *add* 'In Cath. *clouar* is tepidus.'

171. *yn tyan*, better *in tyen* 3162, from *in* (= M. Bret. *ent-*) and *dyen* = M. Br. *dien*.

226. *gvyf* = *guyff* 3700, is *gweff* 1.95,2, superl. *gueffa* Cr. 587, is perhaps cognate with O. Corn. *guaf* 'castus', which has been compared with Neap. *guappo*, Sp. and Port. *guapo*.

254. *dreson* 'over us': cf. *dresos* 'over thee' 3079, *dresof, dresto* Z.682.

273. 2021. *desethys* from *de* + *esedhys*: cf. *yseth-va* 'sedes.'

296. add *omglowugh* 709.

311. add 3155 = W. *craff*, Beitr. II. 174.

313. *moghheys* p. part. p. of the verb (= W. *mwyhau*, Br. *muyhaff*, now *muia*), whence *moghheen* 1265.

323. *aragegh* 'coram (*arak*) vobis': cf. *ragough* P.44.2, *thyragogh* R. 1913.

352. *marrek du*, cf. W. *urdd farchogawl* 'a religious order' (Walters).

395.1050. *pyraga*, like *praga* 1032. 2099. 2236. 2273.3622, P.187.2, is = *prage* O.927 = *pe* + *rak* + *e*, the pronoun being here superfluous. So *pan-a* 642. 1208. 1501, 3461, *pur- a* 1253, *fetl-a* 1357.

397. *lius* = W. *lliaws* f.

399. *ran* = *re*, Z.666 + *an* the definite article.

409. *bo-nyl, bo-neyl* 2461, 3538 : (cf. *pe-neyl* 1257, *bo anneyl* 1918), from *bo* 'sit' ' vel', and *nyl* R. 403.

419. *kerens* late Corn. *keranz* Lh. 50, pl. of *car*, is = W. *ceraint*, Ir. *carait*. So *eskerans* 1176, pl. of *escar*.

428. 572. 1245. 1741, 3184. 3367. *genevy* = *genavy* 1549. 1659. 2568= W. *genyfi* Z. 685. So *ragovy* 2057. *theragovy* 2440, *warnavy* 4000.

440. *pen-noth* = W. *pennoeth*, Ir. *nochtchenn* 'barhaupt' Z. 857. Add to the note at p. 269 '*anhethek, anhethy* O.1722 ; *canhagowe* Cr. 67 *lanherch* Vocab.'

443. *rychys* = *rychyth* 429, 432. where final *s* has become sharp *th*, as in *fath* 944, *spath* 942, *plaeth* 4562, *croyth* 4183.

454. 3417, *hascra, ascra* 1888 (= W. *asgre*, Br. *askre, asgre, askle. asgle*) is *nascra* in R. 486, where (as in Eng. *n.ewt*) the *n* is due to the article.

471. *indellan*, if not a mistake for *indella*, 614, is, by metathesis, for *in-del-na*.

478. *ou herth* from *ou*(s)*kerth* [*ou*(s) ex *mos, Br. *ma*, Goth. *mis* 'mihi.'] So *ou holen* 3585, *ou heskey* 8318, *ou huen* 3913.

The changes of initial *K, T, P* respectively to *H, Th, F* are simply due to the following phonetic laws :
I. *s-k* and *k-k* become *ch* and then *h* :
II. *s-t* and *t-t* become *th* :
III. *s-p* and *p-p* become *ph* and then *f* :

Further illustrations of Law I are *age hense* 2925, *thage herhes* 3288, *na-hen* (= *nak-ken*) 505, 608, 2082, *na-kyns* 1932.

Illustrations of Law II are : *ou thays* 349, *ou threys* 2398, *ou threst* 3195, *age therry* 3806.

Illustrations of Law III are *ou fehas* (peccatum) 2131, *ou fehosou* 1826, *o*(*u*) *fen-treg-se* 2215, *ou fobyl* (populus) 2437, 2489, *ou fresmer* 3730, *iij ferson* 1318. *thy fesy* 3589, *dre-fen* (-dres + pen) 1303, 1707, *ke-fris* (kes-pris) 998, *ke-ke-frys* 1528, *na felle* (= nep-pelle) 2488, *na fella* 1746, 1885. The effect of *s* on *p* is most clearly seen in the compound *calys-feyn* 'hard pain' P. 196. 4 : compare the French *nèfle* from *mespilum*.

The changes of initial *G, D, B* respectively to *K, T* and *P* are due to the following laws :
IV. *th-g* and *s-g* become *k*, or (before *u*) *q*.
V. *th-d* and *s-d* become *t*.
VI. *th-b* and *s-b* become *p*.

Illustrations of Law IV are *ou cuthel* (orth-guthel) 785, *cul* 1162, *colowhy* 3714, *cortes* 3655, *quandra* 1203, 1880, *queras* 3154, *quan-rewardya* 3261, *y-crasseeff* 3892, *a callen* 2587 (as-gallen), *a qurelles* 2613, *mara kyllyn* 1339, *kylla* 1503, *calla* 2109, *qureth* 2441. *mar kyssys* (=mara gyssys) 218, *crons* 2085, *kyl* 2168, *corthyyth* 2379, *cothens* 1383, *kyllyn* 1347, 1876, *kyllyth* 3812, *kyl* 2168, *qureth* 904 etc. *quregh* 1225, *quelogh* 2087, *quelyth* 3230. The effect of *th* on *g* is clearly shewn by *byth-queth*, 204, that of *s* on *g* by *dys-crasiis* 1405, *vynnas quelas* P. 164. 4 ; and cf. *nan*(s) *quelse* P.85.4, *can*(s)*quyth* D. 574.

Illustrations of Law V are *ou tyberth* (=orth dyberth) 510, *teberth* 3478, *tustruya* 2060, *terevel* 602 = *trehevel* 2103, *toys* 4476, *y terfensa* (= yth derfensa) 185, *tegoth* 1299, *tuth* 2148, *tuth*-*e* 2274, *trehevys* 4431, *teserya* 2696, *troff* 2730, *o tyweth* 4255, *to-ta* 1675 (toth-da) [cf. mod. Corn. *benetu* = *beneth-du*] ,*may teffo* 1712, *teffons* 1738, *tevera* 2608, *mara tue* 1106, *tuen* 3476, *tuny* 3907. *kyn teffo*, 251, *teseryas* 2579, *mar tegen* 61, *tuth* 746, 2908, *tuff* 3365, *tur* 1163. *in-tefry* 2222 (ins-defry). The effect of *th* on *d* is clearly shewn by *yth torn*, O. 1455. In *as-teve* 1590, *as-tefe* 1935, *as-tevyth* 765, *as-teveth* 1199, *may-s-tefons*, 4287, *nys-tufons* 2785, the *t* is due to the effect of the preceding *s* on the *d* of the root.

Illustrations of Law VI are *ou pewe* (=orth bewe) 2006, *a-ppeua* (= as-beva) 686, *mara peya* 186, *pewy* 194, *mar pethen* 420, 2159, *peth* 422, *pewaff* 1864= *pewa* 2124.

The apparent changes of initial *G* to *H* and of *B* and *M* to *F* are really illustrations of the following laws :

VII. *th-gh* and *s-gh* become *ch* and then *h*.
VIII. *th-v* and *s-v* become *f*.

Illustrations of Law VII: *may halla* (mayth-ghallaf)13, *hallogh* 2180, *hyllen* 140,4488, *hallen* 630 etc. *hyllyn* 2512, *halla* 543, *hallo* 3385, *hallons* 1556, *y halses* 2639, *halse* 4466, *hylly* 4459, *py halles* 3304 [*yn harow* (yns- gharow P.2. 3], *y (wh)raff* 143, 2176, *y w(h)othen* 309. *may w(h)e thoffsen* 2634. *may (wh)rellen* 3819. *y w(h)othes* 2974. 3649 [cf. *yth wholowys* O. 285] *may w(h)elle* 4006, *y (wh)ra* 4021, *kyn w(h)yske* 4442, *gans w(h)eres* 1991.

Illustrations of Law VIII: First, when the *v* is an infected *b*:—*y fetheth* (= yth vedheth) 1242 [cf. *y ret(h) flamyas* 'they blamed thee' P. 92.2], *fyen* 311, *feth* 725. 1218, *fuff* 2154, *fueff* 4393. *may fo* 1007, *festa* 1710, *fe* 1090, *fegh* 2162, *kyn feny* 892, *fo-ve* 976, *feste*, 2046, *fewy* 4568; *in fyu* (= ens-vyu) 1784, *guel-fos* (guels-vos) 1127. Secondly, when the *v* is an infected *m*: *y fensyn* 2728, *fyn* 2304, *fynnas* 869, *fannaf* 173, *fanna* 520, *fannavy* 2123, *infays* (ins-vays, *mâs*) 1743, 3973: cf. *guit(h)-fil* Vocab.

Besides these provections, which have been treated by Ebel, Beitr. v. 162—189, we find a few instances in which *k g, t-d* and *p-b* respectively become *kk, tt* (and then *th*) and *pp*. Thus *drok-coleth* 1768, *preytha* 1410, 1417 (from *pryt-ta, pryt-da*), *map pron* O. 1983. In *pub tezoll* P. 228. 1, *p-d* has become *p-t*.

493. *am anvoth vy*, lit. 'of my unwill': cf. *ay anvoth* P. 175.1, W. *anfodd*. The simplex *both* occurs in 584. 595. 614.

503. *kemynna*: cf. *a tas yntre the thule my a gymmyn ow spyrys*, D. 2986.

508. *dore* (so in 3685), for the usual *doro*.

509. 4184. 4232. *assoff* 'ut sum'= *asoma, assoma* 2522. 4181, *asota* 'ut es' 230. *assyu* 'ut est' 4467. *assus* 757. *asson* 'ut sumus' 1120. 4526. *asogh* 'ut estis' 1237 (see Z. 549), *asevya* 'ut esset' 685 : see Z. 795, and cf. *as wrussogh cam tremene* R. 40.

510. *the orthys, the orthugh* 545, for *dheworthys, dheworthugh*, Z. 683,684.

514. *tanou*, cf. *ow len-grysy tus yw tanow* R. 2462, *ow howetha ew tanow* 'my comrades are few' Cr. 121, where it is wrongly rendered.

521.529. *ordys* pl. of *ord* (*orth* ?) = W. *urdd* pl. *urddau* (eglwys).

523. *venystra* a mutation of *menystra* = Br. *ministraff*: cf. O. Corn. *menistror* (gl. pincerna).

528. literally 'of thee speech of much goodness'.

536. *alusyon* = *alusyen* 3118, seems the pl. of *alus* = W. *elusen*, pl. *elusenau*, Br. *aluson* pl. *alusennou*, Ir. *almsan*, all borrowed from *eleemosyna*. Another form *alesonou* (pl. of *aleson*) occurs in 1829.

542. add W. *cronen* f. a globe. As to *in* cf. Z. 617.

579. The verb *ens* 'sunt' is for *yns* as in 1280.

580.3743. *hagis*, a combination of the conjunction *hag* and the possessive pronoun *agis*. So *ham* 54. 480. 711, *hau* 597, *hath* 491. 827. 830, *hay* 852.

592. *thagys* a combination of the prep. *the* and the possessive pronoun *agis*. So *thum* 725, *theth, dheth, thethe* 705. 65. 64, *thagen* 674.

599. 1108. 1269. *at eve* = *at eva* 1121, 1408. 4198 =*ottefe, otteve* R. 1901. O.2513. 2567. Other such forms are *atta hy* 3944. 3953: *attens?* 3447 (= *a wottense* P. 203, 2). *attonsy* 1278 (= *otensy* D. 601),

atte ty 1832. *at oma* 1332. *atomma* 1464. *atte* 3792. *atta* 1444, 4091. 4538.

650. *add* ' So *orthen* 1023 = *orth* + *an.*'

662. *add* ' in *effen* as in *godhaffsen* 2634, and *proffse* 1427.

668. *add* in brevi spatio.

678. 727. 3814. *pendrama* = *pendra wrama* R 2219, from *pe* + *an* + *tra* + *graf* + *ma* : cf. *pendra raff* 3099.

709. *add* ' The simplex occurs in O.1990 : *ny glewsyug....sawor an parma* ' non sentiistis odorem huius similem).'

746. *an n-ur* : cf. *zen n-ezyn* P.206.3, *zen n-empynnyon* P.134.3. *han n ohan* Cr. 1069.

778. *iouden* generally *jaudyn, joudyn,* a term of reproach. Is it a corruption of the English *jordan* formerly *jourden* ? ' why you will allow us nere a *jourden* and then we leake in your chimney', Shakspere, Hen. iv. Part I. Act II. sc. i.

821. 1204. 3447. *enos* seems formed like the O.Corn. adverbs *isot* (gl. deorsum), *huchot* (gl. sursum).

853. *weder* a mutation of *gweder, gwedyr* 1445 = W. *gwydyr,* M. Br. *guezr,* from *vitrum.*

857. *mostye, mostya* 3863, p.part. p. *mostyys* D.867, R. 1927, is cognate with Eng. musty, Fr. moisir, Lat. mucidus.

906. *pan deffen ha moys*. Here the second verb is in the infinitive. So it is in 1001 and 3476. See Z.934 and my note on P.175.2.

915. 1229. *mylwyth,* like *unwyth* 110, is compounded with *gwyth* = W. *gwaeth,* M. Br. *guez,* Ir. *fecht.*

923. 1241. *cloghprennyer,* lit. ' bellbeams', is Lhuyd's *clochprednier.* Were Cornish belfries used as prisons ?

936. the *clap* sens = sens the *clap* R. 1113.

947. 1163. *napel* for *nep-pell,* as *napyth* 3570 for *neppyth.*

948. *hardygrath* is perhaps *har* + *dygrath* ' disgrace'=Br. *digracc.*

953. *ny (w)regh vry,* cf. *ny wraf vry* D. 2244.

955. *mogh,* like W. *mooio,* is connected with Eng. *mock,* Fr. *moquer,* Sp. *muecar.*

960. *tannegh* pl. of *tan* 1464. O.206. 504. 540.

961. *frappia* from Fr. *frapper.*

975. *pegh* 2d pl. imperat. of *pea* or *pe* D.1557 : cf. *me an pe dhen hebyhors* 1061.

980. *quartron, quartren* 1541, is in meaning the Fr. *quartier,* in form the Fr. *quarteron.* In 1548 *quarton* (leg. *quartron* ?) means *quarta pars.* The verb *quartrona* occurs in 1918. 3608.

1004. *sewagya* = a Fr. *souagier,* a Latin *suaviare.*

1020. 3439. *bener* = *byner* O.583, *vyner* O.2196, *bydnar* Cr. 1161. Z. 621.

1045. 3734. *methou,* Lhuyd's *medho,* W. *meddw,* M. Br. *mezu,* root MADH, whence also Gr. *methusos, methuô,* Skr. *madhu.*

1102. *trohe (troha* 2780) = the prep. *troha* Z.690, with the suffixed personal pron. of the 3d pl.

1104. *blyth, bleit* (gl. lupus), *bligh* Cr. 1149. *blaidh* Lh.82 b. W. *blaidd,* M. Br. *bleiz* ' lupus', *bleizes* ' lupa' Cath.

1121. 4104. *kepar hag on* ' ut agnus'. So in O.894, where it is wrongly rendered.

1145. *yne* for *yeyn* 3042, *iein* (gl. frig[id]us), M. Br. *yen,* W. *iain* ' icy', all derived from *$ia(g)i$, Ir. *aig* = O. N. *jaki.*

1166. *meule*, Mid. W. *meuel* Laws i.92, *mefyl*, O. Ir. *nebul*, cognate perhaps with Gr. *me-m-phomai*.

1148. 1480. *byteweth* = *bys* + *deweth*.

1190. *ornogh*, for *ordnogh*, as *ornas* Cr. 630, for *ordnas*.

1205. *fysmens (fysmant* Cr. 527) = *fantysm*, Ital. *fantasima*, *phantasma*.

1255. 1728. 3679. *degeys* compounded of *de-*, *dy-* Z.904 and *kês* = Br. *kaêet* fermé. Cf. O.W. *en kayu e dressou* 'to shut the doors' and A.S. *caeg*, Eng. *key*.

1272. *pottis* pl. of *pot* 'pudding' (W.), here used for entrails. W. *potten*.

273. *felge* (= W. *hyllt* 'findit' Z.508) 3d sg. pres. of Lhuyd's *feldzha* ex *felta*, root *SPALT*.

1274. *ompynnen* = *impinion* (gl. cerebrum), *ympynnyon* R. 1011.

1280. 1281. cf. myl wyth dyghtys ages brogh gans nep mylgy, D 2926.

1282. *cosker* : cf. *den cosgor* (gl. cliens vel clientulus), W. *cosgordd* Z. 1062, M. Br. *coscor* 'familia'.

1309. *in neys* = W. *yn nes* (tyred yn nês).

1312. For the *Gesugh* of the ms. we should certainly read *Pesugh* 'pray ye' : cf. 151. 2160. 4220.

1331. 1758. *regen* = *re* + *'gen*. So *regys* 3031 = *re 'gys*.

1352. *draylys* = Br. *dralet* 'coupé en morceaux' : cf. *dral ha dral* O.2782, M. Br. *draillaff* 'laniare.'

1355. *covya* Fr. *couver*, Ital. *covare*.

1402. *pendrus wer*, 1412. *pendrus werys* : cf. bos trest thywhy *pendra wher* R.1255. Adam *pandra whear* thywhy. Cr. 1222. Root *SVAR*, Skr. *svar, svarati*, Zend *qara* 'a wound,' Nhg. *schwaere*, W. *chwarel*.

1403. *in poynt da* = en bon point. So R. 1383.1756. M. Br. *poent* 'status.'

1406. *drethon* a new form of *dre* with suffixed pron. Z. 666.

1450. *warvan* 'sursum' = *war* + *ban* (Ir. *benn* 'mountain') as *warnans* 'deorsum' = *war* + *nans* (W. *nant* 'valley'). So *yn ban, yn nans*.

1475, 1476. 'By my faith, I cannot spare a bit (?). Fairer payment, it is now a month,' etc.

Here *wesse* is for *vês*, the vocalic mutation of *mês*, caused by *yu*, as in *nag yu vas* 2519 : cf. *nansyu meys* 3918, *nansyu tremmys* 1491.

1482. *ny thereff* for *ny dhreff*, from the Engl. *thrive*, as *drushen* from the Eng. *thresh*.

1483. *losowen* a singulative form, Z. 295-6, = W. *llysiewyn*, Br. *lousouen*. The pl. *losow* frequently occurs. Ir. *lus*. Other singulative forms are *dagren* (Gr. *dakru*) 3319. *fuven* 2407. 3481 (Lat. *faba*), *guelen* 3294 pl. *guelynny* 3298.

1491. *tremmys* : note the assimilation of the *s* of *tris* : so in *tremmyl* 1516. 1539, *treffer* 2191, *treddeth* 3895.

1535. *flehyggyou* for *flehyjow, flehysow* pl. of *flogh*, M. Br. *floch*, from Lat. *floccus*.

1546. *achy the try blythy* 'within three years'. So *achy the kernou* 2234. *achy thum tyr* 2260, *agy the ewhe* R. 275, *agy then yet*, O.3065.

1548. 3162. *meyny*, also in O.1018, *mayny*, Cr. 465, O. Fr. *mesgnée*, Ital. *masnada*.

1557. *porhel* = *porchel* (gl. porcellus), pl. *porhelli* Lh., M. Br. *porchell*. *lugh* = *loch* (gl. vitulus), Ir. *liacc*.

1602. *an clergy* 'the clergy' : cf. 1773.

1625. 3418. *bogh* = *boch* (gl. caper), M. Br. *bouch*, Ir. *bocc*, A.S. *bucca*, Beitr. II. 174.

1626. *nycoth* from *nyth goth* as *y coth* 1934 from *yth goth*.

1675. *mammethou* pl. of *mammeth* = mamaid (gl. altrix v. nutrix).

1778. *tum*, later *tubm* = *toim* (gl. calidam), M. Br. *toem*, W. *twym*.

1784. *in fyu* 'alive', W. *yn fyw*, Z. 614.

1785. *noswyth* = W. *noswaith* 'a certain night.' So *dethwyth* 2145 'on a certain day.'

1845. *sollebreys* = *solabrys* Z. 621. So *solladeth* 2940.

1384. *geyn* a mutation of *keyn* = *chein* (gl. dorsum), M. Br. *queyn*, W. *cefn*, Gaulish *Cebenna*, Glück 57, where the Teutonic *Bacenis* is compared.

1901. *mage sery avel hok* cf. 466. 863. D.1790. I suppose *sery* to be for *serhy* and compare W. *serchawg*.

1902. *gon* = W. *gwn*, Ir. *fuan* (gl. lacerna) Z. 22.1039. The Italian *gonna*, O. Fr. *gone*, Eng. *gown* are cognate.

1994. 3389. *sempel*, *pur sempel* 2459.2567. *sempel-los* 2256, Br. *sempl'* 'faible', M. Br. *sembl*, *sembldet*, *semplat*, *semplaff*.

2069. *wehes* = W. *chweched*. The ordinary form is *wheffes* = Br. *chouec'hved*. The other ordinals in this play are *kynse* 2071 *(an kensa* 4304), *secund* 2198, *tresse* 2376. 2200. 4051. 4083, viii *ves* (leg. *ethves*) 2197.

2076. *guyngala* = *guyn* + *cala(mus)* 'white straw', M. Br. *guenngoloff*.

2102. *nynsyu eff lemen an lor* 'it is nothing but the moon'. (W). So in R. 1363 : *Iohan nynsos lemyn flogh* 'John, thou art nothing but a child.'

2112. 3951. *ancumbra*, hence the p. part. p. *ancombrys* P. 34.1, where it is wrongly rendered.

2152: *truethek*, *trewethek* 3823, is = in form the Br. *truézek* 'qui est enclin à la pitié,' in meaning, the W. *trueddus*, Br. *truezus* M. C. 90.

2158. *ameys* (cf. *ameys of ow predery* O. 193) is the O. Fr. *esmaié*, *esmoyé* from *ex-magatus*.

2279. 'Whither is best for us to hold.'

2285. 2289. 2584. *For* This *read* That (*honna*).

2291. *harber* (A.S. *hereberge*), here perhaps used in its old sense of statio militaris.

2296. *dyspletyogh* 2d. pl. imper. of *dyspleytya* = a Lat. *displictiare* (where plictiare, Fr. *plisser*, is a deriv. from *plicare*) as *feytour* 3436 is from *fictor*.

2338. 3370. *monfras*. The first syllable of this name is perhaps the Br. *mon* 'excrement.'

2351. *sul voy ... the larchya* : cf. the Bret. *seul moy ...... seul muy* Z.931.

2353, *for* that *read* this.

2373. *nythus* (non tibi est) : cf. *nathues* R. 1391.

2385. *reyu* from *re-gou* 'too false'?

2431. literally 'To help thee shall be little.'

2438. *pys* (so in O.2641) is from Lat. *pistus*.

2455. *hynways* (i.e. *henwas*) : cf. *taklays* 3094, *benegays* 3149, and *benegas*, *malegas* Z.532,

2503. *remenant* = O. Fr. *remanant, remainant*, part. pres. of *remanoir*, Corn. *remaynya*.

2505. 4560. *guary* used for 'players', as *pow* 4476 for oountry-folk.

2554. read 'I am a blind man : I see thee not.'

2582. *guertha* should have been rendered 'to sell', M. Br. *guerzaff*, W. *gwerthu*, from *gwerth* 'worth' 'price', Ir. *firt* in *esirt, esfeirt* (ex-verti), 'one who deserts his land', Goth. *vairths*.

2884. 2885, more literally thus : 'The company I ask earnestly If ye will go to Vannes ?'

2752. For 'Turn' read 'That ye turn.'

2837. For 'every' read 'some.'

2964. *gerennou*, for the usual *geryou*, 3001 seems the pl. of a singulative form, Z. 299. So *denerennou* 3404.

2979. *medel* for the organic *medhel* O.928, W. *meddal*, Br. *mezel*. Ir. *medhal* (gl. panca).

2981. *dewysyou* for *devysyou*, later *devidgyow* Cr. 1770, a pl. of *davas, davat* (gl. ovis), W. *dafad*, M. Br. *davat*.

2994. *grogon* a mutation of *crogon* = *crogen* (gl. concha). M. Br. *croguenn an penn* (gl. craneum).

2998. lit. 'I would be beseeching you,' *orth* omitted before *agys*.

3055. *yrgh* = *irch* (gl. nix), W. *eira*, Br. *erc'h* : cf. Lat. *algor, algeo, algidus* : *clehy*, Lhuyd's *klihi*, borrowed from *glacies*.

3071. *goheles, gohelas* 4213 = W. *gochelyd* 'to avoid,' 'to shun.'

3085. *poder* W. *pwdyr*, Lat. *putris*. Cognate are *podrek* 3048, *podrethek* 541, 3061, 4205, *podren* 3323 = *poddren* 2290.

3144. cf. *yn kyk nag in knes* O. 659 (Engl. 'flesh and fell'), *y kyk hay knes* D. 2941. *yn kyc in kneus*, R.199, 231, where *knes, kneus* are misprinted *kues, kueus*. So *gnas* (W. *gnawd*, Ir. *gnáth*) D.2969, [*a peue den drok y gnas ny alse ...cafus mar mur ras* 'if he were a man of evil habit he could not have so much grace'] is there misprinted *guas*.

3166. *mylguen* (= Ir. *mílchoin*), pl. of *mylgy* D. 2957, Ir. *mílchú* : *rechys* pl. of *rech* = Fr. *rets*, as *lych*, 2832, = *lits, list*.

3225. *depse* should be *deprse* : cf. *debre* 3984, *deppro* P. 44. 4. M. Br. *dibriff*, O. W. *diprim*.

3302. *nyth* is the *neid* (gl. nidus) of the Vocab. M. Br. *ness*, W. *nyth*, O. Ir. *net* : *oy* (= *wy* ?), the *uy* (gl. ovum) of the Vocab. and Cath.

3309. read 'They are : very red their mouths.' cf. 3408.

3311. A friend would translate 'Order from them each his coat' (*pous*). 4. But *bous* is from *bout* (Br. *bout* M.C., 232, Fr. *bout* properly a 'blow' : all, like Fr. *bouter*, Ital. *bottare*, M. Bret. *boutaff*, from Mhg. *bōzen to beat*), and *rag* after the verb *ordna* always means 'for' not 'from' : cf. P. 152. 3 and R. 1986.

3372. *for* had I read would I have

3375. *for* they read who

3395. *horth* (gl. aries) Vocab. W. *hwrdd*.

3403. add M. Br. *squezrenn* 'estelle de bois' Cath.

3404. omit nine *and cf. note on* 2964.

3406. *iovyn* = Lat. *Iovem*. Latin loanwords from the accusative are frequent in the neo-celtic tongues, e.g. W. *Moesen*, Corn. *Sareptyn, Baraban*, Ir. *Moysen, Eufraten, Iordanen*. See Diez Gr. II. 9.

3414. add M. Br. *logodenn* 'mus'.

3427. *add* ' A Borea omne malum.'

3436. *feytour, faytowre* fictor, simulator; faytowre that feynyth sekeness for truandise, vagius 'Pr. P. cf. fandi *fictor* Ulixes.

3437. *read* ' Whom it would be wished to lay hold of. '

3453. Is *ewyas* for *ewhyas*, and may we compare W. *echwa* ' to ride' ?

3527. *plosethes* formed from *plos* as *mostethes* ' filth' from *most* and perhaps *negethys* 777, *nygythys* 3972, *nygethys* O. 914 from *nyg*, Fr. *nique, niche*, whence M. Br. *nichiff* ' nuire.'

3574. 4098, *guaya* 'to move' may be cognate with Lat. *vago* (' arbores vento *vagant*' Ennius), *vagus, veho*, Eng. *wag*, Skr. *vah*.

3578. *deves* to be read *deues (dewes* 3603) pl. *dewosow* 1473, O. Corn. *diot*. W. *diawd*.

3606. 3612. 3982. In *an vorou* (cf. M. Br. *en beure*, W. *yn fore* ' mane,' Ir. *imbarach*) we have a mutation of *borou* = W. *boreu* : cf. *a-vorou* (gl. cras). M.W. *avory*.

3610. *goleys* is = Br. *goullôet* : cf. O.W. *gwollung* (gl. vacuum).

3642. *malys*, better *maylys*, p. part. p. of *maylye*, cogn. with Fr. *maillot*, Eng. *mail*, Lat. *macula* the mesh of a net.

3643. *cofyr*, Fr. *coffre*, from *cophinus*, whence M. Br. *coffin*.

3649. *da- lour* = *lour yn ta* O. 2507.

3680. *for* now, to me *read* it was.

3710. 4024. *askevy* = W. *anghofio*, M. Br. *ancouffhat*. In 3710 *for* will *read* would.

3722. *drogathla :* can this be a corruption of *drok-whethlow* ' bad tidings' ?

3740. *goulya* ' perjury' (W. *geu-lw*, Br. *gwall-lê*, Ir. *bras-luighe*) compounded of *gou* = W. *gau*, Ir. *gô* and *ly* = W. *llw*, Br. *lê*, Ir. *luighe*. The final *a* is added for rhyme's sake, as in *neffre- a* 2078 and *a thue - a* 3902 : With *heb ty vyth na goulya* cf. *heb oun oma na truath* 1627.

3751. *add* W. *llesteir* ' impedimentum' Z. 826, from AS. *läst* 'onus.' So Fr. *lester* ' to ballast' from Ohg. *hlast*.

3757. cf. ' Our hostess keeps her state ; but *in best time* We will require her welcome.' *Macbeth* III. 4.

3772. *degolmas* pret. of *degelmy* 3842, M. Br. *digolmaff*, from *de* and *kelmy*, M. W. *cylymu*, M. Br. *coulmaff*.

3782, 3783, *read* ' If she will help, At the end (one) will not be deceived.'

3913. In the text *after* me *insert* ny

3944. *defethys* from *de* and *fethys* p. part. p. of *fethe* 4021, 4033, M. Br. *faezaff* ' vincere' from SPAC-TAM, SPAGTAMA. Cognate with Gr. *sphazô*, root SPHAG.

3949. *gonsy* (sic) is probably a scribe's error for *gensy* 304. 4011.

3835. *add* ' So *gueres-vy* 2628, *guyth- ny* 4073, *toul -e* 1445.'

3959. *add* ' Hence *brentyn* 1650. Cr. 2241 = W. *brennhin*.'

4007. *rydome* (ms. *ry dome*) from A.S. *rîcedôm* ' regnum.'

4036. *ha gueres ad* seems for *hag ad (ath) weres*.

4024. *add* M. Br. *alasn*.

4120. *omgellys* for *omwhelys, omhelys* 4190. With *war dor omgellys* cf. *war doer lemyn umhelaf* Cr. 1211.

4253. 4341. 4511 *deleth* = M. W. *deleed* (pl. *deleelyon* ' debita' Z. 289), Ir. *dliged*.

4303. *add* ' M. Br. *mezeuen*, Ir. *meitheamh*.'

4348. *beys* from A.S. *bídan*, Eng. *bide*. With *in ioy a beys* cf. *an ioy a thur* 1293.

4487. *geler* = W. *gelor (ar yr eler* 'in feretro' Z.513), M. Br. *gueler* bière a porter les mors, Cath.

4406. *han*. This must be a mistake for *ha*.

4538. Here *orth* is omitted before the pronoun, as in 245, 1997, 2998.

4546. add W. *hebof, heboch*.

W. S.

August 22, 1872.

Rebacked S Holliday
2/1995

Lightning Source UK Ltd.
Milton Keynes UK
UKOW07f0930260715

255824UK00006B/89/P